Machine Learning with R Cookbook

Explore over 110 recipes to analyze data and build
predictive models with the simple and easy-to-use R code

Yu-Wei, Chiu (David Chiu)

[PACKT] open source*
community experience distilled

PUBLISHING

BIRMINGHAM - MUMBAI

Machine Learning with R Cookbook

First published: March 2015

Production reference: 1240315

Published by Packt Publishing Ltd.
Livery Place
35 Livery Street
Birmingham B3 2PB, UK.

ISBN 978-1-78398-204-2

www.packtpub.com

Credits

Author

Yu-Wei, Chiu (David Chiu)

Reviewers

Tarek Amr

Abir Datta (data scientist)

Saibal Dutta

Ratanlal Mahanta
(senior quantitative analyst)

Ricky Shi

Jithin S.L

Commissioning Editor

Akram Hussain

Acquisition Editor

James Jones

Content Development Editor

Arvind Koul

Technical Editors

Tanvi Bhatt

Shashank Desai

Copy Editor

Sonia Cheema

Project Coordinator

Nikhil Nair

Proofreaders

Simran Bhogal

Joanna McMahon

Jonathan Todd

Indexer

Mariammal Chettiyar

Graphics

Sheetal Aute

Abhinash Sahu

Production Coordinator

Melwyn D'sa

Cover Work

Melwyn D'sa

About the Author

Yu-Wei, Chiu (David Chiu) is the founder of LargitData (www.LargitData.com). He has previously worked for Trend Micro as a software engineer, with the responsibility of building big data platforms for business intelligence and customer relationship management systems. In addition to being a start-up entrepreneur and data scientist, he specializes in using Spark and Hadoop to process big data and apply data mining techniques for data analysis. Yu-Wei is also a professional lecturer and has delivered lectures on Python, R, Hadoop, and tech talks at a variety of conferences.

In 2013, Yu-Wei reviewed *Bioinformatics with R Cookbook, Packt Publishing*. For more information, please visit his personal website at www.ywchiu.com.

I have immense gratitude for my family and friends for supporting and encouraging me to complete this book. I would like to sincerely thank my mother, Ming-Yang Huang (Miranda Huang); my mentor, Man-Kwan Shan; the proofreader of this book, Brendan Fisher; Taiwan R User Group; Data Science Program (DSP); and other friends who have offered their support.

About the Reviewers

Tarek Amr currently works as a data scientist at bidx in the Netherlands. He has an MSc degree from the University of East Anglia in knowledge discovery and data mining. He also volunteers at the Open Knowledge Foundation and School of Data, where he works on projects related to open data and gives training in the field of data journalism and data visualization. He has reviewed another book, *Python Data Visualization Cookbook, Packt Publishing*, and is currently working on writing a new book on data visualization using D3.js.

You can find out more about him at `http://tarekamr.appspot.com/`.

Abir Datta (data scientist) has been working as a data scientist in Cognizant Technology Solutions Ltd. in the fields of insurance, financial services, and digital analytics verticals. He has mainly been working in the fields of analytics, predictive modeling, and business intelligence/analysis in designing and developing end-to-end big data integrated analytical solutions for different verticals to cater to a client's analytical business problems. He has also developed algorithms to identify the latent characteristics of customers so as to take channelized strategic decisions for much more effective business success.

Abir is also involved in risk modeling and has been a part of the team that developed a model risk governance platform for his current organization, which has been widely recognized across the banking and financial service industry.

Saibal Dutta is presently researching in the field of data mining and machine learning at the Indian Institute of Technology, Kharagpur, India. He also holds a master's degree in electronics and communication from the National Institute of Technology, Rourkela, India. He has also worked at HCL Technologies Limited, Noida, as a software consultant. In his 4 years of consulting experience, he has been associated with global players such as IKEA (in Sweden), Pearson (in the U.S.), and so on. His passion for entrepreneurship has led him to start his own start-up in the field of data analytics, which is in the bootstrapping stage. His areas of expertise include data mining, machine learning, image processing, and business consultation.

Ratanlal Mahanta (senior quantitative analyst) holds an MSc in computational finance and is currently working at the GPSK Investment Group as a senior quantitative analyst. He has 4 years of experience in quantitative trading and strategy developments for sell-side and risk consultation firms. He is an expert in high frequency and algorithmic trading.

He has expertise in the following areas:

- Quantitative trading: FX, equities, futures, options, and engineering on derivatives
- Algorithms: Partial differential equations, Stochastic Differential Equations, Finite Difference Method, Monte-Carlo, and Machine Learning
- Code: R Programming, C++, MATLAB, HPC, and Scientific Computing
- Data analysis: Big-Data-Analytic [EOD to TBT], Bloomberg, Quandl, and Quantopian
- Strategies: Vol-Arbitrage, Vanilla and Exotic Options Modeling, trend following, Mean reversion, Co-integration, Monte-Carlo Simulations, ValueatRisk, Stress Testing, Buy side trading strategies with high Sharpe ratio, Credit Risk Modeling, and Credit Rating

He has already reviewed two books for Packt Publishing: *Mastering Scientific Computing with R* and *Mastering Quantitative Finance with R*.

Currently, he is reviewing a book for Packt Publishing: *Mastering Python for Data Science.*

Ricky Shi is currently a quantitative trader and researcher, focusing on large-scale machine learning and robust prediction techniques. He obtained a PhD in the field of machine learning and data mining with big data. Concurrently, he conducts research in applied math. With the objective to apply academic research to real-world practice, he has worked with several research institutes and companies, including Yahoo! labs, AT&T Labs, Eagle Seven, Morgan Stanley Equity Trading Lab (ETL), and Engineers Gate Manager LP, supervised by Professor Philip S. Yu.

His research interest covers the following topics:

- Correlation among heterogeneous data, such as social advertising from both the users' demographic features and users' social networks
- Correlation among evolving time series objects, such as finding dynamic correlations, finding the most influential financial products (shaker detection, cascading graph), and using the correlation in hedging and portfolio management
- Correlation among learning tasks, such as transfer learning

Jithin S.L completed his BTech in information technology from Loyola Institute of Technology and Science. He started his career in the field of analytics and then moved to various verticals of big data technology. He has worked with reputed organizations, such as Thomson Reuters, IBM, and Flytxt, under different roles. He has worked in the banking, energy, healthcare, and telecom domains and has handled global projects on big data technology.

He has submitted many research papers on technology and business at national and international conferences.

His motto in life is that learning is always a neverending process that helps in understanding, modeling, and presenting new concepts to the modern world.

I surrender myself to God almighty who helped me to review this book in an effective way. I dedicate my work on this book to my dad, Mr. N. Subbian Asari, my lovable mom, Mrs. M. Lekshmi, and my sweet sister, Ms. S.L Jishma, for coordinating and encouraging me to write this book.

Last but not least, I would like to thank all my friends.

www.PacktPub.com

Support files, eBooks, discount offers, and more

For support files and downloads related to your book, please visit www.PacktPub.com.

Did you know that Packt offers eBook versions of every book published, with PDF and ePub files available? You can upgrade to the eBook version at www.PacktPub.com and as a print book customer, you are entitled to a discount on the eBook copy. Get in touch with us at service@packtpub.com for more details.

At www.PacktPub.com, you can also read a collection of free technical articles, sign up for a range of free newsletters and receive exclusive discounts and offers on Packt books and eBooks.

https://www2.packtpub.com/books/subscription/packtlib

Do you need instant solutions to your IT questions? PacktLib is Packt's online digital book library. Here, you can search, access, and read Packt's entire library of books.

Why subscribe?

- ▶ Fully searchable across every book published by Packt
- ▶ Copy and paste, print, and bookmark content
- ▶ On demand and accessible via a web browser

Free access for Packt account holders

If you have an account with Packt at www.PacktPub.com, you can use this to access PacktLib today and view 9 entirely free books. Simply use your login credentials for immediate access.

Table of Contents

Preface

Big data has become a popular buzzword across many industries. An increasing number of people have been exposed to the term and are looking at how to leverage big data in their own businesses, to improve sales and profitability. However, collecting, aggregating, and visualizing data is just one part of the equation. Being able to extract useful information from data is another task, and much more challenging.

Traditionally, most researchers perform statistical analysis using historical samples of data. The main downside of this process is that conclusions drawn from statistical analysis are limited. In fact, researchers usually struggle to uncover hidden patterns and unknown correlations from target data. Aside from applying statistical analysis, machine learning has emerged as an alternative. This process yields a more accurate predictive model with the data inserted into a learning algorithm. Through machine learning, the analysis of business operations and processes is not limited to human-scale thinking. Machine-scale analysis enables businesses to discover hidden values in big data.

The most widely used tool for machine learning and data analysis is the R language. In addition to being the most popular language used by data scientists, R is open source and is free for use for all users. The R programming language offers a variety of learning packages and visualization functions, which enable users to analyze data on the fly. Any user can easily perform machine learning with R on their dataset without knowing every detail of the mathematical models behind the analysis.

Machine Learning with R Cookbook takes a practical approach to teaching you how to perform machine learning with R. Each of the 12 chapters are introduced to you by dividing this topic into several simple recipes. Through the step-by-step instructions provided in each recipe, the reader can construct a predictive model by using a variety of machine learning packages.

In this book, readers are first directed how to set up the R environment and use simple R commands to explore data. The next topic covers how to perform statistical analysis with machine learning analysis and assessing created models, which are covered in detail later on in the book. There is also content on learning how to integrate R and Hadoop to create a big data analysis platform. The detailed illustrations provide all the information required to start applying machine learning to individual projects.

With *Machine Learning with R Cookbook*, users will feel that machine learning has never been easier.

What this book covers

Chapter 1, Practical Machine Learning with R, describes how to create a ready-to-use R environment. Furthermore, we cover all the basic R operations, from reading data into R, manipulating data, and performing simple statistics, to visualizing data.

Chapter 2, Data Exploration with RMS Titanic, provides you an opportunity to perform exploratory analysis in R. In this chapter, we walk you through the process of transforming, analyzing, and visualizing the RMS Titanic data. We conclude by creating a prediction model to identify the possible survivors of the Titanic tragedy.

Chapter 3, R and Statistics, begins with an emphasis on data sampling and probability distribution. Subsequently, the chapter demonstrates how to perform descriptive statistics and inferential statistics on data.

Chapter 4, Understanding Regression Analysis, analyzes the linear relationship between a dependent (response) variable and one or more independent (predictor) sets of explanatory variables. You will learn how to use different regression models to make sense of numeric relationships, and further apply a fitted model to data for continuous value prediction.

Chapter 5, Classification (I) – Tree, Lazy, Probabilistic, teaches you how to fit data into a tree-based classifier, k-nearest neighbor classifier, logistic regression classifier, or the Naïve Bayes classifier. In order to understand how classification works, we provide an example with the purpose of identifying possible customer churns from a telecom dataset.

Chapter 6, Classification (II) – Neural Network, SVM, introduces two complex but powerful classification methods: neural networks and support vector machines. Despite the complex nature of these methods, this chapter shows how easy it is to make an accurate prediction using these algorithms in R.

Chapter 7, Model Evaluation, reveals some measurements that you can use to evaluate the performance of a fitted model. With these measurements, we can select the optimum model that accurately predicts responses for future subjects.

Chapter 8, Ensemble Learning, introduces how to use the power of ensemble learners to produce better classification and regression results, as compared to a single learner. As an ensemble learner is frequently the winning approach in many data prediction competitions; you should know how to apply ensemble learners to your projects.

Chapter 9, Clustering, explores different types of clustering methods. Clustering can group similar points of data together. In this chapter, we demonstrate how to apply the clustering technique to segment customers and further compare differences between each clustering method.

Chapter 10, Association Analysis and Sequence Mining, exposes you to the common methods used to discover associated items and underlying frequent patterns from transaction data. This chapter is a must read for those of you interested in finding out how researchers discovered the famous association between customers that purchase beer and those who purchase diapers.

Chapter 11, Dimension Reduction, teaches you how to select and extract features from original variables. With this technique, we can remove the effect from redundant features, and reduce the computational cost to avoid overfitting. For a more concrete example, this chapter reveals how to compress and restore an image with the dimension reduction approach.

Chapter 12, Big Data Analysis (R and Hadoop), reveals how you can use RHadoop, which allows R to leverage the scalability of Hadoop, so as to process and analyze big data. We cover all the steps, from setting up the RHadoop environment to actual big data processing and machine learning on big data. Lastly, we explore how to deploy an RHadoop cluster using Amazon EC2.

Appendix A, Resources for R and Machine Learning, will provide you with all the resources for R and machine learning.

Appendix B, Dataset – Survival of Passengers on the Titanic, shows you the dataset for survival of passengers on the Titanic.

What you need for this book

To follow the book's examples, you will need a computer with access to the Internet and the ability to install the R environment. You can download R from `http://www.cran.r-project.org/`. Detailed installation instructions are available in the first chapter.

The examples provided in this book were coded and tested with R Version 3.1.2 on a computer with Microsoft Windows installed on it. These examples should also work with any recent version of R installed on either MAC OSX or a Unix-like OS.

Who this book is for

This book is ideal for those of you who want to learn how to use R for machine learning and gain insights from data. Regardless of your level of experience, this book covers the basics of applying R to machine learning through advanced techniques. While it is helpful if you are familiar with basic programming or machine learning concepts, you do not require prior experience to benefit from this book.

Sections

In this book, you will find several headings that appear frequently (Getting ready, How to do it, How it works, There's more, and See also).

To give clear instructions on how to complete a recipe, we use these sections as follows:

Getting ready

This section tells you what to expect in the recipe, and describes how to set up any software or any preliminary settings required for the recipe.

How to do it...

This section contains the steps required to follow the recipe.

How it works...

This section usually consists of a detailed explanation of what happened in the previous section.

There's more...

This section consists of additional information about the recipe in order to make the reader more knowledgeable about the recipe.

See also

This section provides helpful links to other useful information for the recipe.

Conventions

This book contains a number of styles of text that distinguish between different kinds of information. Here are some examples of these styles, and an explanation of their meaning.

Code words in text, database table names, folder names, filenames, file extensions, pathnames, dummy URLs, user input, and Twitter handles are shown as follows: "Use the `rpart` function to build a classification tree model."

A block of code is set as follows:

```
> churn.rp = rpart(churn ~ ., data=trainset)
```

Any command-line input or output is written as follows:

```
$ sudo R CMD INSTALL rmr2_3.3.0.tar.gz
```

New terms and **important words** are shown in bold. Words that you see on the screen, in menus or dialog boxes for example, appear in text in the following format: "In R, a missing value is noted with the symbol **NA (not available)**, and an impossible value is **NaN (not a number)**."

Warnings or important notes appear in a box like this.

Tips and tricks appear like this.

Reader feedback

Feedback from our readers is always welcome. Let us know what you think about this book— what you liked or disliked. Reader feedback is important for us as it helps us develop titles that you will really get the most out of.

To send us general feedback, simply e-mail feedback@packtpub.com, and mention the book's title in the subject of your message.

If there is a topic that you have expertise in and you are interested in either writing or contributing to a book, see our author guide at www.packtpub.com/authors.

Customer support

Now that you are the proud owner of a Packt book, we have a number of things to help you to get the most from your purchase.

Downloading the example code

You can download the example code files from your account at `http://www.packtpub.com` for all the Packt Publishing books you have purchased. If you purchased this book elsewhere, you can visit `http://www.packtpub.com/support` and register to have the files e-mailed directly to you.

Errata

Although we have taken every care to ensure the accuracy of our content, mistakes do happen. If you find a mistake in one of our books—maybe a mistake in the text or the code—we would be grateful if you could report this to us. By doing so, you can save other readers from frustration and help us improve subsequent versions of this book. If you find any errata, please report them by visiting `http://www.packtpub.com/submit-errata`, selecting your book, clicking on the **Errata Submission Form** link, and entering the details of your errata. Once your errata are verified, your submission will be accepted and the errata will be uploaded to our website or added to any list of existing errata under the Errata section of that title.

To view the previously submitted errata, go to `https://www.packtpub.com/books/content/support` and enter the name of the book in the search field. The required information will appear under the **Errata** section.

Piracy

Piracy of copyrighted material on the Internet is an ongoing problem across all media. At Packt, we take the protection of our copyright and licenses very seriously. If you come across any illegal copies of our works in any form on the Internet, please provide us with the location address or website name immediately so that we can pursue a remedy.

Please contact us at `copyright@packtpub.com` with a link to the suspected pirated material.

We appreciate your help in protecting our authors and our ability to bring you valuable content.

Questions

If you have a problem with any aspect of this book, you can contact us at `questions@packtpub.com`, and we will do our best to address the problem.

1

Practical Machine Learning with R

In this chapter, we will cover the following topics:

- ▶ Downloading and installing R
- ▶ Downloading and installing RStudio
- ▶ Installing and loading packages
- ▶ Reading and writing data
- ▶ Using R to manipulate data
- ▶ Applying basic statistics
- ▶ Visualizing data
- ▶ Getting a dataset for machine learning

Introduction

The aim of machine learning is to uncover hidden patterns, unknown correlations, and find useful information from data. In addition to this, through incorporation with data analysis, machine learning can be used to perform predictive analysis. With machine learning, the analysis of business operations and processes is not limited to human scale thinking; machine scale analysis enables businesses to capture hidden values in big data.

Machine learning has similarities to the human reasoning process. Unlike traditional analysis, the generated model cannot evolve as data is accumulated. Machine learning can learn from the data that is processed and analyzed. In other words, the more data that is processed, the more it can learn.

R, as a dialect of GNU-S, is a powerful statistical language that can be used to manipulate and analyze data. Additionally, R provides many machine learning packages and visualization functions, which enable users to analyze data on the fly. Most importantly, R is open source and free.

Using R greatly simplifies machine learning. All you need to know is how each algorithm can solve your problem, and then you can simply use a written package to quickly generate prediction models on data with a few command lines. For example, you can either perform Naïve Bayes for spam mail filtering, conduct k-means clustering for customer segmentation, use linear regression to forecast house prices, or implement a hidden Markov model to predict the stock market, as shown in the following screenshot:

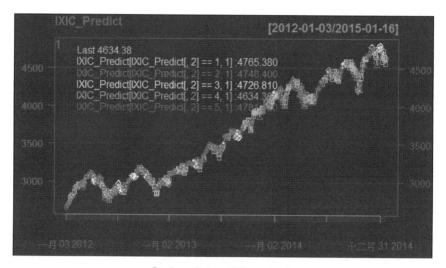

Stock market prediction using R

Moreover, you can perform nonlinear dimension reduction to calculate the dissimilarity of image data, and visualize the clustered graph, as shown in the following screenshot. All you need to do is follow the recipes provided in this book.

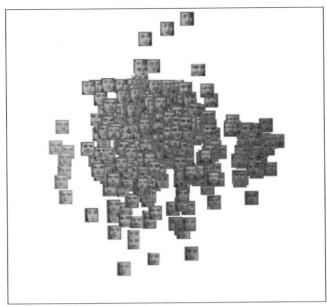

A clustered graph of face image data

This chapter serves as an overall introduction to machine learning and R; the first few recipes introduce how to set up the R environment and integrated development environment, RStudio. After setting up the environment, the following recipe introduces package installation and loading. In order to understand how data analysis is practiced using R, the next four recipes cover data read/write, data manipulation, basic statistics, and data visualization using R. The last recipe in the chapter lists useful data sources and resources.

Downloading and installing R

To use R, you must first install it on your computer. This recipe gives detailed instructions on how to download and install R.

Getting ready

If you are new to the R language, you can find a detailed introduction, language history, and functionality on the official website (http://www.r-project.org/). When you are ready to download and install R, please access the following link: http://cran.r-project.org/.

How to do it...

Please perform the following steps to download and install R for Windows and Mac users:

1. Go to the R CRAN website, `http://www.r-project.org/`, and click on the **download R** link, that is, `http://cran.r-project.org/mirrors.html`):

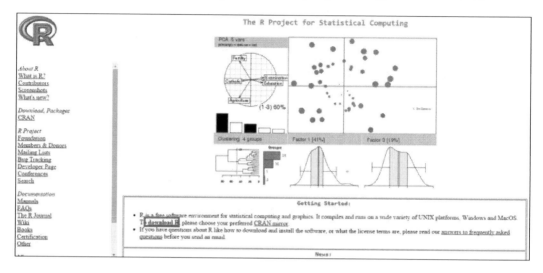

2. You may select the mirror location closest to you:

CRAN mirrors

3. Select the correct download link based on your operating system:

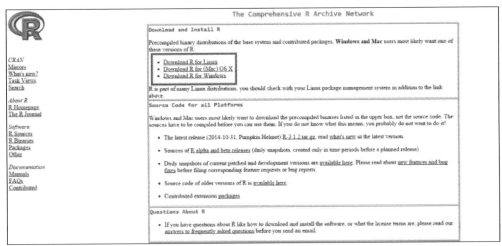

Click on the download link based on your OS

As the installation of R differs for Windows and Mac, the steps required to install R for each OS are provided here.

For Windows users:

1. Click on **Download R for Windows**, as shown in the following screenshot, and then click on **base**:

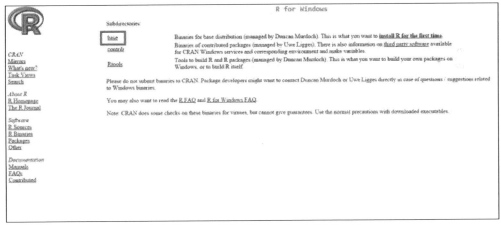

Go to "Download R for Windows" and click "base"

2. Click on **Download R 3.x.x for Windows**:

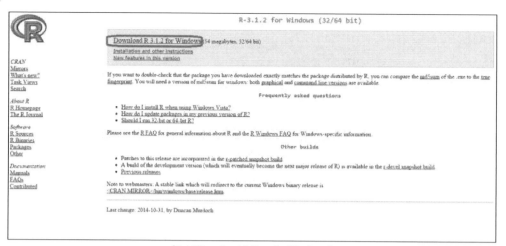

Click "Download R 3.x.x for Windows"

3. The installation file should be downloaded. Once the download is finished, you can double-click on the installation file and begin installing R:

4. The Windows installation of R is quite straightforward; the installation GUI may instruct you on how to install the program step by step (public license, destination location, select components, startup options, startup menu folder, and select additional tasks). Leave all the installation options as the default settings if you do not want to make any changes.

5. After successfully completing the installation, a shortcut to the R application will appear in your Start menu, which will open the R Console:

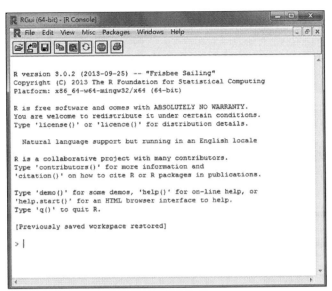

The Windows R Console

For Mac OS X users:

1. Go to **Download R for (Mac) OS X,** as shown in this screenshot.

2. Click on the latest version (.pkg file extension) according to your Mac OS version:

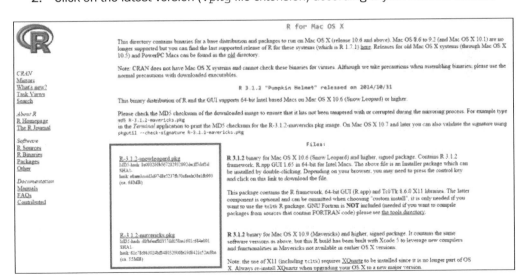

3. Double-click on the downloaded installation file (.pkg extension) and begin to install R. Leave all the installation options as the default settings if you do not want to make any changes:

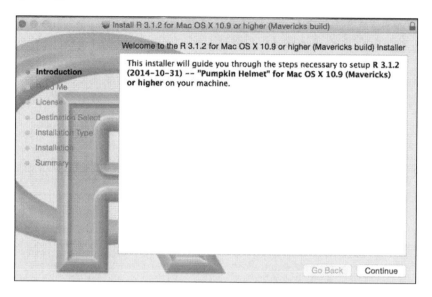

4. Follow the onscreen instructions, **Introduction**, **Read Me**, **License**, **Destination Select**, **Installation Type**, **Installation**, **Summary**, and click on **continue** to complete the installation.

5. After the file is installed, you can use **Spotlight Search** or go to the application folder to find R:

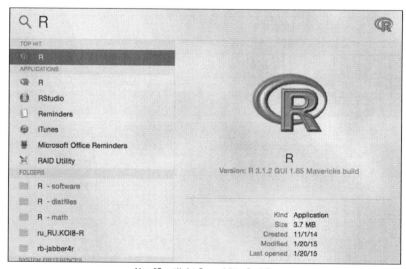

Use "Spotlight Search" to find R

6. Click on R to open **R Console**:

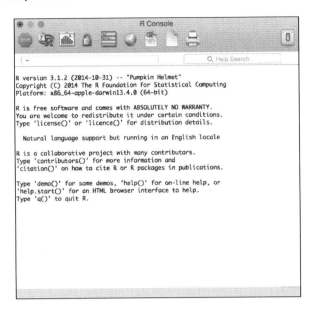

As an alternative to downloading a Mac `.pkg` file to install R, Mac users can also install R using Homebrew:

1. Download `XQuartz-2.X.X.dmg` from `https://xquartz.macosforge.org/landing/`.

2. Double-click on the `.dmg` file to mount it.

3. Update brew with the following command line:

    ```
    $ brew update
    ```

4. Clone the repository and symlink all its formulae to `homebrew/science`:

    ```
    $ brew tap homebrew/science
    ```

5. Install gfortran:

    ```
    $ brew install gfortran
    ```

6. Install R:

    ```
    $ brew install R
    ```

For Linux users, there are precompiled binaries for Debian, Red Hat, SUSE, and Ubuntu. Alternatively, you can install R from a source code. Besides downloading precompiled binaries, you can install R for Linux through a package manager. Here are the installation steps for CentOS and Ubuntu.

Downloading and installing R on Ubuntu:

1. Add the entry to the `/etc/apt/sources.list` file:

   ```
   $ sudo sh -c "echo 'deb http:// cran.stat.ucla.edu/bin/linux/
   ubuntu precise/' >> /etc/apt/sources.list"
   ```

2. Then, update the repository:

   ```
   $ sudo apt-get update
   ```

3. Install R with the following command:

   ```
   $ sudo apt-get install r-base
   ```

4. Start R in the command line:

   ```
   $ R
   ```

Downloading and installing R on CentOS 5:

1. Get rpm CentOS5 RHEL EPEL repository of CentOS5:

   ```
   $ wget http://dl.fedoraproject.org/pub/epel/5/x86_64/epel-
   release-5-4.noarch.rpm
   ```

2. Install CentOS5 RHEL EPEL repository:

   ```
   $ sudo rpm -Uvh epel-release-5-4.noarch.rpm
   ```

3. Update the installed packages:

   ```
   $ sudo yum update
   ```

4. Install R through the repository:

   ```
   $ sudo yum install R
   ```

5. Start R in the command line:

   ```
   $ R
   ```

Downloading and installing R on CentOS 6:

1. Get rpm CentOS5 RHEL EPEL repository of CentOS6:

   ```
   $ wget http://dl.fedoraproject.org/pub/epel/6/x86_64/epel-
   release-6-8.noarch.rpm
   ```

2. Install the CentOS5 RHEL EPEL repository:

   ```
   $ sudo rpm -Uvh epel-release-6-8.noarch.rpm
   ```

3. Update the installed packages:

   ```
   $ sudo yum update
   ```

4. Install R through the repository:

```
$ sudo yum install R
```

5. Start R in the command line:

```
$ R
```

How it works...

CRAN provides precompiled binaries for Linux, Mac OS X, and Windows. For Mac and Windows users, the installation procedures are straightforward. You can generally follow onscreen instructions to complete the installation. For Linux users, you can use the package manager provided for each platform to install R or build R from the source code.

See also

▶ For those planning to build R from the source code, refer to **R Installation and Administration** (http://cran.r-project.org/doc/manuals/R-admin.html), which illustrates how to install R on a variety of platforms.

Downloading and installing RStudio

To write an R script, one can use R Console, R commander, or any text editor (EMACS, VIM, or sublime). However, the assistance of RStudio, an **integrated development environment** (**IDE**) for R, can make development a lot easier.

RStudio provides comprehensive facilities for software development. Built-in features such as syntax highlighting, code completion, and smart indentation help maximize productivity. To make R programming more manageable, RStudio also integrates the main interface into a four-panel layout. It includes an interactive R Console, a tabbed source code editor, a panel for the currently active objects/history, and a tabbed panel for the file browser/plot window/package install window/R help window. Moreover, RStudio is open source and is available for many platforms, such as Windows, Mac OS X, and Linux. This recipe shows how to download and install RStudio.

Getting ready

RStudio requires a working R installation; when RStudio loads, it must be able to locate a version of R. You must therefore have completed the previous recipe with R installed on your OS before proceeding to install RStudio.

How to do it...

Perform the following steps to download and install RStudio for Windows and Mac users:

1. Access RStudio's official site by using the following URL: `http://www.rstudio.com/products/RStudio/`.

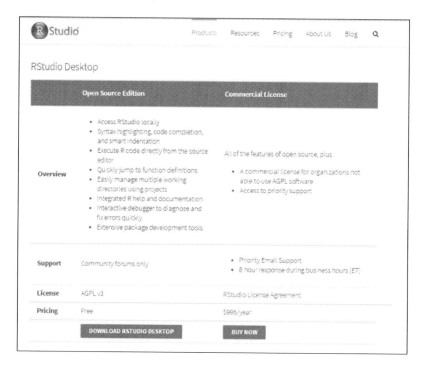

2. For a desktop version installation, click on **Download RStudio Desktop** (`http://www.rstudio.com/products/rstudio/download/`) and choose the RStudio recommended for your system. Download the relevant packages:

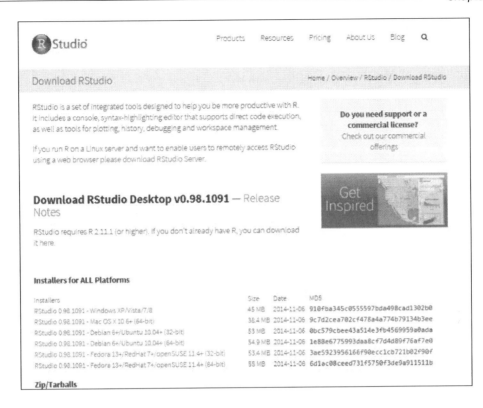

3. Install RStudio by double-clicking on the downloaded packages. For Windows users, follow the onscreen instruction to install the application:

4. For Mac users, simply drag the RStudio icon to the `Applications` folder:

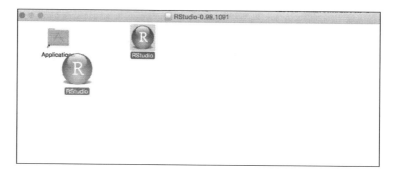

5. Start RStudio:

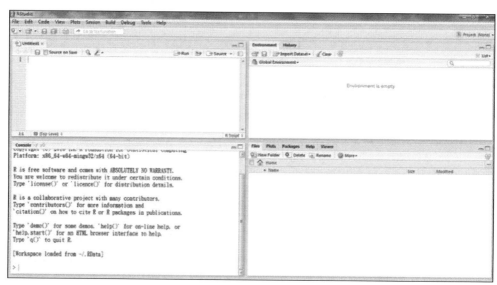

The RStudio console

Perform the following steps for downloading and installing RStudio for Ubuntu/Debian and RedHat/Centos users:

For Debian(6+)/Ubuntu(10.04+) 32-bit:

```
$ wget http://download1.rstudio.org/rstudio-0.98.1091-i386.deb
$ sudo gdebi rstudio-0.98. 1091-i386.deb
```

For Debian(6+)/Ubuntu(10.04+) 64-bit:

```
$ wget http://download1.rstudio.org/rstudio-0.98. 1091-amd64.deb
$ sudo gdebi rstudio-0.98. 1091-amd64.deb
```

For RedHat/CentOS(5,4+) 32 bit:

```
$ wget http://download1.rstudio.org/rstudio-0.98. 1091-i686.rpm
$ sudo yum install --nogpgcheck rstudio-0.98. 1091-i686.rpm
```

For RedHat/CentOS(5,4+) 64 bit:

```
$ wget http://download1.rstudio.org/rstudio-0.98. 1091-x86_64.rpm
$ sudo yum install --nogpgcheck rstudio-0.98. 1091-x86_64.rpm
```

How it works

The RStudio program can be run on the desktop or through a web browser. The desktop version is available for Windows, Mac OS X, and Linux platforms with similar operations across all platforms. For Windows and Mac users, after downloading the precompiled package of RStudio, follow the onscreen instructions, shown in the preceding steps, to complete the installation. Linux users may use the package management system provided for installation.

See also

- In addition to the desktop version, users may install a server version to provide access to multiple users. The server version provides a URL that users can access to use the RStudio resources. To install RStudio, please refer to the following link: http://www.rstudio.com/ide/download/server.html. This page provides installation instructions for the following Linux distributions: Debian (6+), Ubuntu (10.04+), RedHat, and CentOS (5.4+).
- For other Linux distributions, you can build RStudio from the source code.

Installing and loading packages

After successfully installing R, users can download, install, and update packages from the repositories. As R allows users to create their own packages, official and non-official repositories are provided to manage these user-created packages. **CRAN** is the official R package repository. Currently, the CRAN package repository features 6,379 available packages (as of 02/27/2015). Through the use of the packages provided on CRAN, users may extend the functionality of R to machine learning, statistics, and related purposes. CRAN is a network of FTP and web servers around the world that store identical, up-to-date versions of code and documentation for R. You may select the closest CRAN mirror to your location to download packages.

Getting ready

Start an R session on your host computer.

How to do it...

Perform the following steps to install and load R packages:

1. To load a list of installed packages:

   ```
   > library()
   ```

2. Setting the default CRAN mirror:

   ```
   > chooseCRANmirror()
   ```

R will return a list of CRAN mirrors, and then ask the user to either type a mirror ID to select it, or enter zero to exit:

1. Install a package from CRAN; take package e1071 as an example:

   ```
   > install.packages("e1071")
   ```

2. Update a package from CRAN; take package e1071 as an example:

   ```
   > update.packages("e1071")
   ```

3. Load the package the package:

   ```
   > library(e1071)
   ```

4. If you would like to view the documentation of the package, you can use the `help` function:

   ```
   > help(package ="e1071")
   ```

5. If you would like to view the documentation of the function, you can use the `help` function:

   ```
   > help(svm, e1071)
   ```

6. Alternatively, you can use the help shortcut, ?, to view the help document for this function:

   ```
   > ?e1071::svm
   ```

7. If the function does not provide any documentation, you may want to search the supplied documentation for a given keyword. For example, if you wish to search for documentation related to svm:

   ```
   > help.search("svm")
   ```

8. Alternatively, you can use ?? as the shortcut for `help.search`:

   ```
   > ??svm
   ```

9. To view the argument taken for the function, simply use the `args` function. For example, if you would like to know the argument taken for the `lm` function:

   ```
   > args(lm)
   ```

10. Some packages will provide examples and demos; you can use `example` or `demo` to view an example or demo. For example, one can view an example of the `lm` package and a demo of the `graphics` package by typing the following commands:

```
> example(lm)
> demo(graphics)
```

11. To view all the available demos, you may use the demo function to list all of them:

```
> demo()
```

How it works

This recipe first introduces how to view loaded packages, install packages from CRAN, and load new packages. Before installing packages, those of you who are interested in the listing of the CRAN package can refer to `http://cran.r-project.org/web/packages/available_packages_by_name.html`.

When a package is installed, documentation related to the package is also provided. You are, therefore, able to view the documentation or the related help pages of installed packages and functions. Additionally, demos and examples are provided by packages that can help users understand the capability of the installed package.

See also

- Besides installing packages from CRAN, there are other R package repositories, including Crantastic, a community site for rating and reviewing CRAN packages, and R-Forge, a central platform for the collaborative development of R packages. In addition to this, Bioconductor provides R packages for the analysis of genomic data.

- If you would like to find relevant functions and packages, please visit the list of task views at `http://cran.r-project.org/web/views/`, or search for keywords at `http://rseek.org`.

Reading and writing data

Before starting to explore data, you must load the data into the R session. This recipe will introduce methods to load data either from a file into the memory or use the predefined data within R.

Getting ready

First, start an R session on your machine. As this recipe involves steps toward the file IO, if the user does not specify the full path, read and write activity will take place in the current working directory.

You can simply type `getwd()` in the R session to obtain the current working directory location. However, if you would like to change the current working directory, you can use `setwd("<path>")`, where `<path>` can be replaced as your desired path, to specify the working directory.

How to do it...

Perform the following steps to read and write data with R:

1. To view the built-in datasets of R, type the following command:

   ```
   > data()
   ```

2. R will return a list of datasets in a `dataset` package, and the list comprises the name and description of each dataset.

3. To load the dataset `iris` into an R session, type the following command:

   ```
   > data(iris)
   ```

4. The dataset iris is now loaded into the data frame format, which is a common data structure in R to store a data table.

5. To view the data type of iris, simply use the `class` function:

   ```
   > class(iris)
   [1] "data.frame"
   ```

6. The `data.frame` console print shows that the `iris` dataset is in the structure of data frame.

7. Use the save function to store an object in a file. For example, to save the loaded iris data into `myData.RData`, use the following command:

   ```
   > save(iris, file="myData.RData")
   ```

8. Use the load function to read a saved object into an R session. For example, to load iris data from `myData.RData`, use the following command:

   ```
   > load("myData.RData")
   ```

9. In addition to using built-in datasets, R also provides a function to import data from text into a data frame. For example, the `read.table` function can format a given text into a data frame:

   ```
   > test.data = read.table(header = TRUE, text = "
   + a b
   + 1 2
   + 3 4
   + ")
   ```

10. You can also use `row.names` and `col.names` to specify the names of columns and rows:

```
> test.data = read.table(text = "
+ 1 2
+ 3 4",
+ col.names=c("a","b"),
+ row.names = c("first","second"))
```

11. View the class of the `test.data` variable:

```
> class(test.data)
[1] "data.frame"
```

12. The `class` function shows that the `test.data` variable contains a data frame.

13. In addition to importing data by using the `read.table` function, you can use the `write.table` function to export data to a text file:

```
> write.table(test.data, file = "test.txt" , sep = " ")
```

14. The `write.table` function will write the content of `test.data` into `test.txt` (the written path can be found by typing `getwd()`), with a separation delimiter as white space.

15. Similar to `write.table`, `write.csv` can also export data to a file. However, `write.csv` uses a comma as the default delimiter:

```
> write.csv(test.data, file = "test.csv")
```

16. With the `read.csv` function, the `csv` file can be imported as a data frame. However, the last example writes column and row names of the data frame to the `test.csv` file. Therefore, specifying header to `TRUE` and row names as the first column within the function can ensure the read data frame will not treat the header and the first column as values:

```
> csv.data = read.csv("test.csv", header = TRUE, row.names=1)
> head(csv.data)
  a b
1 1 2
2 3 4
```

How it works

Generally, data for collection may be in multiple files and different formats. To exchange data between files and RData, R provides many built-in functions, such as `save`, `load`, `read.csv`, `read.table`, `write.csv`, and `write.table`.

This example first demonstrates how to load the built-in dataset iris into an R session. The iris dataset is the most famous and commonly used dataset in the field of machine learning. Here, we use the iris dataset as an example. The recipe shows how to save RData and load it with the `save` and `load` functions. Furthermore, the example explains how to use `read.table`, `write.table`, `read.csv`, and `write.csv` to exchange data from files to a data frame. The use of the R IO function to read and write data is very important as most of the data sources are external. Therefore, you have to use these functions to load data into an R session.

See also

For the `load`, `read.table`, and `read.csv` functions, the file to be read can also be a complete URL (for supported URLs, use `?url` for more information).

On some occasions, data may be in an Excel file instead of a flat text file. The `WriteXLS` package allows writing an object into an Excel file with a given variable in the first argument and the file to be written in the second argument:

1. Install the `WriteXLS` package:

   ```
   > install.packages("WriteXLS")
   ```

2. Load the `WriteXLS` package:

   ```
   > library("WriteXLS")
   ```

3. Use the `WriteXLS` function to write the data frame iris into a file named `iris.xls`:

   ```
   > WriteXLS("iris", ExcelFileName="iris.xls")
   ```

Using R to manipulate data

This recipe will discuss how to use the built-in R functions to manipulate data. As data manipulation is the most time consuming part of most analysis procedures, you should gain knowledge of how to apply these functions on data.

Getting ready

Ensure you have completed the previous recipes by installing R on your operating system.

How to do it...

Perform the following steps to manipulate the data with R.

Subset the data using the bracelet notation:

1. Load the dataset iris into the R session:

   ```
   > data(iris)
   ```

2. To select values, you may use a bracket notation that designates the indices of the dataset. The first index is for the rows and the second for the columns:

   ```
   > iris[1,"Sepal.Length"]
   [1] 5.1
   ```

3. You can also select multiple columns using c():

   ```
   > Sepal.iris = iris[, c("Sepal.Length", "Sepal.Width")]
   ```

4. You can then use `str()` to summarize and display the internal structure of `Sepal.iris`:

   ```
   > str(Sepal.iris)
   'data.frame':  150 obs. of  2 variables:
    $ Sepal.Length: num  5.1 4.9 4.7 4.6 5 5.4 4.6 5 4.4 4.9 ...
    $ Sepal.Width : num  3.5 3 3.2 3.1 3.6 3.9 3.4 3.4 2.9 3.1 ..
   ```

5. To subset data with the rows of given indices, you can specify the indices at the first index with the bracket notation. In this example, we show you how to subset data with the top five records with the `Sepal.Length` column and the `Sepal.Width` selected:

   ```
   > Five.Sepal.iris = iris[1:5, c("Sepal.Length", "Sepal.Width")]
   > str(Five.Sepal.iris)
   'data.frame': 5 obs. of  2 variables:
    $ Sepal.Length: num  5.1 4.9 4.7 4.6 5
    $ Sepal.Width : num  3.5 3 3.2 3.1 3.6
   ```

6. It is also possible to set conditions to filter the data. For example, to filter returned records containing the setosa data with all five variables. In the following example, the first index specifies the returning criteria, and the second index specifies the range of indices of the variable returned:

   ```
   > setosa.data = iris[iris$Species=="setosa",1:5]
   > str(setosa.data)
   'data.frame': 50 obs. of  5 variables:
    $ Sepal.Length: num  5.1 4.9 4.7 4.6 5 5.4 4.6 5 4.4 4.9 ...
    $ Sepal.Width : num  3.5 3 3.2 3.1 3.6 3.9 3.4 3.4 2.9 3.1 ...
    $ Petal.Length: num  1.4 1.4 1.3 1.5 1.4 1.7 1.4 1.5 1.4 1.5 ...
    $ Petal.Width : num  0.2 0.2 0.2 0.2 0.2 0.4 0.3 0.2 0.2 0.1 ...
    $ Species      : Factor w/ 3 levels "setosa","versicolor",..: 1 1 1 1 1 1 1 1 1 1 ...
   ```

7. Alternatively, the `which` function returns the indexes of satisfied data. The following example returns indices of the iris data containing species equal to `setosa`:

```
> which(iris$Species=="setosa")
 [1]  1  2  3  4  5  6  7  8  9 10 11 12 13 14 15 16 17 18
[19] 19 20 21 22 23 24 25 26 27 28 29 30 31 32 33 34 35 36
[37] 37 38 39 40 41 42 43 44 45 46 47 48 49 50
```

8. The indices returned by the operation can then be applied as the index to select the iris containing the setosa species. The following example returns the setosa with all five variables:

```
> setosa.data = iris[which(iris$Species=="setosa"),1:5]
> str(setosa.data)
'data.frame': 50 obs. of  5 variables:
 $ Sepal.Length: num  5.1 4.9 4.7 4.6 5 5.4 4.6 5 4.4 4.9 ...
 $ Sepal.Width : num  3.5 3 3.2 3.1 3.6 3.9 3.4 3.4 2.9 3.1 ...
 $ Petal.Length: num  1.4 1.4 1.3 1.5 1.4 1.7 1.4 1.5 1.4 1.5 ...
 $ Petal.Width : num  0.2 0.2 0.2 0.2 0.2 0.4 0.3 0.2 0.2 0.1 ...
 $ Species     : Factor w/ 3 levels "setosa","versicolor",..: 1 1
1 1 1 1 1 1 ...
```

Subset data using the `subset` function:

1. Besides using the bracket notation, R provides a `subset` function that enables users to subset the data frame by observations with a logical statement.

2. First, subset species, sepal length, and sepal width out of the iris data. To select the sepal length and width out of the iris data, one should specify the column to be subset in the `select` argument:

```
> Sepal.data = subset(iris, select=c("Sepal.Length", "Sepal.
Width"))
> str(Sepal.data)
'data.frame': 150 obs. of  2 variables:
 $ Sepal.Length: num  5.1 4.9 4.7 4.6 5 5.4 4.6 5 4.4 4.9 ...
 $ Sepal.Width : num  3.5 3 3.2 3.1 3.6 3.9 3.4 3.4 2.9 3.1 ...
```

This reveals that `Sepal.data` contains 150 objects with the `Sepal.Length` variable and `Sepal.Width`.

1. On the other hand, you can use a subset argument to get subset data containing setosa only. In the second argument of the subset function, you can specify the subset criteria:

```
> setosa.data = subset(iris, Species =="setosa")
> str(setosa.data)
'data.frame': 50 obs. of  5 variables:
 $ Sepal.Length: num  5.1 4.9 4.7 4.6 5 5.4 4.6 5 4.4 4.9 ...
 $ Sepal.Width : num  3.5 3 3.2 3.1 3.6 3.9 3.4 3.4 2.9 3.1 ...
 $ Petal.Length: num  1.4 1.4 1.3 1.5 1.4 1.7 1.4 1.5 1.4 1.5 ...
 $ Petal.Width : num  0.2 0.2 0.2 0.2 0.2 0.4 0.3 0.2 0.2 0.1 ...
 $ Species     : Factor w/ 3 levels "setosa","versicolor",..: 1 1
 1 1 1 1 1 1 ...
```

2. Most of the time, you may want to apply a union or intersect a condition while subsetting data. The OR and AND operations can be further employed for this purpose. For example, if you would like to retrieve data with `Petal.Width >=0.2` and `Petal.Length < = 1.4`:

```
> example.data= subset(iris, Petal.Length <=1.4 & Petal.Width >=
0.2, select=Species )
> str(example.data)
'data.frame': 21 obs. of  1 variable:
 $ Species: Factor w/ 3 levels "setosa","versicolor",..: 1 1 1 1 1
 1 1 1 1 1 ...
```

Merging data: merging data involves joining two data frames into a merged data frame by a common column or row name. The following example shows how to merge the `flower.type` data frame and the first three rows of the iris with a common row name within the `Species` column:

```
> flower.type = data.frame(Species = "setosa", Flower = "iris")
> merge(flower.type, iris[1:3,], by ="Species")
  Species Flower Sepal.Length Sepal.Width Petal.Length Petal.Width
1 setosa   iris          5.1         3.5          1.4         0.2
2 setosa   iris          4.9         3.0          1.4         0.2
3 setosa   iris          4.7         3.2          1.3         0.2
```

Ordering data: the `order` function will return the index of a sorted data frame with a specified column. The following example shows the results from the first six records with the sepal length ordered (from big to small) iris data

```
> head(iris[order(iris$Sepal.Length, decreasing = TRUE),])
    Sepal.Length Sepal.Width Petal.Length Petal.Width   Species
132          7.9         3.8          6.4         2.0 virginica
118          7.7         3.8          6.7         2.2 virginica
```

119	7.7	2.6	6.9	2.3 virginica
123	7.7	2.8	6.7	2.0 virginica
136	7.7	3.0	6.1	2.3 virginica
106	7.6	3.0	6.6	2.1 virginica

How it works

Before conducting data analysis, it is important to organize collected data into a structured format. Therefore, we can simply use the R data frame to subset, merge, and order a dataset. This recipe first introduces two methods to subset data: one uses the bracket notation, while the other uses the `subset` function. You can use both methods to generate the subset data by selecting columns and filtering data with the given criteria. The recipe then introduces the `merge` function to merge data frames. Last, the recipe introduces how to use `order` to sort the data.

There's more...

The `sub` and `gsub` functions allow using regular expression to substitute a string. The `sub` and `gsub` functions perform the replacement of the first and all the other matches, respectively:

```
> sub("e", "q", names(iris))
[1] "Sqpal.Length" "Sqpal.Width"  "Pqtal.Length" "Pqtal.Width"  "Spqcies"
> gsub("e", "q", names(iris))
[1] "Sqpal.Lqngth" "Sqpal.Width"  "Pqtal.Lqngth" "Pqtal.Width"  "Spqciqs"
```

Applying basic statistics

R provides a wide range of statistical functions, allowing users to obtain the summary statistics of data, generate frequency and contingency tables, produce correlations, and conduct statistical inferences. This recipe covers basic statistics that can be applied to a dataset.

Getting ready

Ensure you have completed the previous recipes by installing R on your operating system.

How to do it...

Perform the following steps to apply statistics on a dataset:

1. Load the iris data into an R session:

    ```
    > data(iris)
    ```

2. Observe the format of the data:

```
> class(iris)
  [1] "data.frame"
```

3. The iris dataset is a data frame containing four numeric attributes: petal length, petal width, sepal width, and sepal length. For numeric values, you can perform descriptive statistics, such as mean, sd, var, min, max, median, range, and quantile. These can be applied to any of the four attributes in the dataset:

```
> mean(iris$Sepal.Length)
[1] 5.843333
> sd(iris$Sepal.Length)
[1] 0.8280661
> var(iris$Sepal.Length)
[1] 0.6856935
> min(iris$Sepal.Length)
[1] 4.3
> max(iris$Sepal.Length)
[1] 7.9
> median(iris$Sepal.Length)
[1] 5.8
> range(iris$Sepal.Length)
[1] 4.3 7.9
> quantile(iris$Sepal.Length)
   0%   25%   50%   75%  100%
  4.3   5.1   5.8   6.4   7.9
```

4. The preceding example demonstrates how to apply descriptive statistics on a single variable. In order to obtain summary statistics on every numeric attribute of the data frame, one may use sapply. For example, to apply the mean on the first four attributes in the iris data frame, ignore the na value by setting na.rm as TRUE:

```
> sapply(iris[1:4], mean, na.rm=TRUE)
Sepal.Length  Sepal.Width Petal.Length  Petal.Width
    5.843333     3.057333     3.758000     1.199333
```

5. As an alternative to using sapply to apply descriptive statistics on given attributes, R offers the summary function that provides a full range of descriptive statistics. In the following example, the summary function provides the mean, median, 25th and 75th quartiles, min, and max of every iris dataset numeric attribute:

```
> summary(iris)
Sepal.Length    Sepal.Width    Petal.Length    Petal.Width
Species
```

```
Min.    :4.300     Min.    :2.000     Min.    :1.000     Min.    :0.100
setosa    :50
1st Qu.:5.100     1st Qu.:2.800     1st Qu.:1.600     1st Qu.:0.300
versicolor:50
Median :5.800     Median :3.000     Median :4.350     Median :1.300
virginica :50
Mean    :5.843     Mean    :3.057     Mean    :3.758     Mean    :1.199
3rd Qu.:6.400     3rd Qu.:3.300     3rd Qu.:5.100     3rd Qu.:1.800
Max.    :7.900     Max.    :4.400     Max.    :6.900     Max.    :2.500
```

6. The preceding example shows how to output the descriptive statistics of a single variable. R also provides the correlation for users to investigate the relationship between variables. The following example generates a 4x4 matrix by computing the correlation of each attribute pair within the iris:

```
> cor(iris[,1:4])
             Sepal.Length Sepal.Width Petal.Length Petal.Width
Sepal.Length    1.0000000   -0.1175698    0.8717538    0.8179411
Sepal.Width    -0.1175698    1.0000000   -0.4284401   -0.3661259
Petal.Length    0.8717538   -0.4284401    1.0000000    0.9628654
Petal.Width     0.8179411   -0.3661259    0.9628654    1.0000000
```

7. R also provides a function to compute the covariance of each attribute pair within the iris:

```
> cov(iris[,1:4])
             Sepal.Length Sepal.Width Petal.Length Petal.Width
Sepal.Length    0.6856935   -0.0424340    1.2743154    0.5162707
Sepal.Width    -0.0424340    0.1899794   -0.3296564   -0.1216394
Petal.Length    1.2743154   -0.3296564    3.1162779    1.2956094
Petal.Width     0.5162707   -0.1216394    1.2956094    0.5810063
```

8. Statistical tests are performed to access the significance of the results; here we demonstrate how to use a t-test to determine the statistical differences between two samples. In this example, we perform a t.test on the petal width an of an iris in either the setosa or versicolor species. If we obtain a p-value less than 0.5, we can be certain that the petal width between the setosa and versicolor will vary significantly:

```
> t.test(iris$Petal.Width[iris$Species=="setosa"],
+        iris$Petal.Width[iris$Species=="versicolor"])


    Welch Two Sample t-test
```

```
data:  iris$Petal.Width[iris$Species == "setosa"] and iris$Petal.
Width[iris$Species == "versicolor"]

t = -34.0803, df = 74.755, p-value < 2.2e-16

alternative hypothesis: true difference in means is not equal to 0

95 percent confidence interval:

 -1.143133 -1.016867

sample estimates:

mean of x mean of y

     0.246     1.326
```

9. Alternatively, you can perform a correlation test on the sepal length to the sepal width of an iris, and then retrieve a correlation score between the two variables. The stronger the positive correlation, the closer the value is to 1. The stronger the negative correlation, the closer the value is to -1:

```
> cor.test(iris$Sepal.Length, iris$Sepal.Width)


    Pearson's product-moment correlation


data:  iris$Sepal.Length and iris$Sepal.Width
t = -1.4403, df = 148, p-value = 0.1519
alternative hypothesis: true correlation is not equal to 0
95 percent confidence interval:
 -0.27269325  0.04351158
sample estimates:
       cor
-0.1175698
```

How it works...

R has a built-in statistics function, which enables the user to perform descriptive statistics on a single variable. The recipe first introduces how to apply mean, sd, var, min, max, median, range, and quantile on a single variable. Moreover, in order to apply the statistics on all four numeric variables, one can use the sapply function. In order to determine the relationships between multiple variables, one can conduct correlation and covariance. Finally, the recipe shows how to determine the statistical differences of two given samples by performing a statistical test.

There's more...

If you need to compute an aggregated summary statistics against data in different groups, you can use the aggregate and reshape functions to compute the summary statistics of data subsets:

1. Use `aggregate` to calculate the mean of each iris attribute group by the species:

    ```
    > aggregate(x=iris[,1:4],by=list(iris$Species),FUN=mean)
    ```

2. Use `reshape` to calculate the mean of each iris attribute group by the species:

    ```
    >   library(reshape)
    >   iris.melt <- melt(iris,id='Species')
    >   cast(Species~variable,data=iris.melt,mean,
            subset=Species %in% c('setosa','versicolor'),
            margins='grand_row')
    ```

For information on reshape and aggregate, refer to the help documents by using `?reshape` or `?aggregate`.

Visualizing data

Visualization is a powerful way to communicate information through graphical means. Visual presentations make data easier to comprehend. This recipe presents some basic functions to plot charts, and demonstrates how visualizations are helpful in data exploration.

Getting ready

Ensure that you have completed the previous recipes by installing R on your operating system.

How to do it...

Perform the following steps to visualize a dataset:

1. Load the iris data into the R session:

    ```
    > data(iris)
    ```

2. Calculate the frequency of species within the iris using the `table` command:

    ```
    > table.iris = table(iris$Species)
    > table.iris

        setosa versicolor  virginica
            50         50         50
    ```

3. As the frequency in the table shows, each species represents 1/3 of the iris data. We can draw a simple pie chart to represent the distribution of species within the iris:

```
> pie(table.iris)
```

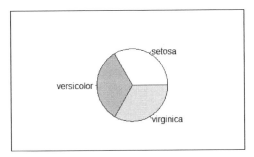

The pie chart of species distribution

4. The histogram creates a frequency plot of sorts along the x-axis. The following example produces a histogram of the sepal length:

```
> hist(iris$Sepal.Length)
```

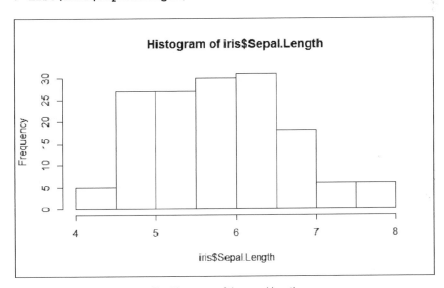

The histogram of the sepal length

5. In the histogram, the x-axis presents the sepal length and the y-axis presents the count for different sepal lengths. The histogram shows that for most irises, sepal lengths range from 4 cm to 8 cm.

6. Boxplots, also named box and whisker graphs, allow you to convey a lot of information in one simple plot. In such a graph, the line represents the median of the sample. The box itself shows the upper and lower quartiles. The whiskers show the range:

```
> boxplot(Petal.Width ~ Species, data = iris)
```

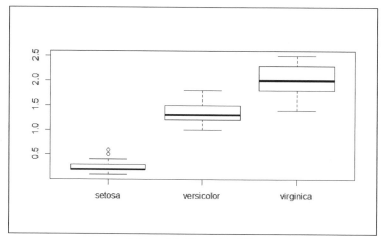

The boxplot of the petal width

7. The preceding screenshot clearly shows the median and upper range of the petal width of the setosa is much shorter than versicolor and virginica. Therefore, the petal width can be used as a substantial attribute to distinguish iris species.

8. A scatter plot is used when there are two variables to plot against one another. This example plots the petal length against the petal width and color dots in accordance to the species it belongs to:

```
> plot(x=iris$Petal.Length, y=iris$Petal.Width, col=iris$Species)
```

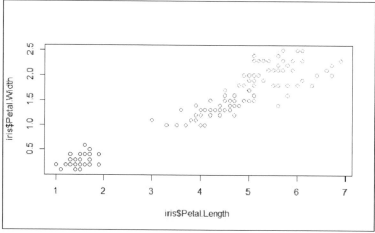

The scatter plot of the sepal length

9. The preceding screenshot is a scatter plot of the petal length against the petal width. As there are four attributes within the iris dataset, it takes six operations to plot all combinations. However, R provides a function named `pairs`, which can generate each subplot in one figure:

```
> pairs(iris[1:4], main = "Edgar Anderson's Iris Data", pch = 21,
bg = c("red", "green3", "blue")[unclass(iris$Species)])
```

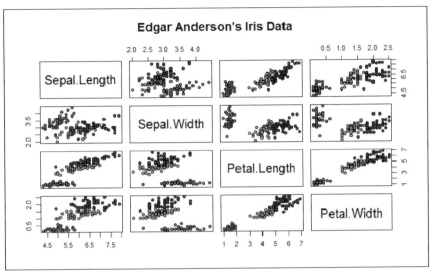

Pairs scatterplot of iris data

How it works...

R provides many built-in plot functions, which enable users to visualize data with different kinds of plots. This recipe demonstrates the use of pie charts that can present category distribution. A pie chart of an equal size shows that the number of each species is equal. A histogram plots the frequency of different sepal lengths. A box plot can convey a great deal of descriptive statistics, and shows that the petal width can be used to distinguish an iris species. Lastly, we introduced scatter plots, which plot variables on a single plot. In order to quickly generate a scatter plot containing all the pairs of iris data, one may use the `pairs` command.

See also

▶ ggplot2 is another plotting system for R, based on the implementation of Leland Wilkinson's grammar of graphics. It allows users to add, remove, or alter components in a plot with a higher abstraction. However, the level of abstraction results is slow compared to lattice graphics. For those of you interested in the topic of ggplot, you can refer to this site: http://ggplot2.org/.

Getting a dataset for machine learning

While R has a built-in dataset, the sample size and field of application is limited. Apart from generating data within a simulation, another approach is to obtain data from external data repositories. A famous data repository is the UCI machine learning repository, which contains both artificial and real datasets. This recipe introduces how to get a sample dataset from the UCI machine learning repository.

Getting ready

Ensure that you have completed the previous recipes by installing R on your operating system.

How to do it...

Perform the following steps to retrieve data for machine learning:

1. Access the UCI machine learning repository: `http://archive.ics.uci.edu/ml/`.

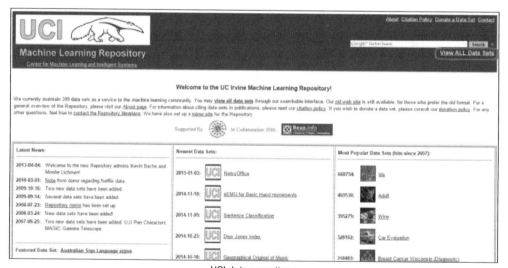

UCI data repository

2. Click on **View ALL Data Sets**. Here you will find a list of datasets containing field names, such as **Name**, **Data Types**, **Default Task**, **Attribute Types**, **# Instances**, **# Attributes**, and **Year**:

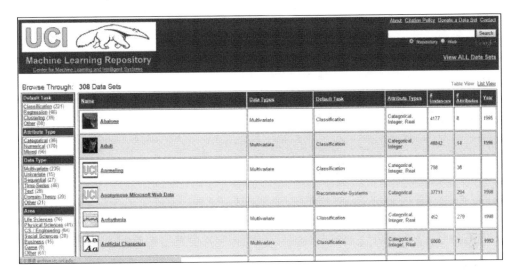

3. Use *Ctrl + F* to search for **Iris**:

4. Click on **Iris**. This will display the data folder and the dataset description:

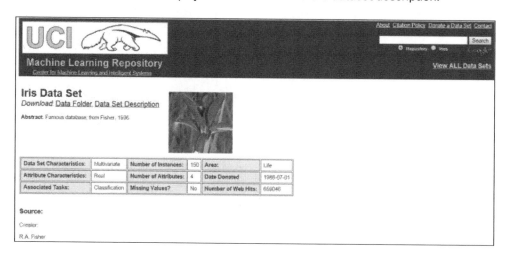

5. Click on **Data Folder**, which will display a directory containing the iris dataset:

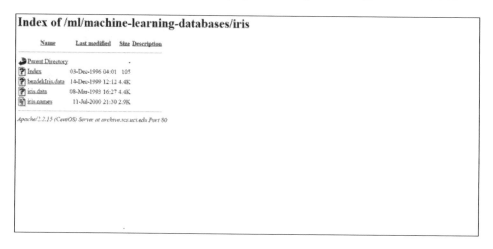

6. You can then either download `iris.data` or use the `read.csv` function to read the dataset:

```
> iris.data = read.csv(url("http://archive.ics.uci.edu/ml/machine-
learning-databases/iris/iris.data"), header = FALSE,  col.names =
c("Sepal.Length", "Sepal.Width", "Petal.Length", "Petal.Width",
"Species"))
```

```
> head(iris.data)
```

	Sepal.Length	Sepal.Width	Petal.Length	Petal.Width	Species
1	5.1	3.5	1.4	0.2	Iris-setosa
2	4.9	3.0	1.4	0.2	Iris-setosa
3	4.7	3.2	1.3	0.2	Iris-setosa
4	4.6	3.1	1.5	0.2	Iris-setosa
5	5.0	3.6	1.4	0.2	Iris-setosa
6	5.4	3.9	1.7	0.4	Iris-setosa

How it works...

Before conducting data analysis, it is important to collect your dataset. However, to collect an appropriate dataset for further exploration and analysis is not easy. We can, therefore, use the prepared dataset with the UCI repository as our data source. Here, we first access the UCI dataset repository and then use the iris dataset as an example. We can find the iris dataset by using the browser's find function (*Ctrl + F*), and then enter the file directory. Last, we can download the dataset and use the R IO function, `read.csv`, to load the iris dataset into an R session.

See also

 ▶ KDnuggets (`http://www.kdnuggets.com/datasets/index.html`) offers a resourceful list of datasets for data mining and data science. You can explore the list to find the data that satisfies your requirements.

2
Data Exploration with RMS Titanic

In this chapter, we will cover the following recipes:

- ▸ Reading a Titanic dataset from a CSV file
- ▸ Converting types on character variables
- ▸ Detecting missing values
- ▸ Imputing missing values
- ▸ Exploring and visualizing data
- ▸ Predicting passenger survival with a decision tree
- ▸ Validating the power of prediction with a confusion matrix
- ▸ Assessing performance with the ROC curve

Introduction

Data exploration helps a data consumer to focus on searching for information, with a view to forming a true analysis from the gathered information. Furthermore, with the completion of the steps of data munging, analysis, modeling, and evaluation, users can generate insights and valuable points from their focused data.

In a real data exploration project, there are six steps involved in the exploration process. They are as follows:

1. Asking the right questions.
2. Data collection.
3. Data munging.

4. Basic exploratory data analysis.

5. Advanced exploratory data analysis.

6. Model assessment.

A more detailed explanation of these six steps is provided here:

1. **Asking the right questions**: When the user presents their question, for example "What are my expected findings after the exploration is finished?", or "What kind of information can I extract through the exploration?," different results will be given. Therefore, asking the right question is essential in the first place, for the question itself determines the objective and target of the exploration.

2. **Data collection**: Once the goal of exploration is determined, the user can start collecting or extracting relevant data from the data source, with regard to the exploration target. Mostly, data collected from disparate systems appears unorganized and diverse in format. Clearly, the original data may be from different sources, such as files, databases, or the Internet. To retrieve data from these sources requires the assistance of the file IO function, JDBC/ODBC, web crawler, and so on. This extracted data is called **raw data**, which is because it has not been subjected to processing, or been through any other manipulation. Most raw data is not easily consumed by the majority of analysis tools or visualization programs.

3. **Data munging**: The next phase is data munging (or wrangling), a step to help map raw data into a more convenient format for consumption. During this phase, there are many processes, such as data parsing, sorting, merging, filtering, missing value completion, and other processes to transform and organize the data, and enable it to fit into a consume structure. Later, the mapped data can be further utilized for data aggregation, analysis, or visualization.

4. **Basic exploratory data analysis**: After the data munging phase, users can conduct further analysis toward data processing. The most basic analysis is to perform exploratory data analysis. Exploratory data analysis involves analyzing a dataset by summarizing its characteristics. Performing basic statistical, aggregation, and visual methods are also crucial tasks to help the user understand data characteristics, which are beneficial for the user to capture the majority, trends, and outliers easily through plots.

5. **Advanced exploratory data analysis**: Until now, the descriptive statistic gives a general description of data features. However, one would like to generate an inference rule for the user to predict data features based on input parameters. Therefore, the application of machine learning enables the user to generate an inferential model, where the user can input a training dataset to generate a predictive model. After this, the prediction model can be utilized to predict the output value or label based on given parameters.

6. **Model assessment**: Finally, to assess whether the generating model performs the best in the data estimation of a given problem, one must perform a model selection. The selection method here involves many steps, including data preprocessing, tuning parameters, and even switching the machine learning algorithm. However, one thing that is important to keep in mind is that the simplest model frequently achieves the best results in predictive or exploratory power; whereas complex models often result in over fitting.

For the following example, we would like to perform a sample data exploration based on the dataset of passengers surviving the Titanic shipwreck. The steps we demonstrate here follow how to collect data from the online source, Kaggle; clean data through data munging; perform basic exploratory data analysis to discover important attributes that might give a prediction of the survival rate; perform advanced exploratory data analysis using the classification algorithm to predict the survival rate of the given data; and finally, perform model assessment to generate a prediction model.

Reading a Titanic dataset from a CSV file

To start the exploration, we need to retrieve a dataset from Kaggle (https://www.kaggle.com/). We had look at some of the samples in *Chapter 1, Practical Machine Learning with R*. Here, we introduce methods to deal with real-world problems.

Getting ready

To retrieve data from Kaggle, you need to first sign up for a Kaggle account (https://www.kaggle.com/account/register). Then, log in to the account for further exploration:

Kaggle.com

How to do it...

Perform the following steps to read the Titanic dataset from the CSV file:

1. Go to `http://www.kaggle.com/c/titanic-gettingStarted/data` to retrieve the data list.

2. You can see a list of data files for download, as shown in the following table:

Filename	Available formats
`train`	`.csv` (59.76 kb)
`genderclassmodel`	`.py` (4.68 kb)
`myfirstforest`	`.csv` (3.18 kb)
`myfirstforest`	`.py` (3.83 kb)
`gendermodel`	`.csv` (3.18 kb)
`genderclassmodel`	`.csv` (3.18 kb)
`test`	`.csv` (27.96 kb)
`gendermodel`	`.py` (3.58 kb)

3. Download the training data (`https://www.kaggle.com/c/titanic-gettingStarted/download/train.csv`) to a local disk.

4. Then, make sure the downloaded file is placed under the current directory. You can use the `getwd` function to check the current working directory. If the downloaded file is not located in the working directory, move the file to the current working directory. Or, you can use `setwd()` to set the working directory to where the downloaded files are located:

```
> getwd()

[1] "C:/Users/guest"
```

5. Next, one can use `read.csv` to load data into the data frame. Here, one can use the `read.csv` function to read `train.csv` to frame the data with the variable names set as `train.data`. However, in order to treat the blank string as `NA`, one can specify that `na.strings` equals either `"NA"` or an empty string:

```
> train.data = read.csv("train.csv", na.strings=c("NA", ""))
```

6. Then, check the loaded data with the `str` function:

```
> str(train.data)

'data.frame': 891 obs. of  12 variables:

 $ PassengerId: int  1 2 3 4 5 6 7 8 9 10 ...

 $ Survived   : int  0 1 1 1 0 0 0 0 1 1 ...

 $ Pclass     : int  3 1 3 1 3 3 1 3 3 2 ...
```

```
$ Name       : Factor w/ 891 levels "Abbing, Mr. Anthony",..: 109
191 358 277 16 559 520 629 417 581 ...

$ Sex        : Factor w/ 2 levels "female","male": 2 1 1 1 2 2 2
2 1 1 ...

$ Age        : num   22 38 26 35 35 NA 54 2 27 14 ...

$ SibSp      : int   1 1 0 1 0 0 0 3 0 1 ...

$ Parch      : int   0 0 0 0 0 0 0 1 2 0 ...

$ Ticket     : Factor w/ 681 levels "110152","110413",..: 524 597
670 50 473 276 86 396 345 133 ...

$ Fare       : num   7.25 71.28 7.92 53.1 8.05 ...

$ Cabin      : Factor w/ 148 levels "","A10","A14",..: 1 83 1 57
1 1 131 1 1 1 ...

$ Embarked   : Factor w/ 4 levels "","C","Q","S": 4 2 4 4 4 3 4 4
4 2 ...
```

How it works...

To begin the data exploration, we first downloaded the Titanic dataset from Kaggle, a website containing many data competitions and datasets. To load the data into the data frame, this recipe demonstrates how to apply the `read.csv` function to load the dataset with the `na.strings` argument, for the purpose of converting blank strings and `"NA"` to NA values. To see the structure of the dataset, we used the `str` function to compactly display `train.data`; you can find the dataset contains demographic information and survival labels of the passengers. The data collected here is good enough for beginners to practice how to process and analyze data.

There's more...

On Kaggle, much of the data on science is related to competitions, which mostly refer to designing a machine learning method to solve real-world problems.

Most competitions on Kaggle are held by either academia or corporate bodies, such as Amazon or Facebook. In fact, they create these contests and provide rewards, such as bonuses, or job prospects (see `https://www.kaggle.com/competitions`). Thus, there are many data scientists who are attracted to registering for a Kaggle account to participate in competitions. A beginner in a pilot exploration can participate in one of these competitions, which will help them gain experience by solving real-world problems with their machine learning skills.

To create a more challenging learning environment as a competitor, a participant needs to submit their output answer and will receive the assessment score, so that each one can assess their own rank on the leader board.

Converting types on character variables

In R, since nominal, ordinal, interval, and ratio variable are treated differently in statistical modeling, we have to convert a nominal variable from a character into a factor.

Getting ready

You need to have the previous recipe completed by loading the Titanic training data into the R session, with the `read.csv` function and assigning an argument of `na.strings` equal to NA and the blank string (""). Then, assign the loaded data from `train.csv` into the `train.data` variables.

How to do it...

Perform the following steps to convert the types on character variables:

1. Use the `str` function to print the overview of the Titanic data:

```
> str(train.data)
'data.frame':  891 obs. of  12 variables:
 $ PassengerId: int  1 2 3 4 5 6 7 8 9 10 ...
 $ Survived   : int  0 1 1 1 0 0 0 0 1 1 ...
 $ Pclass     : int  3 1 3 1 3 3 1 3 3 2 ...
 $ Name       : Factor w/ 891 levels "Abbing, Mr. Anthony",..: 109
191 358 277 16 559 520 629 417 581 ...
 $ Sex        : Factor w/ 2 levels "female","male": 2 1 1 1 2 2 2
2 1 1 ...
 $ Age        : num  22 38 26 35 35 NA 54 2 27 14 ...
 $ SibSp      : int  1 1 0 1 0 0 0 3 0 1 ...
 $ Parch      : int  0 0 0 0 0 0 0 1 2 0 ...
 $ Ticket     : Factor w/ 681 levels "110152","110413",..: 524 597
670 50 473 276 86 396 345 133 ...
 $ Fare       : num  7.25 71.28 7.92 53.1 8.05 ...
 $ Cabin      : Factor w/ 147 levels "A10","A14","A16",..: NA 82
NA 56 NA NA 130 NA NA NA ...
 $ Embarked   : Factor w/ 3 levels "C","Q","S": 3 1 3 3 3 2 3 3 3
1 ...
```

2. To transform the variable from the `int` numeric type to the `factor` categorical type, you can cast `factor`:

```
> train.data$Survived = factor(train.data$Survived)
> train.data$Pclass = factor(train.data$Pclass)
```

3. Print out the variable with the `str` function and again, you can see that `Pclass` and `Survived` are now transformed into the factor as follows:

```
> str(train.data)
'data.frame':  891 obs. of  12 variables:
 $ PassengerId: int  1 2 3 4 5 6 7 8 9 10 ...
 $ Survived   : Factor w/ 2 levels "0","1": 1 2 2 2 1 1 1 1 2 2
...
 $ Pclass     : Factor w/ 3 levels "1","2","3": 3 1 3 1 3 3 1 3 3
2 ...
 $ Name       : Factor w/ 891 levels "Abbing, Mr. Anthony",..: 109
191 358 277 16 559 520 629 417 581 ...
 $ Sex        : Factor w/ 2 levels "female","male": 2 1 1 1 2 2 2
2 1 1 ...
 $ Age        : num  22 38 26 35 35 NA 54 2 27 14 ...
 $ SibSp      : int  1 1 0 1 0 0 0 3 0 1 ...
 $ Parch      : int  0 0 0 0 0 0 0 1 2 0 ...
 $ Ticket     : Factor w/ 681 levels "110152","110413",..: 524 597
670 50 473 276 86 396 345 133 ...
 $ Fare       : num  7.25 71.28 7.92 53.1 8.05 ...
 $ Cabin      : Factor w/ 147 levels "A10","A14","A16",..: NA 82
NA 56 NA NA 130 NA NA NA ...
 $ Embarked   : Factor w/ 3 levels "C","Q","S": 3 1 3 3 3 2 3 3 3
1 ...
```

How it works...

Talking about statistics, there are four measurements: nominal, ordinal, interval, and ratio. Nominal variables are used to label variables, such as gender and name; ordinal variables, and are measures of non-numeric concepts, such as satisfaction and happiness. Interval variables shows numeric scales, which tell us not only the order but can also show the differences between the values, such as temperatures in Celsius. A ratio variable shows the ratio of a magnitude of a continuous quantity to a unit magnitude. Ratio variables provide order, differences between the values, and a true zero value, such as weight and height. In R, different measurements are calculated differently, so you should perform a type conversion before applying descriptive or inferential analytics toward the dataset.

In this recipe, we first display the structure of the train data using the `str` function. From the structure of data, you can find the attribute name, data type, and the first few values contained in each attribute. From the `Survived` and `Pclass` attribute, you can see the data type as `int`. As the variable description listed in Chart 1 (*Preface*), you can see that `Survived` (0 = No; 1 = Yes) and `Pclass` (1 = 1st; 2 = 2nd; 3 = 3rd) are categorical variables. As a result, we transform the data from a character to a factor type via the `factor` function.

There's more...

Besides factor, there are more type conversion functions. For numeric types, there are `is.numeric()` and `as.numeric()`; for character, there are: `is.character()` and `as.character()`. For vector, there are: `is.vector()` and `as.vector()`; for matrix, there are `is.matrix()` and `as.matrix()`. Finally, for data frame, there are: `is.data.frame()` and `as.data.frame()`.

Detecting missing values

Missing values reduce the representativeness of the sample, and furthermore, might distort inferences about the population. This recipe will focus on detecting missing values within the Titanic dataset.

Getting ready

You need to have completed the previous recipes by the `Pclass` attribute and `Survived` to a factor type.

In R, a missing value is noted with the symbol **NA (not available)**, and an impossible value is **NaN (not a number)**.

How to do it...

Perform the following steps to detect the missing value:

1. The `is.na` function is used to denote which index of the attribute contains the NA value. Here, we apply it to the `Age` attribute first:

   ```
   > is.na(train.data$Age)
   ```

2. The `is.na` function indicates the missing value of the `Age` attribute. To get a general number of how many missing values there are, you can perform a `sum` to calculate this:

   ```
   > sum(is.na(train.data$Age) == TRUE)
   [1] 177
   ```

3. To calculate the percentage of missing values, one method adopted is to count the number of missing values against nonmissing values:

```
> sum(is.na(train.data$Age) == TRUE) / length(train.data$Age)
[1] 0.1986532
```

4. To get a percentage of the missing value of the attributes, you can use `sapply` to calculate the percentage of all the attributes:

```
> sapply(train.data, function(df) {
+                sum(is.na(df)==TRUE)/ length(df);
+                })
PassengerId     Survived      Pclass         Name          Sex
Age
0.000000000 0.000000000 0.000000000 0.000000000 0.000000000
0.198653199
      SibSp        Parch       Ticket         Fare        Cabin
Embarked
0.000000000 0.000000000 0.000000000 0.000000000 0.771043771
0.002244669
```

5. Besides simply viewing the percentage of missing data, one may also use the `Amelia` package to visualize the missing values. Here, we use `install.packages` and `require` to install `Amelia` and load the package. However, before the installation and loading of the `Amelia` package, you are required to install `Rcpp`, beforehand:

```
> install.packages("Amelia")
> require(Amelia)
```

6. Then, use the `missmap` function to plot the missing value map:

```
> missmap(train.data, main="Missing Map")
```

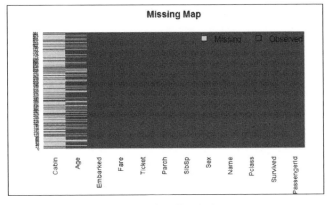

Missing map of the Titanic dataset

How it works...

In R, a missing value is often noted with the `"NA"` symbol, which stands for not available. Most functions (such as `mean` or `sum`) may output NA while encountering an NA value in the dataset. Though you can assign an argument such as `na.rm` to remove the effect of NA, it is better to impute or remove the missing data in the dataset to prevent propagating the effect of the missing value. To find out the missing value in the Titanic dataset, we first sum up all the NA values and divide them by the number of values within each attribute, Then, we apply the calculation to all the attributes with `sapply`.

In addition to this, to display the calculation results using a table, you can utilize the `Amelia` package to plot the missing value map of every attribute on one chart. The visualization of missing values enables users to get a better understanding of the missing percentage within each dataset. From the preceding screenshot, you may have observed that the missing value is beige colored, and its observed value is dark red. The x-axis shows different attribute names, and the y-axis shows the recorded index. Clearly, most of the cabin shows missing data, and it also shows that about 19.87 percent of the data is missing when counting the `Age` attribute, and two values are missing in the `Embarked` attribute.

There's more...

To handle the missing values, we introduced `Amelia` to visualize them. Apart from typing console commands, you can also use the interactive GUI of `Amelia` and `AmeliaView`, which allows users to load datasets, manage options, and run `Amelia` from a windowed environment.

To start running `AmeliaView`, simply type `AmeliaView()` in the R Console:

```
> AmeliaView()
```

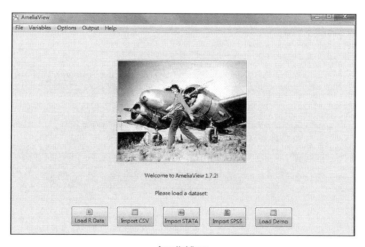

AmeliaView

Imputing missing values

After detecting the number of missing values within each attribute, we have to impute the missing values since they might have a significant effect on the conclusions that can be drawn from the data.

Getting ready

This recipe will require `train.data` loaded in the R session and have the previous recipe completed by converting `Pclass` and `Survived` to a factor type.

How to do it...

Perform the following steps to impute the missing values:

1. First, list the distribution of **Port of Embarkation**. Here, we add the `useNA = "always"` argument to show the number of NA values contained within `train.data`:

   ```
   > table(train.data$Embarked, useNA = "always")
   ```

   ```
        C    Q    S  <NA>
       168   77  644    2
   ```

2. Assign the two missing values to a more probable port (that is, the most counted port), which is Southampton in this case:

   ```
   > train.data$Embarked[which(is.na(train.data$Embarked))] = 'S';
   > table(train.data$Embarked, useNA = "always")
   ```

   ```
        C    Q    S  <NA>
       168   77  646    0
   ```

3. In order to discover the types of titles contained in the names of `train.data`, we first tokenize `train.data$Name` by blank (a regular expression pattern as `"\\s+"`), and then count the frequency of occurrence with the `table` function. After this, since the name title often ends with a period, we use the regular expression to grep the word containing the period. In the end, `sort` the table in decreasing order:

   ```
   > train.data$Name = as.character(train.data$Name)
   > table_words = table(unlist(strsplit(train.data$Name, "\\s+")))
   > sort(table_words [grep('\\.',names(table_words))],
   decreasing=TRUE)
   ```

Mr.	Miss.	Mrs.	Master.
517	182	125	40
Dr.	Rev.	Col.	Major.
7	6	2	2
Mlle.	Capt.	Countess.	Don.
2	1	1	1
Jonkheer.	L.	Lady .	Mme.
1	1	1	1
Ms.	Sir.		
1	1		

4. To obtain which title contains missing values, you can use `str_match` provided by the `stringr` package to get a substring containing a period, then bind the column together with `cbind`. Finally, by using the table function to acquire the statistics of missing values, you can work on counting each title:

```
> library(stringr)
> tb = cbind(train.data$Age, str_match(train.data$Name, "
[a-zA-Z]+\\."))
> table(tb[is.na(tb[,1]),2])
```

Dr.	Master.	Miss.	Mr.	Mrs.
1	4	36	119	17

5. For a title containing a missing value, one way to impute data is to assign the mean value for each title (not containing a missing value):

```
> mean.mr = mean(train.data$Age[grepl(" Mr\\.", train.data$Name) &
!is.na(train.data$Age)])

> mean.mrs = mean(train.data$Age[grepl(" Mrs\\.", train.data$Name)
& !is.na(train.data$Age)])

> mean.dr = mean(train.data$Age[grepl(" Dr\\.", train.data$Name) &
!is.na(train.data$Age)])

> mean.miss = mean(train.data$Age[grepl(" Miss\\.", train.
data$Name) & !is.na(train.data$Age)])

> mean.master =  mean(train.data$Age[grepl(" Master\\.", train.
data$Name) & !is.na(train.data$Age)])
```

6. Then, assign the missing value with the mean value of each title:

```
> train.data$Age[grepl(" Mr\\.", train.data$Name) & is.na(train.
data$Age)] = mean.mr

> train.data$Age[grepl(" Mrs\\.", train.data$Name) & is.na(train.
data$Age)] = mean.mrs
```

```
> train.data$Age[grepl(" Dr\\.", train.data$Name) & is.na(train.
data$Age)] = mean.dr

> train.data$Age[grepl(" Miss\\.", train.data$Name) & is.na(train.
data$Age)] = mean.miss

> train.data$Age[grepl(" Master\\.", train.data$Name) &
is.na(train.data$Age)] = mean.master
```

How it works...

To impute the missing value of the `Embarked` attribute, we first produce the statistics of the embarked port with the `table` function. The `table` function counts two NA values in `train.data`. From the dataset description, we recognize C, Q, and S(C = Cherbourg, Q = Queenstown, S = Southampton). Since we do not have any knowledge about which category these two missing values are in, one possible way is to assign the missing value to the most likely port, which is `Southampton`.

As for another attribute, `Age`, though about 20 percent of the value is missing, users can still infer the missing value with the title of each passenger. To discover how many titles there are within the name of the dataset, we suggest the method of counting segmented words in the `Name` attribute, which helps to calculate the number of missing values of each given title. The resultant word table shows common titles such as `Mr`, `Mrs`, `Miss`, and `Master`. You may reference an English honorific entry from Wikipedia to get the description of each title.

Considering the missing data, we reassign the mean value of each title to the missing value with the corresponding title. However, for the `Cabin` attribute, there are too many missing values, and we cannot infer the value from any referencing attribute. Therefore, we find it does not work by trying to use this attribute for further analysis.

There's more...

Here we list the honorific entry from Wikipedia for your reference. According to it (http://en.wikipedia.org/wiki/English_honorific):

- ▶ **Mr**: This is used for a man, regardless of his marital status
- ▶ **Master**: This is used for young men or boys, especially used in the UK
- ▶ **Miss**: It is usually used for unmarried women, though also used by married female entertainers
- ▶ **Mrs**: It is used for married women
- ▶ **Dr**: It is used for a person in the US who owns his first professional degree

Exploring and visualizing data

After imputing the missing values, one should perform an exploratory analysis, which involves using a visualization plot and an aggregation method to summarize the data characteristics. The result helps the user gain a better understanding of the data in use. The following recipe will introduce how to use basic plotting techniques with a view to help the user with exploratory analysis.

Getting ready

This recipe needs the previous recipe to be completed by imputing the missing value in the age and Embarked attribute.

How to do it...

Perform the following steps to explore and visualize data:

1. First, you can use a bar plot and histogram to generate descriptive statistics for each attribute, starting with passenger survival:

   ```
   > barplot(table(train.data$Survived), main="Passenger Survival",
   names= c("Perished", "Survived"))
   ```

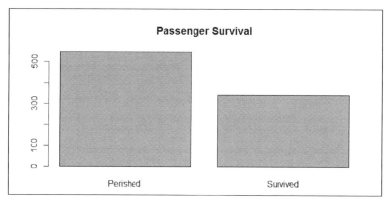

Passenger survival

2. We can generate the bar plot of passenger class:

```
> barplot(table(train.data$Pclass), main="Passenger Class",
names= c("first", "second", "third"))
```

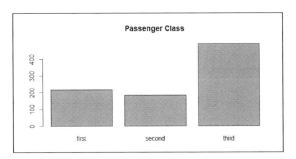

Passenger class

3. Next, we outline the gender data with the bar plot:

```
> barplot(table(train.data$Sex), main="Passenger Gender")
```

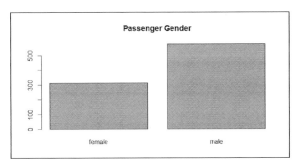

Passenger gender

4. We then plot the histogram of the different ages with the `hist` function:

```
> hist(train.data$Age, main="Passenger Age", xlab = "Age")
```

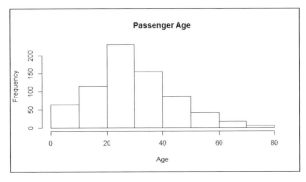

Passenger age

5. We can plot the bar plot of sibling passengers to get the following:

```
> barplot(table(train.data$SibSp), main="Passenger Siblings")
```

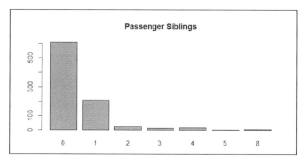

Passenger siblings

6. Next, we can get the distribution of the passenger parch:

```
> barplot(table(train.data$Parch), main="Passenger Parch")
```

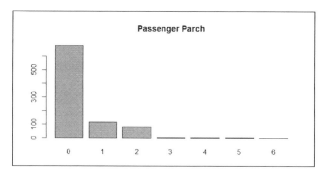

Passenger parch

7. Next, we plot the histogram of the passenger fares:

```
> hist(train.data$Fare, main="Passenger Fare", xlab = "Fare")
```

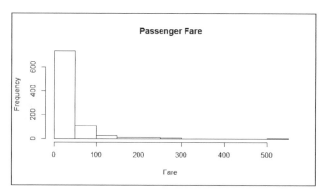

Passenger fares

8. Finally, one can look at the port of embarkation:

```
> barplot(table(train.data$Embarked), main="Port of Embarkation")
```

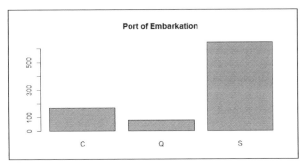

Port of embarkation

9. Use `barplot` to find out which gender is more likely to perish during shipwrecks:

```
> counts = table( train.data$Survived, train.data$Sex)
> barplot(counts,  col=c("darkblue","red"), legend = c("Perished",
"Survived"), main = "Passenger Survival by Sex")
```

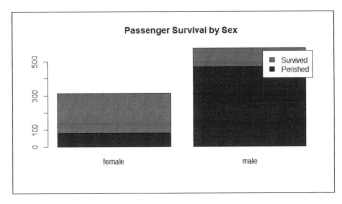

Passenger survival by sex

10. Next, we should examine whether the `Pclass` factor of each passenger may affect the survival rate:

```
> counts = table( train.data$Survived, train.data$Pclass)
```

```
> barplot(counts,  col=c("darkblue","red"), legend =c("Perished",
"Survived"), main= "Titanic Class Bar Plot" )
```

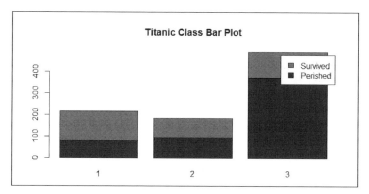

Passenger survival by class

11. Next, we examine the gender composition of each `Pclass`:

```
> counts = table( train.data$Sex, train.data$Pclass)
```

```
> barplot(counts,  col=c("darkblue","red"), legend =
rownames(counts), main= "Passenger Gender by Class")
```

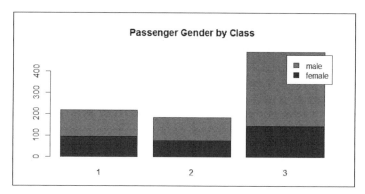

Passenger gender by class

12. Furthermore, we examine the histogram of passenger ages:

```
> hist(train.data$Age[which(train.data$Survived == "0")], main=
"Passenger Age Histogram", xlab="Age", ylab="Count", col ="blue",
breaks=seq(0,80,by=2))
```

```
> hist(train.data$Age[which(train.data$Survived == "1")], col
="red", add = T, breaks=seq(0,80,by=2))
```

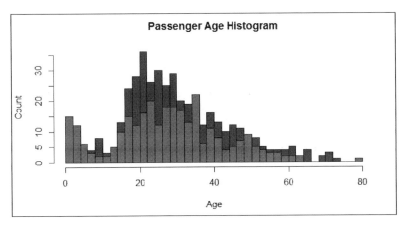

Passenger age histogram

13. To examine more details about the relationship between the age and survival rate, one can use a boxplot:

```
> boxplot(train.data$Age ~ train.data$Survived,
+          main="Passenger Survival by Age",
+          xlab="Survived", ylab="Age")
```

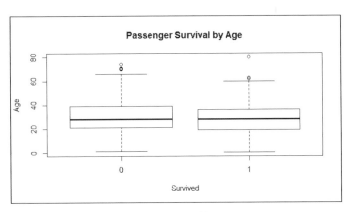

Passenger survival by age

14. To categorize people with different ages into different groups, such as children (below 13), youths (13 to 19), adults (20 to 65), and senior citizens (above 65), execute the following commands:

```
>train.child = train.data$Survived[train.data$Age < 13]
> length(train.child[which(train.child == 1)] ) / length(train.
child)
  [1] 0.5797101


> train.youth = train.data$Survived[train.data$Age >= 15 & train.
data$Age < 25]
> length(train.youth[which(train.youth == 1)] ) / length(train.
youth)
  [1] 0.4285714


> train.adult  = train.data$Survived[train.data$Age >= 20 & train.
data$Age < 65]
> length(train.adult[which(train.adult == 1)] ) / length(train.
adult)
  [1] 0.3659218


> train.senior  = train.data$Survived[train.data$Age >= 65]
> length(train.senior[which(train.senior == 1)] ) / length(train.
senior)
  [1] 0.09090909
```

How it works...

Before we predict the survival rate, one should first use the aggregation and visualization method to examine how each attribute affects the fate of the passengers. Therefore, we begin the examination by generating a bar plot and histogram of each attribute.

The plots from the screenshots in the preceding list give one an outline of each attribute of the Titanic dataset. As per the first screenshot, more passengers perished than survived during the shipwreck. Passengers in the third class made up the biggest number out of the three classes on board, which also reflects the truth that the third class was the most economical class on the Titanic (step 2). For the sex distribution, there were more male passengers than female (step 3). As for the age distribution, the screenshot in step 4 shows that most passengers were aged between 20 to 40. According to the screenshot in step 5, most passengers had one or fewer siblings. The screenshot in step 6 shows that most of the passengers have 0 to 2 parch.

In the screenshot in step 7, the fare histogram shows there were fare differences, which may be as a result of the different passenger classes on the Titanic. At last, the screenshot in step 8 shows that the boat made three stops to pick up passengers.

As we began the exploration from the `sex` attribute, and judging by the resulting bar plot, it clearly showed that female passengers had a higher rate of survival than males during the shipwreck (step 9). In addition to this, the Wikipedia entry for RMS Titanic (`http://en.wikipedia.org/wiki/RMS_Titanic`) explains that 'A *disproportionate number of men were left aboard because of a "women and children first" protocol followed by some of the officers loading the lifeboats'*. Therefore, it is reasonable that the number of female survivors outnumbered the male survivors. In other words, simply using `sex` can predict whether a person will survive with a high degree of accuracy.

Then, we examined whether the passenger class affected the survival rate (step 10). Here, from the definition of `Pclass`, the fares for each class were priced accordingly with the quality; high fares for first class, and low fares for third class. As the class of each passenger seemed to indicate their social and financial status, it is fair to assume that the wealthier passengers may have had more chances to survive.

Unfortunately, there was no correlation between the class and survival rate, so the result does not show the phenomenon we assumed. Nevertheless, after we examined `sex` in the composition of `pclass` (step 11), the results revealed that most third-class passengers were male; the assumption of wealthy people tending to survive more may not be that concrete.

Next, we examined the relationship between the age and passenger fate through a histogram and box plot (step 12). The bar plot shows the age distribution with horizontal columns in which red columns represent the passengers that survived, while blue columns represent those who perished. It is hard to tell the differences in the survival rate from the ages of different groups. The bar plots that we created did not prove that passengers in different age groups were more likely to survive. On the other hand, the plots showed that most people on board were aged between 20 to 40, but does not show whether this group was more likely to survive compared to elderly or young children (step 13). Here, we introduced a box plot, which is a standardized plotting technique that displays the distribution of data with information, such as minimum, first quartile, median, third quartile, maximum, and outliers.

Later, we further examined whether age groups have any relation to passenger fates, by categorizing passenger ages into four groups. The statistics show the the children group (below 13) was more likely to survive than the youths (13 to 20), adults (20 to 65), and senior citizens (above 65). The results showed that people in the younger age groups were more likely to survive the shipwreck. However, we noted that this possibly resulted from the 'women and children first' protocol.

There's more...

Apart from using bar plots, histograms, and boxplots to visualize data, one can also apply `mosaicplot` in the `vcd` package to examine the relationship between multiple categorical variables. For example, when we examine the relationship between the `Survived` and `Pclass` variables, the application is performed as follows:

```
> mosaicplot(train.data$Pclass ~ train.data$Survived,
+            main="Passenger Survival Class", color=TRUE,
+   xlab="Pclass", ylab="Survived")
```

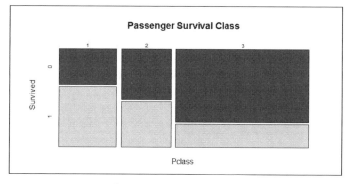

Passenger survival by class

See also

▶ For more information about the shipwreck, one can read the history of RMS Titanic (please refer to the entry *Sinking of the RMS Titanic* in Wikipedia `http://en.wikipedia.org/wiki/Sinking_of_the_RMS_Titanic`), as some of the protocol practiced at that time may have substantially affected the passenger survival rate.

Predicting passenger survival with a decision tree

The exploratory analysis helps users gain insights into how single or multiple variables may affect the survival rate. However, it does not determine what combinations may generate a prediction model, so as to predict the passengers' survival. On the other hand, machine learning can generate a prediction model from a training dataset, so that the user can apply the model to predict the possible labels from the given attributes. In this recipe, we will introduce how to use a decision tree to predict passenger survival rates from the given variables.

Getting ready

We will use the data, `train.data`, that we have already used in our previous recipes.

How to do it...

Perform the following steps to predict the passenger survival with the decision tree:

1. First, we construct a data split `split.data` function with three input parameters: `data`, `p`, and `s`. The `data` parameter stands for the input dataset, the `p` parameter stands for the proportion of generated subset from the input dataset, and the `s` parameter stands for the random seed:

```
> split.data = function(data, p = 0.7, s = 666){
+       set.seed(s)
+       index = sample(1:dim(data)[1])
+       train = data[index[1:floor(dim(data)[1] * p)], ]
+       test = data[index[((ceiling(dim(data)[1] * p)) +
1):dim(data)[1]], ]
+       return(list(train = train, test = test))
+ }
```

2. Then, we split the data, with 70 percent assigned to the training dataset and the remaining 30 percent for the testing dataset:

```
> allset= split.data(train.data, p = 0.7)
> trainset = allset$train
> testset = allset$test
```

3. For the condition tree, one has to use the `ctree` function from the party package; therefore, we install and load the party package:

```
> install.packages('party')
> require('party')
```

4. We then use `Survived` as a label to generate the prediction model in use. After that, we assign the classification tree model into the `train.ctree` variable:

```
> train.ctree = ctree(Survived ~ Pclass + Sex + Age + SibSp + Fare
+ Parch + Embarked, data=trainset)
> train.ctree

        Conditional inference tree with 7 terminal nodes

Response:   Survived
```

```
Inputs:  Pclass, Sex, Age, SibSp, Fare, Parch, Embarked
Number of observations:  623


1) Sex == {male}; criterion = 1, statistic = 173.672
  2) Pclass == {2, 3}; criterion = 1, statistic = 30.951
    3) Age <= 9; criterion = 0.997, statistic = 12.173
      4) SibSp <= 1; criterion = 0.999, statistic = 15.432
        5)* weights = 10
      4) SibSp > 1
        6)* weights = 11
    3) Age > 9
      7)* weights = 282
  2) Pclass == {1}
    8)* weights = 87
1) Sex == {female}
  9) Pclass == {1, 2}; criterion = 1, statistic = 59.504
    10)* weights = 125
  9) Pclass == {3}
    11) Fare <= 23.25; criterion = 0.997, statistic = 12.456
      12)* weights = 85
    11) Fare > 23.25
      13)* weights = 23
```

5. We use a `plot` function to plot the tree:

```
> plot(train.ctree, main="Conditional inference tree of Titanic
Dataset")
```

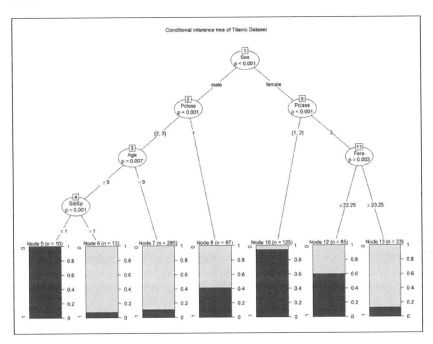

Conditional inference tree of the Titanic dataset

How it works...

This recipe introduces how to use a conditional inference tree, `ctree`, to predict passenger survival. While the conditional inference tree is not the only method to solve the classification problem, it is an easy method to comprehend the decision path to predict passenger survival.

We first split the data into a training and testing set by using our implemented function, `split.data`. So, we can then use the training set to generate a prediction model and later employ the prediction model on the testing dataset in the recipe of the model assessment. Then, we install and load the `party` package, and use `ctree` to build a prediction model, with `Survived` as its label. Without considering any particular attribute, we put attributes such as `Pclass`, `Sex`, `Age`, `SibSp`, `Parch`, `Embarked`, and `Fare` as training attributes, except for `Cabin`, as most of this attribute's values are missing.

After constructing the prediction model, we can either print out the decision path and node in a text mode, or use a plot function to plot the decision tree. From the decision tree, the user can see what combination of variables may be helpful in predicting the survival rate. As per the preceding screenshot, users can find a combination of `Pclass` and `Sex`, which served as a good decision boundary (node 9) to predict the survival rates. This shows female passengers who were in first and second class mostly survived the shipwreck. Male passengers, those in second and third class and aged over nine, almost all perished during the shipwreck. From the tree, one may find that attributes such as `Embarked` and `Parch` are missing. This is because the conditional inference tree regards these attributes as less important during classification.

From the decision tree, the user can see what combination of variables may be helpful in predicting the survival rate. Furthermore, a conditional inference tree is helpful in selecting important attributes during the classification process; one can examine the built tree to see whether the selected attribute matches one's presumption.

There's more...

This recipe covers issues relating to classification algorithms and conditional inference trees. Since we do not discuss the background knowledge of the adapted algorithm, it is better for the user to use the `help` function to view the documents related to `ctree` in the `party` package, if necessary.

There is a similar decision tree based package, named `rpart`. The difference between `party` and `rpart` is that `ctree` in the party package avoids the following variable selection bias of `rpart` and `ctree` in the `party` package, tending to select variables that have many possible splits or many missing values. Unlike the others, `ctree` uses a significance testing procedure in order to select variables, instead of selecting the variable that maximizes an information measure.

Besides `ctree`, one can also use `svm` to generate a prediction model. To load the `svm` function, load the `e1071` package first, and then use the `svm` build to generate this prediction:

```
> install.packages('e1071')
> require('e1071')
> svm.model = svm(Survived ~ Pclass + Sex + Age + SibSp + Fare + Parch +
Embarked, data = trainset, probability = TRUE)
```

Here, we use `svm` to show how easy it is that you can immediately use different machine learning algorithms on the same dataset when using R. For further information on how to use `svm`, please refer to *Chapter 6, Classification (II) – Neural Network, SVM*.

Validating the power of prediction with a confusion matrix

After constructing the prediction model, it is important to validate how the model performs while predicting the labels. In the previous recipe, we built a model with `ctree` and pre-split the data into a training and testing set. For now, users will learn to validate how well `ctree` performs in a survival prediction via the use of a confusion matrix.

Getting ready

Before assessing the prediction model, first be sure that the generated training set and testing dataset are within the R session.

How to do it...

Perform the following steps to validate the prediction power:

1. We start using the constructed `train.ctree` model to predict the survival of the testing set:

   ```
   > ctree.predict = predict(train.ctree, testset)
   ```

2. First, we install the `caret` package, and then load it:

   ```
   > install.packages("caret")
   > require(caret)
   ```

3. After loading `caret`, one can use a confusion matrix to generate the statistics of the output matrix:

   ```
   > confusionMatrix(ctree.predict, testset$Survived)
   Confusion Matrix and Statistics

             Reference
   Prediction   0    1
            0  160   25
            1   16   66

                 Accuracy : 0.8464
                   95% CI : (0.7975, 0.8875)
      No Information Rate : 0.6592
      P-Value [Acc > NIR] : 4.645e-12
   ```

```
                    Kappa : 0.6499
    Mcnemar's Test P-Value : 0.2115

              Sensitivity : 0.9091
              Specificity : 0.7253
            Pos Pred Value : 0.8649
            Neg Pred Value : 0.8049
               Prevalence : 0.6592
           Detection Rate : 0.5993
     Detection Prevalence : 0.6929
        Balanced Accuracy : 0.8172

          'Positive' Class : 0
```

How it works...

After building the prediction model in the previous recipe, it is important to measure the performance of the constructed model. The performance can be assessed by whether the prediction result matches the original label contained in the testing dataset. The assessment can be done by using the confusion matrix provided by the caret package to generate a confusion matrix, which is one method to measure the accuracy of predictions.

To generate a confusion matrix, a user needs to install and load the `caret` package first. The confusion matrix shows that purely using `ctree` can achieve accuracy of up to 84 percent. One may generate a better prediction model by tuning the attribute used, or by replacing the classification algorithm to SVM, `glm`, or random forest.

There's more...

A caret package (*Classification and Regression Training*) helps make iterating and comparing different predictive models very convenient. The package also contains several functions, including:

▶ Data splits

▶ Common preprocessing: creating dummy variables, identifying zero- and near-zero-variance predictors, finding correlated predictors, centering, scaling, and so on

▶ Training (using cross-validation)

▶ Common visualizations (for example, `featurePlot`)

Assessing performance with the ROC curve

Another measurement is by using the ROC curve (this requires the ROCR package), which plots a curve according to its true positive rate against its false positive rate. This recipe will introduce how we can use the ROC curve to measure the performance of the prediction model.

Getting ready

Before applying the ROC curve to assess the prediction model, first be sure that the generated training set, testing dataset, and built prediction model, `ctree.predict`, are within the R session.

How to do it...

Perform the following steps to assess prediction performance:

1. Prepare the probability matrix:

   ```
   > train.ctree.pred = predict(train.ctree, testset)
   > train.ctree.prob =  1- unlist(treeresponse(train.ctree,
   testset), use.names=F)[seq(1,nrow(testset)*2,2)]
   ```

2. Install and load the ROCR package:

   ```
   > install.packages("ROCR")

   > require(ROCR)
   ```

3. Create an ROCR prediction object from probabilities:

   ```
   > train.ctree.prob.rocr = prediction(train.ctree.prob,
   testset$Survived)
   ```

4. Prepare the ROCR performance object for the ROC curve (tpr=true positive rate, fpr=false positive rate) and the area under curve (AUC):

   ```
   > train.ctree.perf = performance(train.ctree.prob.rocr,
   "tpr","fpr")
   > train.ctree.auc.perf =  performance(train.ctree.prob.rocr,
   measure = "auc", x.measure = "cutoff")
   ```

5. Plot the ROC curve, with colorize as TRUE, and put AUC as the title:

```
> plot(train.ctree.perf, col=2,colorize=T, main=paste("AUC:",
train.ctree.auc.perf@y.values))
```

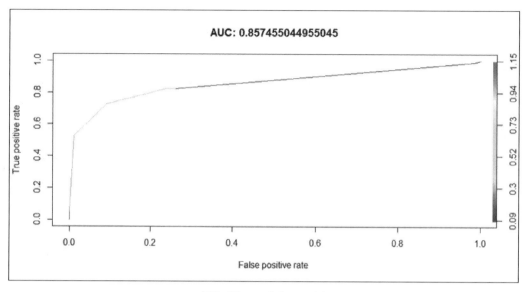

ROC of the prediction model

How it works...

Here, we first create the prediction object from the probabilities matrix, and then prepare the ROCR performance object for the ROC curve (tpr=true positive rate, fpr=false positive rate) and the AUC. Lastly, we use the plot function to draw the ROC curve.

The result drawn in the preceding screenshot is interpreted in the following way: the larger under the curve (a perfect prediction will make AUC equal to 1), the better the prediction accuracy of the model. Our model returns a value of 0.857, which suggests that the simple conditional inference tree model is powerful enough to make survival predictions.

See also

▶ To get more information on the ROCR, you can read the paper *Sing, T., Sander, O., Berenwinkel, N., and Lengauer, T. (2005). ROCR: visualizing classifier performance in R. Bioinformatics, 21(20), 3940-3941.*

3
R and Statistics

In this chapter, we will cover the following topics:

- ▶ Understanding data sampling in R
- ▶ Operating a probability distribution in R
- ▶ Working with univariate descriptive statistics in R
- ▶ Performing correlations and multivariate analysis
- ▶ Operating linear regression and a multivariate analysis
- ▶ Conducting an exact binomial test
- ▶ Performing student's t-test
- ▶ Performing the Kolmogorov-Smirnov test
- ▶ Understanding the Wilcoxon Rank Sum and Signed Rank test
- ▶ Working with Pearson's Chi-squared test
- ▶ Conducting a one-way ANOVA
- ▶ Performing a two-way ANOVA

Introduction

The R language, as the descendent of the statistics language, S, has become the preferred computing language in the field of statistics. Moreover, due to its status as an active contributor in the field, if a new statistical method is discovered, it is very likely that this method will first be implemented in the R language. As such, a large quantity of statistical methods can be fulfilled by applying the R language.

To apply statistical methods in R, the user can categorize the method of implementation into descriptive statistics and inferential statistics:

▸ **Descriptive statistics**: These are used to summarize the characteristics of the data. The user can use mean and standard deviation to describe numerical data, and use frequency and percentages to describe categorical data.

▸ **Inferential statistics**: Based on the pattern within a sample data, the user can infer the characteristics of the population. The methods related to inferential statistics are for hypothesis testing, data estimation, data correlation, and relationship modeling. Inference can be further extended to forecasting, prediction, and estimation of unobserved values either in or associated with the population being studied.

In the following recipe, we will discuss examples of data sampling, probability distribution, univariate descriptive statistics, correlations and multivariate analysis, linear regression and multivariate analysis, Exact Binomial Test, student's t-test, Kolmogorov-Smirnov test, Wilcoxon Rank Sum and Signed Rank test, Pearson's Chi-squared Test, One-way ANOVA, and Two-way ANOVA.

Understanding data sampling in R

Sampling is a method to select a subset of data from a statistical population, which can use the characteristics of the population to estimate the whole population. The following recipe will demonstrate how to generate samples in R.

Getting ready

Make sure that you have an R working environment for the following recipe.

How to do it...

Perform the following steps to understand data sampling in R:

1. In order to generate random samples of a given population, the user can simply use the `sample` function:

   ```
   > sample(1:10)
   ```

2. To specify the number of items returned, the user can set the assigned value to the `size` argument:

   ```
   > sample(1:10, size = 5)
   ```

3. Moreover, the sample can also generate Bernoulli trials by specifying `replace = TRUE` (default is `FALSE`):

   ```
   > sample(c(0,1), 10, replace = TRUE)
   ```

How it works...

As we saw in the preceding demonstration, the `sample` function can generate random samples from a specified population. The returned number from records can be designated by the user simply by specifying the argument of `size`. Assigning the `replace` argument to `TRUE`, you can generate Bernoulli trials (a population with 0 and 1 only).

See also

▸ In R, the default package provides another sample method, `sample.int`, where both n and size must be supplied as integers:

```
> sample.int(20, 12)
```

Operating a probability distribution in R

Probability distribution and statistics analysis are closely related to each other. For statistics analysis, analysts make predictions based on a certain population, which is mostly under a probability distribution. Therefore, if you find that the data selected for prediction does not follow the exact assumed probability distribution in experiment design, the upcoming results can be refuted. In other words, probability provides the justification for statistics. The following examples will demonstrate how to generate probability distribution in R.

Getting ready

Since most distribution functions originate from the `stats` package, make sure the library `stats` are loaded.

How to do it...

Perform the following steps:

1. For a normal distribution, the user can use `dnorm`, which will return the height of a normal curve at 0:

```
> dnorm(0)
[1] 0.3989423
```

2. Then, the user can change the mean and the standard deviation in the argument:

```
> dnorm(0,mean=3,sd=5)
[1] 0.06664492
```

3. Next, plot the graph of a normal distribution with the `curve` function:

```
> curve(dnorm,-3,3)
```

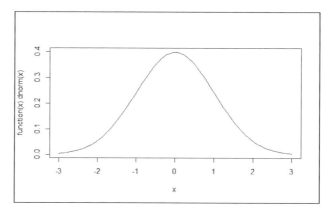

Standard normal distribution

4. In contrast to `dnorm`, which returns the height of a normal curve, the `pnorm` function can return the area under a given value:

```
> pnorm(1.5)
[1] 0.9331928
```

5. Alternatively, to get the area above a certain value, you can specify the option, `lower.tail`, to `FALSE`:

```
> pnorm(1.5, lower.tail=FALSE)
[1] 0.0668072
```

6. To plot the graph of `pnorm`, the user can employ a `curve` function:

```
> curve(pnorm(x), -3,3)
```

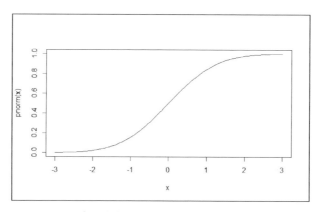

Cumulative density function (pnorm)

7. To calculate the quantiles for a specific distribution, you can use `qnorm`. The function, `qnorm`, can be treated as the inverse of `pnorm`, which returns the Z-score of a given probability:

```
> qnorm(0.5)
[1] 0
> qnorm(pnorm(0))
[1] 0
```

8. To generate random numbers from a normal distribution, one can use the `rnorm` function and specify the number of generated numbers. Also, one can define optional arguments, such as the mean and standard deviation:

```
> set.seed(50)
> x = rnorm(100,mean=3,sd=5)
> hist(x)
```

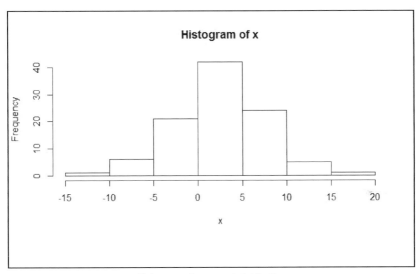

Histogram of a normal distribution

9. To calculate the uniform distribution, the `runif` function generates random numbers from a uniform distribution. The user can specify the range of the generated numbers by specifying variables, such as the minimum and maximum. For the following example, the user generates 100 random variables from 0 to 5:

```
> set.seed(50)
> y = runif(100,0,5)
> hist(y)
```

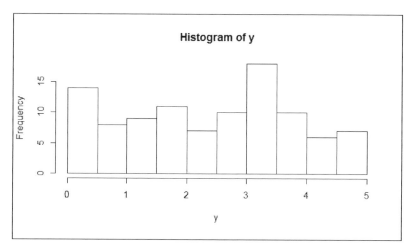

Histogram of a uniform distribution

10. Lastly, if you would like to test the normality of the data, the most widely used test for this is the Shapiro-Wilks test. Here, we demonstrate how to perform a test of normality on both samples from the normal and uniform distributions, respectively:

```
> shapiro.test(x)


        Shapiro-Wilk normality test


data:   x
W = 0.9938, p-value = 0.9319
> shapiro.test(y)


        Shapiro-Wilk normality test


data:   y
W = 0.9563, p-value = 0.002221
```

How it works...

In this recipe, we first introduce dnorm, a probability density function, which returns the height of a normal curve. With a single input specified, the input value is called a standard score or a z-score. Without any other arguments specified, it is assumed that the normal distribution is in use with a mean of zero and a standard deviation of one. We then introduce three ways to draw standard and normal distributions.

After this, we introduce pnorm, a cumulative density function. The function, pnorm, can generate the area under a given value. In addition to this, pnorm can be also used to calculate the p-value from a normal distribution. One can get the p-value by subtracting 1 from the number, or assigning True to the option, lower.tail. Similarly, one can use the plot function to plot the cumulative density.

In contrast to pnorm, qnorm returns the z-score of a given probability. Therefore, the example shows that the application of a qnorm function to a pnorm function will produce the exact input value.

Next, we show you how to use the rnrom function to generate random samples from a normal distribution, and the runif function to generate random samples from the uniform distribution. In the function, rnorm, one has to specify the number of generated numbers and we may also add optional augments, such as the mean and standard deviation. Then, by using the hist function, one should be able to find a bell-curve in figure 3. On the other hand, for the runif function, with the minimum and maximum specifications, one can get a list of sample numbers between the two. However, we can still use the hist function to plot the samples. It is clear that the output figure (shown in the preceding figure) is not in a bell-shape, which indicates that the sample does not come from the normal distribution.

Finally, we demonstrate how to test data normality with the Shapiro-Wilks test. Here, we conduct the normality test on both the normal and uniform distribution samples, respectively. In both outputs, one can find the p-value in each test result. The p-value shows the changes, which show that the sample comes from a normal distribution. If the p-value is higher than 0.05, we can conclude that the sample comes from a normal distribution. On the other hand, if the value is lower than 0.05, we conclude that the sample does not come from a normal distribution.

There's more...

Besides the normal distribution, you can obtain a t distribution, binomial distribution, and Chi-squared distribution by using the built-in functions of R. You can use the help function to access further information about this:

- For a t distribution:

```
> help(TDist)
```

▶ For a binomial distribution:

```
>help(Binomial)
```

▶ For the Chi-squared distribution:

```
>help(Chisquare)
```

To learn more about the distributions in the package, the user can access the `help` function with the keyword `distributions` to find all related documentation on this:

```
> help(distributions)
```

Working with univariate descriptive statistics in R

Univariate descriptive statistics describes a single variable for unit analysis, which is also the simplest form of quantitative analysis. In this recipe, we introduce some basic functions used to describe a single variable.

Getting ready

We need to apply descriptive statistics to a sample data. Here, we use the built-in `mtcars` data as our example.

How to do it...

Perform the following steps:

1. First, load the `mtcars` data into a data frame with a variable named `mtcars`:

```
> data(mtcars)
```

2. To obtain the vector range, the `range` function will return the lower and upper bound of the vector:

```
> range(mtcars$mpg)
[1] 10.4 33.9
```

3. Compute the length of the variable:

```
> length(mtcars$mpg)
[1] 32
```

4. Obtain the mean of mpg:

```
> mean(mtcars$mpg)
[1] 20.09062
```

5. Obtain the median of the input vector:

    ```
    > median(mtcars$mpg)
    [1] 19.2
    ```

6. To obtain the standard deviation of the input vector:

    ```
    > sd(mtcars$mpg)
    [1] 6.026948
    ```

7. To obtain the variance of the input vector:

    ```
    > var(mtcars$mpg)
    [1] 36.3241
    ```

8. The variance can also be computed with the square of standard deviation:

    ```
    > sd(mtcars$mpg) ^ 2
    [1] 36.3241
    ```

9. To obtain the **Interquartile Range (IQR)**:

    ```
    > IQR(mtcars$mpg)
    [1] 7.375
    ```

10. To obtain the quantile:

    ```
    > quantile(mtcars$mpg,0.67)
      67%
    21.4
    ```

11. To obtain the maximum of the input vector:

    ```
    > max(mtcars$mpg)
    [1] 33.9
    ```

12. To obtain the minima of the input vector:

    ```
    > min(mtcars$mpg)
    [1] 10.4
    ```

13. To obtain a vector with elements that are the cumulative maxima:

    ```
    > cummax(mtcars$mpg)
     [1] 21.0 21.0 22.8 22.8 22.8 22.8 22.8 24.4 24.4 24.4 24.4 24.4
    24.4 24.4 24.4 24.4
    [17] 24.4 32.4 32.4 33.9 33.9 33.9 33.9 33.9 33.9 33.9 33.9 33.9
    33.9 33.9 33.9 33.9
    ```

14. To obtain a vector with elements that are the cumulative minima:

```
> cummin(mtcars$mpg)
```

```
 [1] 21.0 21.0 21.0 21.0 18.7 18.1 14.3 14.3 14.3 14.3 14.3 14.3
14.3 14.3 10.4 10.4
```

```
[17] 10.4 10.4 10.4 10.4 10.4 10.4 10.4 10.4 10.4 10.4 10.4 10.4
10.4 10.4 10.4 10.4
```

15. To summarize the dataset, you can apply the `summary` function:

```
> summary(mtcars)
```

16. To obtain a frequency count of the categorical data, take `cyl` of `mtcars` as an example:

```
> table(mtcars$cyl)
```

```
 4   6   8
11   7  14
```

17. To obtain a frequency count of numerical data, you can use a stem plot to outline the data shape; `stem` produces a stem-and-leaf plot of the given values:

```
> stem(mtcars$mpg)
```

```
  The decimal point is at the |

  10 | 44
  12 | 3
  14 | 3702258
  16 | 438
  18 | 17227
  20 | 00445
  22 | 88
  24 | 4
  26 | 03
  28 |
  30 | 44
  32 | 49
```

18. You can use a histogram of ggplot to plot the same stem-and-leaf figure:

```
> library(ggplot2)
> qplot(mtcars$mpg, binwidth=2)
```

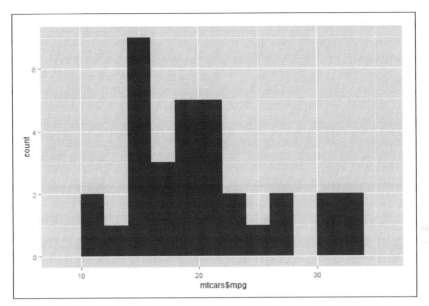

Histogram of mpg of mtcars

How it works...

Univariate descriptive statistics generate the frequency distribution of datasets. Moreover, they can be used to identify the obvious patterns in the data and the characteristics of the variates to provide a better understanding of the data from a holistic viewpoint. Additionally, they can provide information about the central tendency and descriptors of the skewness of individual cases. Therefore, it is common to see that univariate analysis is conducted at the beginning of the data exploration process.

To begin the exploration of data, we first load the dataset, `mtcars`, to an R session. From the data, we apply `range`, `length`, `mean`, `median`, `sd`, `var`, `IQR`, `quantile`, `min`, `max`, `cumin`, and `cumax` to obtain the descriptive statistic of the attribute, `mpg`. Then, we use the `summary` function to obtain summary information about `mtcars`.

Next, we obtain a frequency count of the categorical data (`cyl`). To obtain a frequency count of the numerical data, we use a stem plot to outline the data shape. Lastly, we use a histogram with the `binwidth` argument in 2 to generate a plot similar to the stem-and-leaf plot.

There's more...

One common scenario in univariate descriptive statistics is to find the mode of a vector. In R, there is no built-in function to help the user obtain the mode of the data. However, one can implement the mode function by using the following code:

```
> mode = function(x) {
+ temp = table(x)
+ names(temp)[temp == max(temp)]
+ }
```

By applying the mode function on the vector, mtcars$mpg, you can find the most frequently occurring numeric value or category of a given vector:

```
> x = c(1,2,3,3,3,4,4,5,5,5,6)
> mode(x)
[1] "3" "5"
```

Performing correlations and multivariate analysis

To analyze the relationship of more than two variables, you would need to conduct multivariate descriptive statistics, which allows the comparison of factors. Additionally, it prevents the effect of a single variable from distorting the analysis. In this recipe, we will discuss how to conduct multivariate descriptive statistics using a correlation and covariance matrix.

Getting ready

Ensure that mtcars has already been loaded into a data frame within an R session.

How to do it...

Perform the following steps:

1. Here, you can get the covariance matrix by inputting the first three variables in mtcars to the cov function:

```
> cov(mtcars[1:3])
               mpg        cyl        disp
mpg      36.324103  -9.172379  -633.0972
cyl      -9.172379   3.189516   199.6603
disp  -633.097208 199.660282 15360.7998
```

2. To obtain a correlation matrix of the dataset, we input the first three variables of
   mtcars to the cor function:

```
> cor(mtcars[1:3])
            mpg         cyl        disp
mpg    1.0000000  -0.8521620  -0.8475514
cyl   -0.8521620   1.0000000   0.9020329
disp  -0.8475514   0.9020329   1.0000000
```

How it works...

In this recipe, we have demonstrated how to apply correlation and covariance to discover the
relationship between multiple variables.

First, we compute a covariance matrix of the first three mtcars variables. Covariance can
measure how variables are linearly related. Thus, a positive covariance (for example, cyl
versus mpg) indicates that the two variables are positively linearly related. On the other
hand, a negative covariance (for example, mpg versus disp) indicates the two variables are
negatively linearly related. However, due to the variance of different datasets, the covariance
score of these datasets is not comparable. As a result, if you would like to compare the
strength of the linear relation between two variables in a different dataset, you should use the
normalized score, that is, the correlation coefficient instead of covariance.

Next, we apply a cor function to obtain a correlation coefficient matrix of three variables
within the mtcars dataset. In the correlation coefficient matrix, the numeric element of the
matrix indicates the strength of the relationship between the two variables. If the correlation
coefficient of a variable against itself scores 1, the variable has a positive relationship against
itself. The cyl and mpg variables have a correlation coefficient of -0.85, which means they
have a strong, negative relationship. On the other hand, the disp and cyl variables score
0.90, which may indicate that they have a strong, positive relationship.

See also

▶ You can use `ggplot` to plot the heatmap of the correlation coefficient matrix:

```
> library(reshape2)
> qplot(x=Var1, y=Var2, data=melt(cor(mtcars[1:3])), fill=value,
  geom="tile")
```

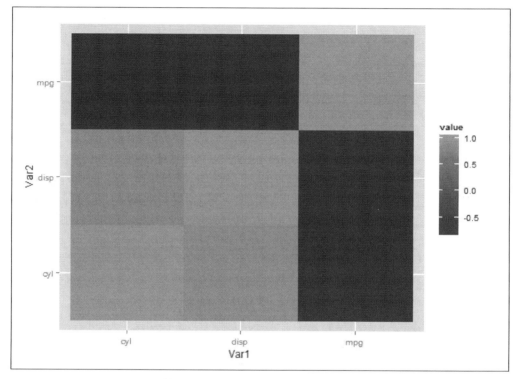

The correlation coefficient matrix heatmap

Operating linear regression and multivariate analysis

Linear regression is a method to assess the association between dependent and independent variables. In this recipe, we will cover how to conduct linear regression for multivariate analysis.

Getting ready

Ensure that `mtcars` has already been loaded into a data frame within an R session.

How to do it...

Perform the following steps:

1. To fit variables into a linear model, you can use the `lm` function:

```
> lmfit = lm(mtcars$mpg ~ mtcars$cyl)
> lmfit


Call:
lm(formula = mtcars$mpg ~ mtcars$cyl)


Coefficients:
(Intercept)    mtcars$cyl
     37.885        -2.876
```

2. To get detailed information on the fitted model, you can use the `summary` function:

```
> summary(lmfit)


Call:
lm(formula = mtcars$mpg ~ mtcars$cyl)


Residuals:
    Min      1Q  Median      3Q     Max
-4.9814 -2.1185  0.2217  1.0717  7.5186


Coefficients:
            Estimate Std. Error t value Pr(>|t|)
(Intercept)  37.8846     2.0738   18.27  < 2e-16 ***
mtcars$cyl   -2.8758     0.3224   -8.92 6.11e-10 ***
---
Signif. codes:  0 '***' 0.001 '**' 0.01 '*' 0.05 '.' 0.1 ' ' 1


Residual standard error: 3.206 on 30 degrees of freedom
Multiple R-squared:  0.7262,  Adjusted R-squared:  0.7171
F-statistic: 79.56 on 1 and 30 DF,  p-value: 6.113e-10
```

3. To create an analysis of a variance table, one can employ the `anova` function:

```
> anova(lmfit)
Analysis of Variance Table

Response: mtcars$mpg
            Df Sum Sq Mean Sq F value    Pr(>F)
mtcars$cyl   1 817.71  817.71  79.561 6.113e-10 ***
Residuals   30 308.33   10.28
---
Signif. codes:  0 '***' 0.001 '**' 0.01 '*' 0.05 '.' 0.1 ' ' 1
```

4. To plot the regression line on a scatter plot of two variables, you first plot `cyl` against `mpg` in it, then use the `abline` function to add a regression line on the plot:

```
> lmfit = lm(mtcars$mpg ~ mtcars$cyl)
> plot(mtcars$cyl, mtcars$mpg)
> abline(lmfit)
```

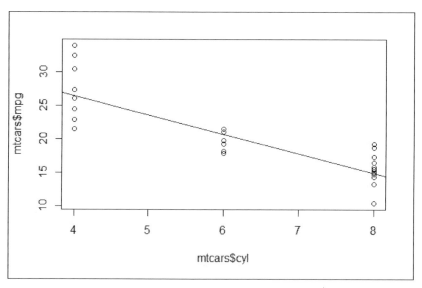

The regression plot of cyl against mpg

How it works...

In this recipe, we apply the linear model function, `lm`, which builds a linear fitted model of two variables and returns the formula and coefficient. Next, we apply the `summary` function to retrieve the detailed information (including F-statistic and P-value) of the model. The purpose of F-statistic is to test the statistical significance of the model. It produces an F-value, which is the ratio of the model mean square to the error mean square. Thus, a large F-value indicates that more of the total variability is accounted for by the regression model. Then, we can use the F-value to support or reject the null hypothesis that all of the regression coefficients are equal to zero. In other words, the null hypothesis is rejected if the F-value is large and shows that the regression model has a predictive capability. On the other hand, P-values of each attribute test the null hypothesis that the coefficient is equal to zero (no effect on the response variable). In other words, a low p-value can reject a null hypothesis and indicates that a change in the predictor's value is related to the value of the response variable.

Next, we apply the `anova` function on the fitted model to determine the variance. The function outputs the sum of squares, which stands for the variability of the model's predicted value. Further, to visualize the linear relationship between two variables, the `abline` function can add a regression line on a scatter plot of `mpg` against `cyl`. From the preceding figure, it is obvious that the `mpg` and `cyl` variables are negatively related.

See also

▸ For more information on how to perform linear and nonlinear regression analysis, please refer to the *Chapter 4, Understanding Regression Analysis*

Conducting an exact binomial test

While making decisions, it is important to know whether the decision error can be controlled or measured. In other words, we would like to prove that the hypothesis formed is unlikely to have occurred by chance, and is statistically significant. In hypothesis testing, there are two kinds of hypotheses: null hypothesis and alternative hypothesis (or research hypothesis). The purpose of hypothesis testing is to validate whether the experiment results are significant. However, to validate whether the alternative hypothesis is acceptable, it is deemed to be true if the null hypothesis is rejected.

In the following recipes, we will discuss some common statistical testing methods. First, we will cover how to conduct an exact binomial test in R.

Getting ready

Since the `binom.test` function originates from the `stats` package, make sure the `stats` library is loaded.

How to do it...

Perform the following step:

1. Assume there is a game where a gambler can win by rolling the number-six-on a dice. As part of the rules, gamblers can bring their own dice. If a gambler tried to cheat in a game, he would use a loaded dice to increase his chance of winning. Therefore, if we observe that the gambler won 92 out of 315 games, we could determine whether the dice was fair by conducting an exact binomial test:

    ```
    > binom.test(x=92, n=315, p=1/6)


        Exact binomial test


    data:   92 and 315
    number of successes = 92, number of trials = 315, p-value =
    3.458e-08
    alternative hypothesis: true probability of success is not equal
    to 0.1666667
    95 percent confidence interval:
     0.2424273 0.3456598
    sample estimates:
    probability of success
              0.2920635
    ```

How it works...

A binomial test uses the binomial distribution to find out whether the true success rate is likely to be *P* for *n* trials with the binary outcome. The formula of the probability, *P*, can be defined in following equation:

$$P(X = k) = \binom{n}{k} p^k q^{n-k}$$

Here, *X* denotes the random variables, counting the number of outcomes of the interest; *n* denotes the number of trials; *k* indicates the number of successes; *p* indicates the probability of success; and *q* denotes the probability of failure.

After we have computed the probability, *P*, we can then perform a sign test to determine whether the success probability is similar to what we expected. If the probability is not equal to what we expected, we can reject the null hypothesis.

By definition, the null hypothesis is a skeptical perspective or a statement about the population parameter that will be tested. The null hypothesis is denoted by H0. An alternative hypothesis is represented by a range of population values, which are not included in the null hypothesis. The alternative hypothesis is denoted by H1. In this case, the null and alternative hypothesis, respectively, are illustrated as:

- **H0 (null hypothesis):** The true probability of success is equal to what we expected
- **H1 (alternative hypothesis):** The true probability of success is not equal to what we expected

In this example, we demonstrate how to use a binomial test to determine the number of times the dice is rolled, the frequency of rolling the number six, and the probability of rolling a six from an unbiased dice. The result of the t-test shows that the p-value = 3.458e-08 (lower than 0.05). For significance, at the five percent level, the null hypothesis (the dice is unbiased) is rejected as too many sixes were rolled (the probability of success = 0.2920635).

See also

- To read more about the usage of the exact binomial test, please use the `help` function to view related documentation on this:

```
> ?binom.test
```

Performing student's t-test

A one sample t-test enables us to test whether two means are significantly different; a two sample t-test allows us to test whether the means of two independent groups are different. In this recipe, we will discuss how to conduct one sample t-test and two sample t-tests using R.

Getting ready

Ensure that `mtcars` has already been loaded into a data frame within an R session. As the `t.test` function originates from the `stats` package, make sure the library, `stats`, is loaded.

How to do it...

Perform the following steps:

1. First, we visualize the attribute, mpg, against am using a boxplot:

    ```
    > boxplot(mtcars$mpg, mtcars$mpg[mtcars$am==0], ylab = "mpg", names=c("overall","automobile"))
    ```

    ```
    > abline(h=mean(mtcars$mpg),lwd=2, col="red")
    ```

    ```
    > abline(h=mean(mtcars$mpg[mtcars$am==0]),lwd=2, col="blue")
    ```

    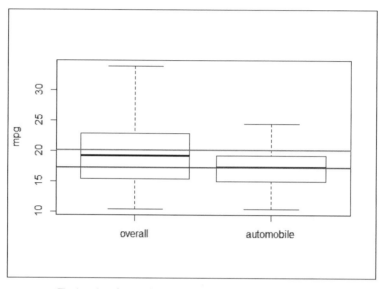

    The boxplot of mpg of the overall population and automobiles

2. We then perform a statistical procedure to validate whether the average mpg of automobiles is lower than the average of the overall mpg:

    ```
    > mpg.mu = mean(mtcars$mpg)
    ```

    ```
    > mpg_am = mtcars$mpg[mtcars$am == 0]
    ```

    ```
    > t.test(mpg_am,mu = mpg.mu)
    ```

    ```
        One Sample t-test

    data:  mpg_am
    t = -3.3462, df = 18, p-value = 0.003595
    alternative hypothesis: true mean is not equal to 20.09062
    95 percent confidence interval:
    ```

```
15.29946 18.99528
```

sample estimates:

mean of x

```
17.14737
```

3. We begin visualizing the data by plotting a boxplot:

    ```
    >boxplot(mtcars$mpg~mtcars$am,ylab='mpg',names=c('automatic','manu
    al'))
    > abline(h=mean(mtcars$mpg[mtcars$am==0]),lwd=2, col="blue")
    > abline(h=mean(mtcars$mpg[mtcars$am==1]),lwd=2, col="red")
    ```

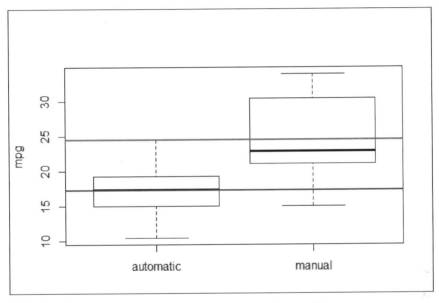

The boxplot of mpg of automatic and manual transmission cars

4. The preceding figure reveals that the mean mpg of automatic transmission cars is lower than the average mpg of manual transmission vehicles:

    ```
    > t.test(mtcars$mpg~mtcars$am)
    ```

    ```
      Welch Two Sample t-test
    ```

    ```
    data:  mtcars$mpg by mtcars$am
    t = -3.7671, df = 18.332, p-value = 0.001374
    alternative hypothesis: true difference in means is not equal to 0
    95 percent confidence interval:
     -11.280194  -3.209684
    ```

```
sample estimates:
mean in group 0 mean in group 1
        17.14737          24.39231
```

How it works...

Student's t-test is where the test statistic follows a normal distribution (the student's t distribution) if the null hypothesis is true. It can be used to determine whether there is a difference between two independent datasets. Student's t-test is best used with the problems associated with an inference based on small samples.

In this recipe, we discuss one sample student's t-test and two sample student's t-tests. In the one sample student's t-test, a research question often asked is, "Is the mean of the population different from the null hypothesis?" Thus, in order to test whether the average mpg of automobiles is lower than the overall average mpg, we first use a boxplot to view the differences between populations without making any assumptions. From the preceding figure, it is clear that the mean of mpg of automobiles (the blue line) is lower than the average mpg (red line) of the overall population. Then, we apply one sample t-test; the low p-value of 0.003595 (< 0.05) suggests that we should reject the null hypothesis that the mean mpg for automobiles is less than the average mpg of the overall population.

As a one sample t-test enables us to test whether two means are significantly different, a two sample t-test allows us to test whether the means of two independent groups are different. Similar to a one sample t-test, we first use a boxplot to see the differences between populations and then apply a two-sample t-test. The test results shows the p-value = 0.01374 ($p< 0.05$). In other words, the test provides evidence that rejects the null hypothesis, which shows the mean mpg of cars with automatic transmission differs from the cars with manual transmission.

See also

▶   To read more about the usage of student's t-test, please use the `help` function to view related documents:

```
> ?t.test
```

Performing the Kolmogorov-Smirnov test

A one-sample Kolmogorov-Smirnov test is used to compare a sample with a reference probability. A two-sample Kolmogorov-Smirnov test compares the cumulative distributions of two datasets. In this recipe, we will demonstrate how to perform the Kolmogorov-Smirnov test with R.

Getting ready

Ensure that `mtcars` has already been loaded into a data frame within an R session. As the `ks.test` function is originated from the `stats` package, make sure the `stats` library is loaded.

How to do it...

Perform the following steps:

1. Validate whether the dataset, x (generated with the `rnorm` function), is distributed normally with a one-sample Kolmogorov-Smirnov test:

    ```
    > x = rnorm(50)
    > ks.test(x,"pnorm")


            One-sample Kolmogorov-Smirnov test

    data:  x
    D = 0.1698, p-value = 0.0994
    alternative hypothesis: two-sided
    ```

2. Next, you can generate uniformly distributed sample data:

    ```
    > set.seed(3)
    > x = runif(n=20, min=0, max=20)

    > y = runif(n=20, min=0, max=20)
    ```

3. We first plot `ecdf` of two generated data samples:

```
> plot(ecdf(x), do.points = FALSE, verticals=T, xlim=c(0, 20))
> lines(ecdf(y), lty=3, do.points = FALSE, verticals=T)
```

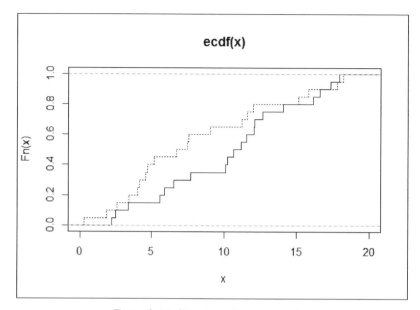

The ecdf plot of two generated data samples

4. Finally, we apply a two-sample Kolmogorov-Smirnov test on two groups of data:

```
> ks.test(x,y)


	Two-sample Kolmogorov-Smirnov test


data:  x and y
D = 0.3, p-value = 0.3356
alternative hypothesis: two-sided
```

How it works...

The **Kolmogorov-Smirnov test** (**K-S test**) is a nonparametric and statistical test, used for the equality of continuous probability distributions. It can be used to compare a sample with a reference probability distribution (a one sample K-S test), or it can directly compare two samples (a two sample K-S test). The test is based on the empirical distribution function (ECDF). Let $x_1, x_2 \cdots x_n$ be a random sample of size, n; the empirical distribution function, $F_n(x)$, is defined as:

$$F_n(x) = \frac{1}{n}\sum_{i=1}^{n} I\{x_i \leq x\}$$

Here, $I\{x_i \leq x\}$ is the indicator function. If $x_i \leq x$, the function equals to 1. Otherwise, the function equals to 0.

The Kolmogorov-Smirnov statistic (D) is based on the greatest (where supx denotes the supremum) vertical difference between F(x) and Fn(x). It is defined as:

$$D_n = \sup{}_x |F_n(x) - F(x)|$$

H_0 is the sample follows the specified distribution. H_1 is the sample does not follow the specified distribution.

If Dn is greater than the critical value obtained from a table, then we reject H_0 at the level of significance α.

We first test whether a random number generated from a normal distribution is normally distributed. At the 5 percent significance level, the p-value of 0.0994 indicates that the input is normally distributed.

Then, we plot an empirical cumulative distribution function (ecdf) plot to show how a two-sample test calculates the maximum distance D (showing 0.3), and apply the two-sample Kolmogorov-Smirnov test to discover whether the two input datasets possibly come from the same distribution.

The p-value is above 0.05, which does not reject the null hypothesis. In other words, it means the two datasets are possibly from the same distribution.

See also

- To read more about the usage of the Kolmogorov-Smirnov test, please use the `help` function to view related documents:

  ```
  > ?ks.test
  ```

- As for the definition of an empirical cumulative distribution function, please refer to the help page of `ecdf`:

  ```
  > ?ecdf
  ```

Understanding the Wilcoxon Rank Sum and Signed Rank test

The Wilcoxon Rank Sum and Signed Rank test (or Mann-Whitney-Wilcoxon) is a nonparametric test of the null hypothesis, which shows that the population distribution of two different groups are identical without assuming that the two groups are normally distributed. This recipe will show how to conduct the Wilcoxon Rank Sum and Signed Rank test in R.

Getting ready

Ensure that mtcars has already been loaded into a data frame within an R session. As the wilcox.test function is originated from the stats package, make sure the library, stats, is loaded.

How to do it...

Perform the following steps:

1. We first plot the data of mtcars with the boxplot function:

    ```
    > boxplot(mtcars$mpg~mtcars$am,ylab='mpg',names=c('automatic','man
    ual'))
    ```

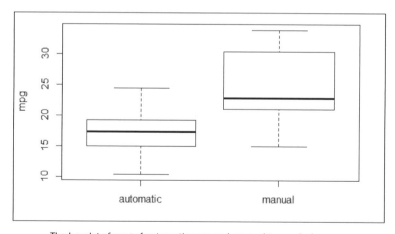

The boxplot of mpg of automatic cars and manual transmission cars

2. Next, we still perform a Wilcoxon Rank Sum test to validate whether the distribution of automatic transmission cars is identical to that of manual transmission cars:

    ```
    > wilcox.test(mpg ~ am, data=mtcars)


    	Wilcoxon rank sum test with continuity correction
    ```

```
data:  mpg by am
W = 42, p-value = 0.001871
alternative hypothesis: true location shift is not equal to 0


Warning message:
In wilcox.test.default(x = c(21.4, 18.7, 18.1, 14.3, 24.4, 22.8,
:
    cannot compute exact p-value with ties
```

How it works...

In this recipe, we discuss a nonparametric test method, the Wilcoxon Rank Sum test (also known as the Mann-Whitney U-test). For student's t-test, it is assumed that the differences between the two samples are normally distributed (and it also works best when the two samples are normally distributed). However, when the normality assumption is uncertain, one can adopt the Wilcoxon Rank Sum Test to test a hypothesis.

Here, we used a Wilcoxon Rank Sum test to determine whether the mpg of automatic and manual transmission cars in the dataset, `mtcars`, is distributed identically. From the test result, we see that the p-value = 0.001871 (< 0.05) rejects the null hypothesis, and also reveals that the distribution of mpg in automatic and manual transmission cars is not identical. When performing this test, you may receive the warning message, "cannot compute exact p-value with ties", which indicates that there are duplicate values within the dataset. The warning message will be cleared once the duplicate values are removed.

See also

▶ To read more about the usage of the Wilcoxon Rank Sum and Signed Rank Test, please use the `help` function to view the concerned documents:

```
> ? wilcox.test
```

Working with Pearson's Chi-squared test

In this recipe, we introduce Pearson's Chi-squared test, which is used to examine whether the distributions of categorical variables of two groups differ. We will discuss how to conduct Pearson's Chi-squared Test in R.

Getting ready

Ensure that `mtcars` has already been loaded into a data frame within an R session. Since the `chisq.test` function is originated from the `stats?` package, make sure the library, `stats`, is loaded.

How to do it

Perform the following steps:

1. To make the counting table, we first use the contingency table built with the inputs of the transmission type and number of forward gears:

   ```
   > ftable = table(mtcars$am, mtcars$gear)
   > ftable
   ```

   ```
       3   4   5
   0  15   4   0
   1   0   8   5
   ```

2. We then plot the mosaic plot of the contingency table:

   ```
   > mosaicplot(ftable, main="Number of Forward Gears Within
   Automatic and Manual Cars", color = TRUE)
   ```

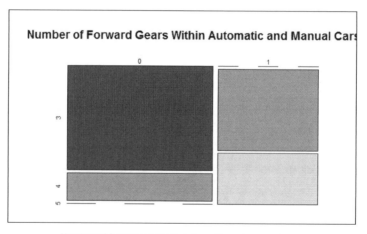

Number of forward gears in automatic and manual cars

3. Next, we perform the Pearson's Chi-squared test on the contingency table to test whether the numbers of gears in automatic and manual transmission cars is the same:

```
> chisq.test(ftable)

	Pearson's Chi-squared test

data:   ftable
X-squared = 20.9447, df = 2, p-value = 2.831e-05

Warning message:
In chisq.test(ftable) : Chi-squared approximation may be incorrect
```

How it works...

Pearson's Chi-squared test is a statistical test used to discover whether there is a relationship between two categorical variables. It is best used for unpaired data from large samples. If you would like to conduct Pearson's Chi-squared test, you need to make sure that the input samples satisfy two assumptions: firstly, the two input variables should be categorical. Secondly, the variable should include two or more independent groups.

In Pearson's Chi-squared test, the assumption is that we have two variables, A and B; we can illustrate the null and alternative hypothesis in the following statements:

▸ H_0: Variable A and variable B are independent
▸ H_1: Variable A and variable B are not independent

To test whether the null hypothesis is correct or incorrect, the Chi-squared test takes these steps.

It calculates the Chi-squared test statistic, X^2:

$$X^2 = \sum_{i=1}^{r} \sum_{j=1}^{c} \frac{\left(O_{i,j} - E_{i,j}\right)^2}{E_{i,j}}$$

Here, r is the number of rows in the contingency table, c is the number of columns in the contingency table, $O_{i,j}$ is the observed frequency count, $E_{i,j}$ is the expected frequency count.

It determines the degrees of freedom, df, of that statistic. The degree of freedom is equal to:

$$df = (r-1) \times (c-1)$$

Here, r is the number of levels for one variable, and c is the number of levels for another variable.

It compares x^2 to the critical value from the Chi-squared distribution with the degrees of freedom.

In this recipe, we use a contingency table and mosaic plot to illustrate the differences in count numbers. It is obvious that the number of forward gears is less in automatic transmission cars than in manual transmission cars.

Then, we perform the Pearson's Chi-squared test on the contingency table to determine whether the gears in automatic and manual transmission cars are the same. The output, p-value = 2.831e-05 (< 0.05), refutes the null hypothesis and shows the number of forward gears is different in automatic and manual transmission cars. However, the output message contains a warning message that Chi-squared approximation may be incorrect, which is because the number of samples in the contingency table is less than five.

There's more...

To read more about the usage of the Pearson's Chi-squared test, please use the help function to view the related documents:

```
> ? chisq.test
```

Besides some common hypothesis testing methods mentioned in previous examples, there are other hypothesis methods provided by R:

 ▸ The Proportional test (prop.test): It is used to test whether the proportions in different groups are the same

 ▸ The Z-test (simple.z.test in the UsingR package): It compares the sample mean with the population mean and standard deviation

 ▸ The Bartlett Test (bartlett.test): It is used to test whether the variance of different groups is the same

 ▸ The Kruskal-Wallis Rank Sum Test (kruskal.test): It is used to test whether the distribution of different groups is identical without assuming that they are normally distributed

 ▸ The Shapiro-Wilk test (shapiro.test): It is used test for normality

Conducting a one-way ANOVA

Analysis of variance (**ANOVA**) investigates the relationship between categorical independent variables and continuous dependent variables. It can be used to test whether the means of several groups are equal. If there is only one categorical variable as an independent variable, you can perform a one-way ANOVA. On the other hand, if there are more than two categorical variables, you should perform a two-way ANOVA. In this recipe, we discuss how to conduct a one-way ANOVA with R.

Getting ready

Ensure that `mtcars` has already been loaded into a data frame within an R session. Since the `oneway.test` and `TukeyHSD` functions originated from the `stats` package, make sure the library, `stats`, is loaded.

How to do it...

Perform the following steps:

1. We begin exploring by visualizing the data with a boxplot:

```
> boxplot(mtcars$mpg~factor(mtcars$gear),xlab='gear',ylab='mpg')
```

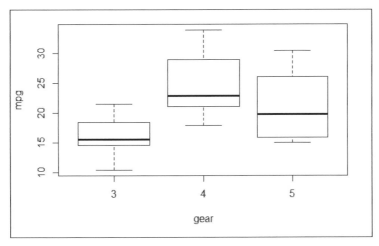

Comparison of mpg of different numbers of forward gears

2. Next, we conduct a one-way ANOVA to examine whether the mean of `mpg` changes with different numbers of forward gears. We use the function, `oneway.test`:

```
> oneway.test(mtcars$mpg~factor(mtcars$gear))


One-way analysis of means (not assuming equal variances)


data:  mtcars$mpg and factor(mtcars$gear)
F = 11.2848, num df = 2.000, denom df = 9.508, p-value = 0.003085
```

3. In addition to `oneway.test`, a standard function, `aov`, is used for the ANOVA analysis:

```
> mtcars.aov = aov(mtcars$mpg ~ as.factor(mtcars$gear))
> summary(mtcars.aov)
                        Df  Sum Sq  Mean Sq  F value   Pr(>F)
as.factor(mtcars$gear)   2   483.2   241.62     10.9 0.000295 ***
Residuals               29   642.8    22.17
---
Signif. codes:  0 '***' 0.001 '**' 0.01 '*' 0.05 '.' 0.1 ' ' 1
```

4. The model generated by the `aov` function can also generate a summary as a fitted table:

```
> model.tables(mtcars.aov, "means")
Tables of means
Grand mean


20.09062


 as.factor(mtcars$gear)
        3      4      5
    16.11  24.53  21.38
rep 15.00  12.00   5.00
```

5. For the `aov` model, one can use `TukeyHSD` for a post hoc comparison test:

```
> mtcars_posthoc =TukeyHSD(mtcars.aov)
> mtcars_posthoc
  Tukey multiple comparisons of means
    95% family-wise confidence level
```

```
Fit: aov(formula = mtcars$mpg ~ as.factor(mtcars$gear))

$`as.factor(mtcars$gear)`
         diff        lwr       upr      p adj
4-3  8.426667  3.9234704 12.929863 0.0002088
5-3  5.273333 -0.7309284 11.277595 0.0937176
5-4 -3.153333 -9.3423846  3.035718 0.4295874
```

6. Further, we can visualize the differences in mean level with a `plot` function:

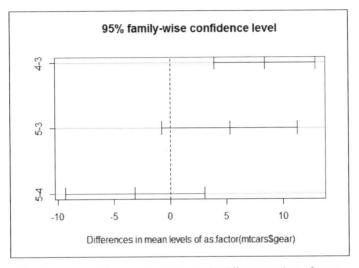

The Tukey mean-difference plot of groups with different numbers of gears

How it works...

In order to understand whether cars with a different number of forward gears have different means in mpg, we first plot the boxplot of mpg by the numbers of forward gears. This offers a simple indication if cars with a different number of forward gears have different means of mpg. We then perform the most basic form of ANOVA, a one-way ANOVA, to test whether the populations have different means.

In R, there are two functions to perform the ANOVA test: `oneway.test` and `aov`. The advantage of `oneway.test` is that the function applies a Welch correction to address the nonhomogeneity of a variance. However, it does not provide as much information as `aov`, and it does not offer a post hoc test. Next, we perform `oneway.test` and `aov` on the independent variable, `gear`, with regard to the dependent variable, `mpg`. Both test results show a small p-value, which rejects the null hypothesis that the mean between cars with a different number of forward gears have the same `mpg` mean.

As the results of ANOVA only suggest that there is a significant difference in the means within overall populations, you may not know which two populations differ in terms of their mean. Therefore, we apply the `TukeyHSD` post hoc comparison test on our ANOVA model. The result shows that cars with four forward gears and cars with three gears have the largest difference, as their confidence interval is the furthest to the right within the plot.

There's more...

ANOVA relies on an F-distribution as the basis of all probability distribution. An F score is obtained by dividing the between-group variance by the in-group variance. If the overall F test was significant, you can conduct a post hoc test (or multiple comparison tests) to measure the differences between groups. The most commonly used post hoc tests are Scheffé's method, the Tukey-Kramer method, and the Bonferroni correction.

In order to interpret the output of ANOVA, you need to have a basic understanding of certain terms, including the degrees of freedom, the sum of square total, the sum of square groups, the sum of square errors, the mean square errors, and the F statistic. If you require more information about these terms, you may refer to *Using multivariate statistics* (Fidell, L. S., & Tabachnick, B. G. (2006) *Boston: Allyn & Bacon.*), or refer to the Wikipedia entry of Analysis of variance (`http://en.wikipedia.org/wiki/Analysis_of_variance#cite_ref-31`).

Performing a two-way ANOVA

A two-way ANOVA can be viewed as the extension of a one-way ANOVA, for the analysis covers more than two categorical variables rather than one. In this recipe, we will discuss how to conduct a two-way ANOVA in R.

Getting ready

Ensure that `mtcars` has already been loaded into a data frame within an R session. Since the `twoway.test`, `TukeyHSD` and `interaction.plot` functions are originated from the `stats` package, make sure the library, `stats`, is loaded.

How to do it...

Perform the following steps:

1. First we plot the two boxplots of factor gears in regard to mpg, with the plot separated from the transmission type:

    ```
    > par(mfrow=c(1,2))
    
    > boxplot(mtcars$mpg~mtcars$gear,subset=(mtcars$am==0),xlab='ge
    ar', ylab = "mpg",main='automatic')
    ```

```
> boxplot(mtcars$mpg~mtcars$gear,subset=(mtcars$am==1),xlab='ge
ar', ylab = "mpg", main='manual')
```

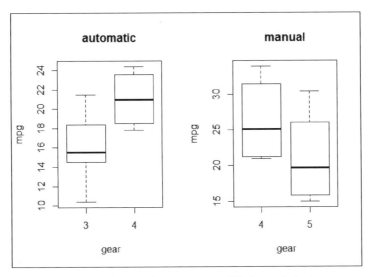

The boxplots of mpg by the gear group and the transmission type

2. Also, you may produce a boxplot of mpg by the number of forward gears * transmission type, with the use of the * operation in the `boxplot` function:

```
> boxplot(mtcars$mpg~factor(mtcars$gear)*
factor(mtcars$am),xlab='gear * transmission', ylab =
"mpg",main='Boxplot of mpg by gear * transmission')
```

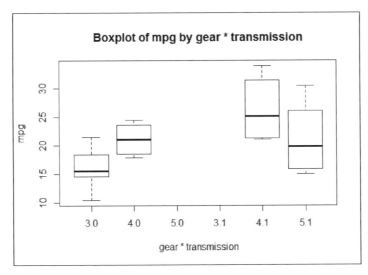

The boxplot of mpg by the gear * transmission type

3. Next, we use an interaction plot to characterize the relationship between variables:

```
> interaction.plot(mtcars$gear, mtcars$am, mtcars$mpg, type="b",
col=c(1:3),leg.bty="o", leg.bg="beige", lwd=2, pch=c(18,24,22),
xlab="Number of Gears", ylab="Mean Miles Per Gallon",
main="Interaction Plot")
```

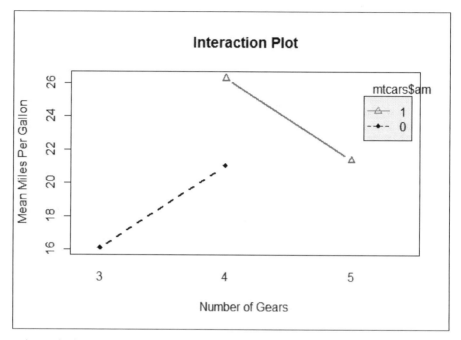

Interaction between the transmission type and the number of gears with the main effects, mpg

4. We then perform a two-way ANOVA on mpg with a combination of the gear and transmission-type factors:

```
> mpg_anova2 = aov(mtcars$mpg~factor(mtcars$gear)*factor(mtcars$
am))
```

```
> summary(mpg_anova2)
```

	Df	Sum Sq	Mean Sq	F value	Pr(>F)	
factor(mtcars$gear)	2	483.2	241.62	11.869	0.000185	***
factor(mtcars$am)	1	72.8	72.80	3.576	0.069001	.
Residuals	28	570.0	20.36			

```
---
```

```
Signif. codes:  0 '***' 0.001 '**' 0.01 '*' 0.05 '.' 0.1 ' ' 1
```

5. Similar to a one-way ANOVA, we can perform a post hoc comparison test to see the results of the two-way ANOVA model:

```
> TukeyHSD(mpg_anova2)
  Tukey multiple comparisons of means
    95% family-wise confidence level


Fit: aov(formula = mtcars$mpg ~ factor(mtcars$gear) *
factor(mtcars$am))


$`factor(mtcars$gear)`
          diff        lwr        upr      p adj
4-3  8.426667  4.1028616 12.750472 0.0001301
5-3  5.273333 -0.4917401 11.038407 0.0779791
5-4 -3.153333 -9.0958350  2.789168 0.3999532


$`factor(mtcars$am)`
         diff        lwr       upr      p adj
1-0 1.805128 -1.521483 5.13174 0.2757926
```

6. We then visualize the differences in mean levels with the `plot` function:

```
> par(mfrow=c(1,2))
```
```
> plot(TukeyHSD(mpg_anova2))
```

The comparison plot of differences in mean levels by the transmission type and the number of gears

How it works...

In this recipe, we perform a two-way ANOVA to examine the influences of the independent variables, gear and am, on the dependent variable, mpg. In the first step, we use a boxplot to examine the mean of mpg by the number of gears and the transmission type. Secondly, we apply an interaction plot to visualize the change in mpg through the different numbers of gears with lines separated by the transmission type.

The resulting plot shows that the number of gears does have an effect on the mean of mpg, but does not show a positive relationship either. Thirdly, we perform a two-way ANOVA with the aov function. The output shows that the p-value of the gear factor rejects the null hypothesis, while the factor, transmission type, does not reject the null hypothesis. In other words, cars with different numbers of gears are more likely to have different means of mpg. Finally, in order to examine which two populations have the largest differences, we perform a post hoc analysis, which reveals that cars with four gears and three gears, respectively, have the largest difference in terms of the mean, mpg.

See also

▸ For multivariate analysis of variances, the function, manova, can be used to examine the effect of multiple independent variables on multiple dependent variables. Further information about MANOVA is included within the help function in R:

```
> ?MANOVA
```

4
Understanding Regression Analysis

In this chapter, we will cover the following recipes:

- ▶ Fitting a linear regression model with lm
- ▶ Summarizing linear model fits
- ▶ Using linear regression to predict unknown values
- ▶ Generating a diagnostic plot of a fitted model
- ▶ Fitting a polynomial regression model with lm
- ▶ Fitting a robust linear regression model with rlm
- ▶ Studying a case of linear regression on SLID data
- ▶ Applying the Gaussian model for generalized linear regression
- ▶ Applying the Poisson model for generalized linear regression
- ▶ Applying the Binomial model for generalized linear regression
- ▶ Fitting a generalized additive model to data
- ▶ Visualizing a generalized additive model
- ▶ Diagnosing a generalized additive model

Introduction

Regression is a supervised learning method, which is employed to model and analyze the relationship between a dependent (response) variable and one or more independent (predictor) variables. One can use regression to build a prediction model, which can first be used to find the best fitted model with minimum squared errors of the fitted values. The fitted model can then be further applied to data for continuous value predictions.

There are many types of regression. If there is only one predictor variable, and the relationship between the response variable and independent variable is linear, we can apply a linear model. However, if there is more than one predictor variable, a multiple linear regression method should be used. When the relationship is nonlinear, one can use a nonlinear model to model the relationship between the predictor and response variables.

In this chapter, we introduce how to fit a linear model into data with the `lm` function. Next, for distribution in other than the normal Gaussian model (for example, Poisson or Binomial), we use the `glm` function with an appropriate link function correspondent to the data distribution. Finally, we cover how to fit a generalized additive model into data using the `gam` function.

Fitting a linear regression model with lm

The simplest model in regression is linear regression, which is best used when there is only one predictor variable, and the relationship between the response variable and the independent variable is linear. In R, we can fit a linear model to data with the `lm` function.

Getting ready

We need to prepare data with one predictor and response variable, and with a linear relationship between the two variables.

How to do it...

Perform the following steps to perform linear regression with `lm`:

1. You should install the `car` package and load its library:

   ```
   > install.packages("car")
   > library(car)
   ```

2. From the package, you can load the `Quartet` dataset:

   ```
   > data(Quartet)
   ```

3. You can use the `str` function to display the structure of the `Quartet` dataset:

   ```
   > str(Quartet)
   'data.frame':    11 obs. of  6 variables:
    $ x : int  10 8 13 9 11 14 6 4 12 7 ...
    $ y1: num  8.04 6.95 7.58 8.81 8.33 ...
    $ y2: num  9.14 8.14 8.74 8.77 9.26 8.1 6.13 3.1 9.13 7.26 ...
    $ y3: num  7.46 6.77 12.74 7.11 7.81 ...
    $ x4: int  8 8 8 8 8 8 8 19 8 8 ...
    $ y4: num  6.58 5.76 7.71 8.84 8.47 7.04 5.25 12.5 5.56 7.91 ...
   ```

4. Draw a scatter plot of the x and y variables with `plot`, and append a fitted line through the `lm` and `abline` function:

```
> plot(Quartet$x, Quartet$y1)
> lmfit = lm(y1~x, Quartet)
> abline(lmfit, col="red")
```

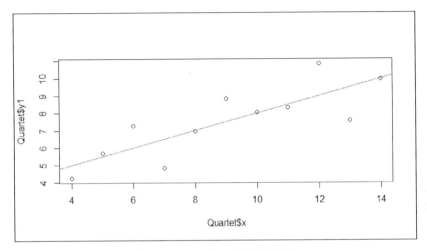

A simple regression plot fitted by lm

5. To view the fit model, execute the following:

```
> lmfit


Call:
lm(formula = y1 ~ x, data = Quartet)


Coefficients:
(Intercept)              x
    3.0001          0.5001
```

How it works...

The regression model has the `response ~ terms` form, where `response` is the response vector, and `terms` is a series of terms that specifies a predictor. We can illustrate a simple regression model in the formula $y=\alpha+\beta x$, where α is the intercept while the slope, β, describes the change in y when x changes. By using the least squares method, we can estimate $\beta = \frac{cov[x,y]}{var[x]}$ and $\alpha = \bar{y} - \beta\bar{x}$ (where $\bar{y}$ indicates the mean value of y and $\bar{x}$ denotes the mean value of x).

To perform linear regression, we first prepare the data that has a linear relationship between the predictor variable and response variable. In this example, we load Anscombe's quartet dataset from the package car. Within the dataset, the x and *y1* variables have a linear relationship, and we prepare a scatter plot of these variables. To generate the regression line, we use the lm function to generate a model of the two variables. Further, we use `abline` to plot a regression line on the plot. As per the previous screenshot, the regression line illustrates the linear relationship of x and *y1* variables. We can see that the coefficient of the fitted model shows the intercept equals 3.0001 and coefficient equals 0.5001. As a result, we can use the intercept and coefficient to infer the response value. For example, we can infer the response value when x at 3 is equal to *4.5103 (3 * 0.5001 + 3.0001)*.

There's more...

Besides the `lm` function, you can also use the `lsfit` function to perform simple linear regression. For example:

```
> plot(Quartet$x, Quartet$y1)
> lmfit2 = lsfit(Quartet$x,Quartet$y1)
> abline(lmfit2, col="red")
```

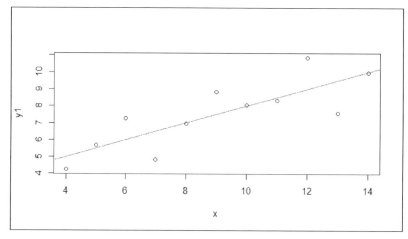

A simple regression fitted by the lsfit function.

Summarizing linear model fits

The `summary` function can be used to obtain the formatted coefficient, standard errors, degree of freedom, and other summarized information of a fitted model. This recipe introduces how to obtain overall information on a model through the use of the `summary` function.

Getting ready

You need to have completed the previous recipe by computing the linear model of the *x* and *y1* variables from the quartet, and have the fitted model assigned to the `lmfit` variable.

How to do it...

Perform the following step to summarize linear model fits:

1. Compute a detailed summary of the fitted model:

```
> summary(lmfit)


Call:
lm(formula = y1 ~ x)


Residuals:
     Min      1Q   Median      3Q     Max
-1.92127 -0.45577 -0.04136  0.70941  1.83882


Coefficients:
            Estimate Std. Error t value Pr(>|t|)
(Intercept)   3.0001     1.1247   2.667  0.02573 *
Quartet$x     0.5001     0.1179   4.241  0.00217 **
---
Signif. codes:  0 '***' 0.001 '**' 0.01 '*' 0.05 '.' 0.1 ' ' 1


Residual standard error: 1.237 on 9 degrees of freedom
Multiple R-squared:  0.6665,    Adjusted R-squared:  0.6295
F-statistic: 17.99 on 1 and 9 DF,  p-value: 0.00217
```

How it works...

The `summary` function is a generic function used to produce summary statistics. In this case, it computes and returns a list of the summary statistics of the fitted linear model. Here, it will output information such as residuals, coefficient standard error R-squared, f-statistic, and a degree of freedom. In the `Call` section, the function called to generate the fitted model is displayed. In the `Residuals` section, it provides a quick summary (min, 1Q, median, 3Q, max) of the distribution.

In the `Coefficients` section, each coefficient is a Gaussian random variable. Within this section, `Estimate` represents the mean distribution of the variable; `Std.Error` displays the standard error of the variable; the `t` value is `Estimate` divided by `Std.Error` and the `p` value indicates the probability of getting a value larger than the `t` value. In this sample, the `p` value of both intercepts (0.002573) and x (0.00217) have a 95 percent level of confidence.

Residual standard error outputs the standard deviation of residuals, while the degree of freedom indicates the differences between the observation in training samples and the number used in the model. Multiple R-squared is obtained by dividing the sum of squares. One can use R-squared to measure how close the data is to fit into the regression line. Mostly, the higher the R-squared, the better the model fits your data. However, it does not necessarily indicate whether the regression model is adequate. This means you might get a good model with a low R-squared or you can have a bad model with a high R-squared. Since multiple R-squared ignore a degree of freedom, the calculated score is biased. To make the calculation fair, an adjusted R-squared (0.6295) uses an unbiased estimate, and will be slightly less than multiple R-squared (0.6665). F-statistic is retrieved by performing an f-test on the model. A p value equal to 0.00217 (< 0.05) rejects the null hypothesis (no linear correlation between variables) and indicates that the observed `F` is greater than the critical `F` value. In other words, the result shows that there is a significant positive linear correlation between the variables.

See also

▸ For more information on the parameters used for obtaining a summary of the fitted model, you can use the `help` function or `?` to view the help page:

```
> ?summary.lm
```

▸ Alternatively, you can use the following functions to display the properties of the model:

```
>  coefficients(lmfit) # Extract model coefficients

>  confint(lmfit, level=0.95)  # Computes confidence intervals for
model parameters.

>  fitted(lmfit) # Extract model fitted values

>  residuals(lmfit) # Extract model residuals

>  anova(lmfit) # Compute analysis of variance tables for fitted
model object

>  vcov(lmfit) # Calculate variance-covariance matrix for a fitted
model object

>  influence(lmfit) # Diagnose quality of regression fits
```

Using linear regression to predict unknown values

With a fitted regression model, we can apply the model to predict unknown values. For regression models, we can express the precision of prediction with a prediction interval and a confidence interval. In the following recipe, we introduce how to predict unknown values under these two measurements.

Getting ready

You need to have completed the previous recipe by computing the linear model of the x and y1 variables from the `quartet` dataset.

How to do it...

Perform the following steps to predict values with linear regression:

1. Fit a linear model with the x and y1 variables:

    ```
    > lmfit = lm(y1~x, Quartet)
    ```

2. Assign values to be predicted into `newdata`:

    ```
    > newdata = data.frame(x = c(3,6,15))
    ```

3. Compute the prediction result using the confidence interval with `level` set as 0.95:

    ```
    > predict(lmfit, newdata, interval="confidence", level=0.95)
             fit      lwr       upr
    1   4.500364 2.691375   6.309352
    2   6.000636 4.838027   7.163245
    3 10.501455 8.692466 12.310443
    ```

4. Compute the prediction result using this prediction interval:

    ```
    > predict(lmfit, newdata, interval="predict")
             fit      lwr       upr
    1   4.500364 1.169022   7.831705
    2   6.000636 2.971271   9.030002
    3 10.501455 7.170113 13.832796
    ```

How it works...

We first build a linear fitted model with x and y1 variables. Next, we assign values to be predicted into a data frame, `newdata`. It is important to note that the generated model is in the form of y1 ~ x.

Next, we compute the prediction result using a confidence interval by specifying `confidence` in the argument interval. From the output of row 1, we get fitted y1 of the x=3 input, which equals to 4.500364, and a 95 percent confidence interval (set 0.95 in the `level` argument) of the y1 mean for x=3 is between 2.691375 and 6.309352. In addition to this, row 2 and 3 give the prediction result of y1 with an input of x=6 and x=15.

Next, we compute the prediction result using a prediction interval by specifying `prediction` in the argument interval. From the output of row 1, we can see fitted y1 of the x=3 input equals to 4.500364, and a 95 percent prediction interval of y1 for x=3 is between 1.169022 and 7.831705. Row 2 and 3 output the prediction result of y1 with an input of x=6 and x=15.

See also

▶ For those who are interested in the differences between prediction intervals and confidence intervals, you can refer to the Wikipedia entry *contrast with confidence intervals* at `http://en.wikipedia.org/wiki/Prediction_interval#Contrast_with_confidence_intervals`.

Generating a diagnostic plot of a fitted model

Diagnostics are methods to evaluate assumptions of the regression, which can be used to determine whether a fitted model adequately represents the data. In the following recipe, we introduce how to diagnose a regression model through the use of a diagnostic plot.

Getting ready

You need to have completed the previous recipe by computing a linear model of the x and y1 variables from the quartet, and have the model assigned to the `lmfit` variable.

How to do it...

Perform the following step to generate a diagnostic plot of the fitted model:

1. Plot the diagnostic plot of the regression model:

```
> par(mfrow=c(2,2))
> plot(lmfit)
```

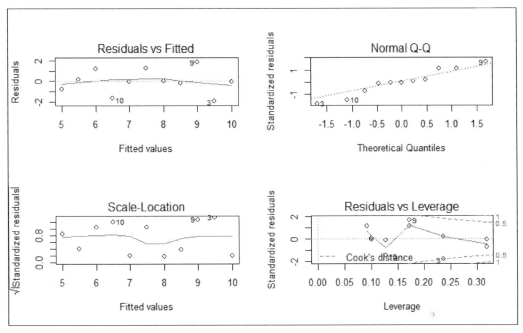

Diagnostic plots of the regression model

How it works...

The plot function generates four diagnostic plots of a regression model:

▸ The upper-left plot shows residuals versus fitted values. Within the plot, residuals represent the vertical distance from a point to the regression line. If all points fall exactly on the regression line, all residuals will fall exactly on the dotted gray line. The red line within the plot is a smooth curve with regard to residuals, and if all the dots fall exactly on the regression line, the position of the red line should exactly match the dotted gray line.

▸ The upper-right shows the normal of residuals. This plot verifies the assumption that residuals were normally distributed. Thus, if the residuals were normally distributed, they should lie exactly on the gray dash line.

- ▶ The **Scale-Location** plot on the bottom-left is used to measure the square root of the standardized residuals against the fitted value. Therefore, if all dots lie on the regression line, the value of *y* should be close to zero. Since it is assumed that the variance of residuals does not change the distribution substantially, if the assumption is correct, the red line should be relatively flat.

- ▶ The bottom-right plot shows standardized residuals versus leverage. The leverage is a measurement of how each data point influences the regression. It is a measurement of the distance from the centroid of regression and level of isolation (measured by whether it has neighbors). Also, you can find the contour of Cook's distance, which is affected by high leverage and large residuals. You can use this to measure how regression would change if a single point is deleted. The red line is smooth with regard to standardized residuals. For a perfect fit regression, the red line should be close to the dashed line with no points over 0.5 in Cook's distance.

There's more...

To see more of the diagnostic plot function, you can use the `help` function to access further information:

```
> ?plot.lm
```

In order to discover whether there are points with large Cook's distance, one can use the `cooks.distance` function to compute the Cook's distance of each point, and analyze the distribution of distance through visualization:

```
> plot(cooks.distance(lmfit))
```

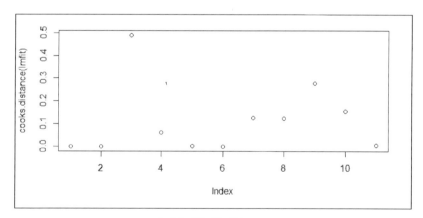

A plot of Cook's distance

In this case, where the point on index 3 shows greater Cook's distance than other points, one can investigate whether this point might be an outlier.

Fitting a polynomial regression model with lm

Some predictor variables and response variables may have a non-linear relationship, and their relationship can be modeled as an *nth* order polynomial. In this recipe, we introduce how to deal with polynomial regression using the lm and `poly` functions.

Getting ready

Prepare the dataset that includes a relationship between the predictor and response variable that can be modeled as an *nth* order polynomial. In this recipe, we will continue to use the Quartet dataset from the car package.

How to do it...

Perform the following steps to fit the polynomial regression model with lm:

1. First, we make a scatter plot of the x and y2 variables:

    ```
    > plot(Quartet$x, Quartet$y2)
    ```

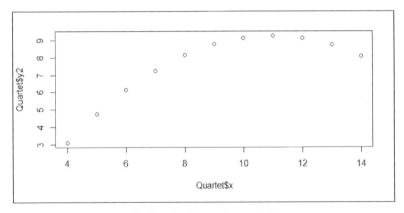

Scatter plot of variables x and y2

2. You can apply the `poly` function by specifying 2 in the argument:

```
> lmfit = lm(Quartet$y2~poly(Quartet$x,2))
> lines(sort(Quartet$x), lmfit$fit[order(Quartet$x)], col = "red")
```

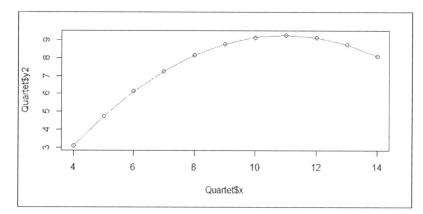

A quardratic fit example of the regression plot of variables x and y2

How it works

We can illustrate the second order polynomial regression model in formula, $y = \alpha + \beta x + cx^2$, where α is the intercept while β, illustrates regression coefficients.

In the preceding screenshot (step 1), the scatter plot of the x and y2 variables does not fit in a linear relationship, but shows a concave downward curve (or convex upward) with the turning point at x=11. In order to model the nonlinear relationship, we apply the `poly` function with an argument of 2 to fit the independent x variable and the dependent y2 variable. The red line in the screenshot shows that the model perfectly fits the data.

There's more...

You can also fit a second order polynomial model with an independent variable equal to the formula of the combined first order x variable and the second order x variable:

```
> plot(Quartet$x, Quartet$y2)
> lmfit = lm(Quartet$y2~ I(Quartet$x)+I(Quartet$x^2))
```

Fitting a robust linear regression model with rlm

An outlier in the dataset will move the regression line away from the mainstream. Apart from removing it, we can apply a robust linear regression to fit datasets containing outliers. In this recipe, we introduce how to apply rlm to perform robust linear regression to datasets containing outliers.

Getting ready

Prepare the dataset that contains an outlier that may move the regression line away from the mainstream. Here, we use the Quartet dataset loaded from the previous recipe.

How to do it...

Perform the following steps to fit the robust linear regression model with rlm:

1. Generate a scatter plot of the x variable against y3:

```
> plot(Quartet$x, Quartet$y3)
```

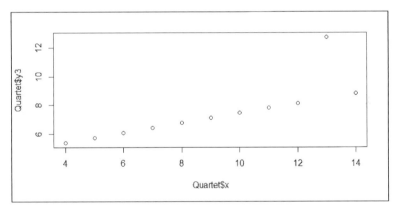

Scatter plot of variables x and y3

2. Next, you should import the MASS library first. Then, you can apply the rlm function to fit the model, and visualize the fitted line with the abline function:

```
> library(MASS)
> lmfit = rlm(Quartet$y3~Quartet$x)
> abline(lmfit, col="red")
```

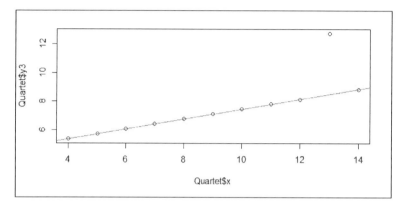

Robust linear regression to variables x and y3

How it works

As per the preceding screenshot (step 1), you may encounter datasets that include outliers away from the mainstream. To remove the effect of an outlier, we demonstrate how to apply a robust linear regression (rlm) to fit the data. In the second screenshot (step 2), the robust regression line ignores the outlier and matches the mainstream.

There's more...

To see the effect of how an outlier can move the regression line away from the mainstream, you may replace the rlm function used in this recipe to lm, and replot the graph:

```
> plot(Quartet$x, Quartet$y3)
> lmfit = lm(Quartet$y3~Quartet$x)
> abline(lmfit, col="red")
```

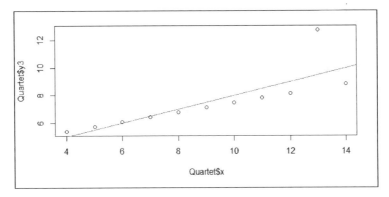

Linear regression on variables x and y3

It is obvious that outlier (x=13) moves the regression line away from the mainstream.

Studying a case of linear regression on SLID data

To summarize the contents of the previous section, we explore more complex data with linear regression. In this recipe, we demonstrate how to apply linear regression to analyze the **Survey of Labor and Income Dynamics (SLID)** dataset.

Getting ready

Check whether the `car` library is installed and loaded, as it is required to access the dataset SLID.

How to do it...

Follow these steps to perform linear regression on SLID data:

1. You can use the `str` function to get an overview of the data:

```
> str(SLID)
'data.frame':   7425 obs. of   5 variables:
 $ wages    : num   10.6 11 NA 17.8 NA ...
 $ education: num   15 13.2 16 14 8 16 12 14.5 15 10 ...
 $ age      : int   40 19 49 46 71 50 70 42 31 56 ...
 $ sex      : Factor w/ 2 levels "Female","Male": 2 2 2 2 2 1 1
 2 1 ...
 $ language : Factor w/ 3 levels "English","French",..: 1 1 3 3 1
 1 1 1 1 1 ..
```

2. First, we visualize the variable wages against language, age, education, and sex:

```
> par(mfrow=c(2,2))
> plot(SLID$wages ~ SLID$language)
> plot(SLID$wages ~ SLID$age)
> plot(SLID$wages ~ SLID$education)
> plot(SLID$wages ~ SLID$sex)
```

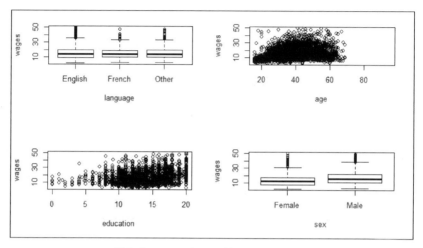

Plot of wages against multiple combinations

3. Then, we can use `lm` to fit the model:

```
> lmfit = lm(wages ~ ., data = SLID)
```

4. You can examine the summary of the fitted model through the `summary` function:

```
> summary(lmfit)


Call:
lm(formula = wages ~ ., data = SLID)


Residuals:
    Min      1Q  Median      3Q     Max
-26.062  -4.347  -0.797   3.237  35.908


Coefficients:
                Estimate Std. Error t value Pr(>|t|)
(Intercept)    -7.888779   0.612263 -12.885   <2e-16 ***
education       0.916614   0.034762  26.368   <2e-16 ***
```

```
age             0.255137   0.008714  29.278   <2e-16 ***
sexMale         3.455411   0.209195  16.518   <2e-16 ***
languageFrench -0.015223   0.426732  -0.036    0.972
languageOther   0.142605   0.325058   0.439    0.661
---
Signif. codes:  0 '***' 0.001 '**' 0.01 '*' 0.05 '.' 0.1 ' ' 1


Residual standard error: 6.6 on 3981 degrees of freedom
  (3438 observations deleted due to missingness)
Multiple R-squared:  0.2973,     Adjusted R-squared:  0.2964
F-statistic: 336.8 on 5 and 3981 DF,  p-value: < 2.2e-16
```

5. Drop the `language` attribute, and refit the model with the `lm` function:

```
> lmfit = lm(wages ~ age + sex + education, data = SLID)
> summary(lmfit)


Call:
lm(formula = wages ~ age + sex + education, data = SLID)


Residuals:
    Min      1Q  Median      3Q     Max
-26.111  -4.328  -0.792   3.243  35.892


Coefficients:
              Estimate Std. Error t value Pr(>|t|)
(Intercept) -7.905243   0.607771  -13.01   <2e-16 ***
age          0.255101   0.008634   29.55   <2e-16 ***
sexMale      3.465251   0.208494   16.62   <2e-16 ***
education    0.918735   0.034514   26.62   <2e-16 ***
---
Signif. codes:  0 '***' 0.001 '**' 0.01 '*' 0.05 '.' 0.1 ' ' 1


Residual standard error: 6.602 on 4010 degrees of freedom
  (3411 observations deleted due to missingness)
Multiple R-squared:  0.2972,     Adjusted R-squared:  0.2967
F-statistic: 565.3 on 3 and 4010 DF,  p-value: < 2.2e-16
```

6. We can then draw a diagnostic plot of `lmfit`:

```
> par(mfrow=c(2,2))
```

```
> plot(lmfit)
```

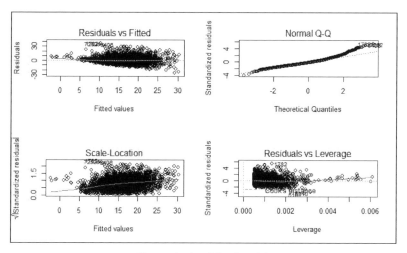

Diagnostic plot of fitted model

7. Next, we take the log of wages and replot the diagnostic plot:

```
> lmfit = lm(log(wages) ~ age + sex + education, data = SLID)
```

```
> plot(lmfit)
```

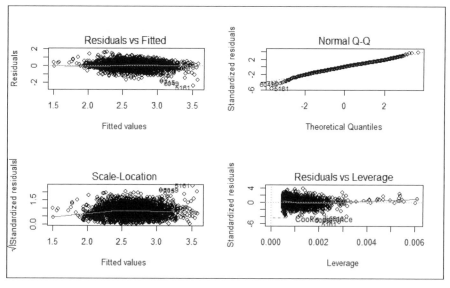

Diagnostic plot of adjusted fitted model

8. Next, you can diagnose the multi-colinearity of the regression model using the `vif` function:

```
> vif(lmfit)
      age       sex education
 1.011613  1.000834  1.012179
> sqrt(vif(lmfit)) > 2
      age       sex education
    FALSE     FALSE     FALSE
```

9. Then, you can install and load the `lmtest` package and diagnose the heteroscedasticity of the regression model with the `bptest` function:

```
> install.packages("lmtest")
> library(lmtest)
> bptest(lmfit)


        studentized Breusch-Pagan test


data:  lmfit
BP = 29.0311, df = 3, p-value = 2.206e-06
```

10. Finally, you can install and load the `rms` package. Then, you can correct standard errors with `robcov`:

```
> install.packages("rms")
> library(rms)
> olsfit = ols(log(wages) ~ age + sex + education, data= SLID, x=
TRUE, y= TRUE)
> robcov(olsfit)


Linear Regression Model


ols(formula = log(wages) ~ age + sex + education, data = SLID,
    x = TRUE, y = TRUE)


Frequencies of Missing Values Due to Each Variable
log(wages)       age       sex education
      3278         0         0       249
```

		Model Likelihood Ratio Test		Discrimination Indexes	
Obs	4014	LR chi2	1486.08	R2	0.309
sigma	0.4187	d.f.	3	R2 adj	0.309
d.f.	4010	Pr(> chi2)	0.0000	g	0.315

Residuals

Min	1Q	Median	3Q	Max
-2.36252	-0.27716	0.01428	0.28625	1.56588

	Coef	S.E.	t	Pr(>|t|)
Intercept	1.1169	0.0387	28.90	<0.0001
age	0.0176	0.0006	30.15	<0.0001
sex=Male	0.2244	0.0132	16.96	<0.0001
education	0.0552	0.0022	24.82	<0.0001

How it works...

This recipe demonstrates how to conduct linear regression analysis on the SLID dataset. First, we load the SLID data and display its structure through the use of the str function. From the structure of the data, we know that there are four independent variables that will affect the wages of the dependent variable.

Next, we explore the relationship of each independent variable to the dependent variable, wages, through visualization; the visualization result is shown in the preceding screenshot (step 2). In the upper-left section of this screenshot, you can find the box plot of three different languages against wages; the correlation between the languages and wages is not obvious. The upper-right section of the screenshot shows that the age appears to have a positive relationship with the dependent variable, wages. In the bottom-left of the screenshot, it is shown that education also appears to have a positive relationship with wages. Finally, the box plot in the bottom-right section of the screenshot shows that the wages of males are slightly higher than females.

Next, we fit all the attributes except for wages to the model as predictor variables. By summarizing the model, it is shown that education, age, and sex show a significance (*p-value* < 0.05). As a result, we drop the insignificant language attribute (which has a p-value greater than 0.05) and fit the three independent variables (education, sex, and age) with regard to the dependent variable (wages) in the linear model. This accordingly raises the f-statistic from 336.8 to 565.3.

Next, we generate the diagnostic plot of the fitted model. Within the diagnostic plot, all the four plots indicate that the regression model follows the regression assumption. However, from residuals versus fitted and scale-location plot, residuals of smaller fitted values are biased toward the regression model. Since wages range over several orders of magnitude, to induce the symmetry, we apply a log transformation to wages and refit the data into a regression model. The red line of residuals versus fitted values plot and the Scale-Location plot are now closer to the gray dashed line.

Next, we would like to test whether multi-colinearity exists in the model. Multi-colinearity takes place when a predictor is highly correlated with others. If multi-colinearity exists in the model, you might see some variables have a high R-squared value but are shown as variables insignificant. To detect multi-colinearity, we can calculate the variance inflation and generalized variance inflation factors for linear and generalized linear models with the `vif` function. If multi-colinearity exists, we should find predictors with the square root of variance inflation factor above 2. Then, we may remove redundant predictors or use a principal component analysis to transform predictors to a smaller set of uncorrelated components.

Finally, we would like to test whether **heteroscedasticity** exists in the model. Before discussing the definition of heteroscedasticity, we first have to know that in classic assumptions, the ordinary regression model assumes that the variance of the error is constant or homogeneous across observations. On the contrary, heteroscedasticity means that the variance is unequal across observations. As a result, heteroscedasticity may be biased toward the standard errors of our estimates and, therefore, mislead the testing of the hypothes. To detect and test heteroscedasticity, we can perform the **Breusch-Pagan** test for heteroscedasticity with the `bptest` function within the `lmtest` package. In this case, the p-value shows 2.206e-06 (<0.5), which rejects the null hypothesis of homoscedasticity (no heteroscedasticity). Here, it implies that the standard errors of the parameter estimates are incorrect. However, we can use robust standard errors to correct the standard error (do not remove the heteroscedasticity) and increase the significance of truly significant parameters with `robcov` from the `rms` package. However, since it only takes the fitted model from the `rms` series as an input, we have to fit the ordinary least squares model beforehand.

See also

▸ For more information about the SLID dataset, you can use the `help` function to view the related documentation:

```
>   ?SLID
```

Applying the Gaussian model for generalized linear regression

Generalized linear model (GLM) is a generalization of linear regression, which can include a link function to make a linear prediction. As a default setting, the family object for `glm` is Gaussian, which makes the `glm` function perform exactly the same as `lm`. In this recipe, we first demonstrate how to fit the model into the data using the `glm` function, and then show that `glm` with a Gaussian model performs exactly the same as `lm`.

Getting ready

Check whether the `car` library is installed and loaded as we require the SLID dataset from this package.

How to do it...

Perform the following steps to fit a generalized linear regression model with the Gaussian model:

1. Fit the independent variables, `age`, `sex`, and `education`, and dependent variable wages to `glm`:

```
> lmfit1 = glm(wages ~ age + sex + education, data = SLID,
family=gaussian)
> summary(lmfit1)


Call:
glm(formula = wages ~ age + sex + education, family = gaussian,
    data = SLID)


Deviance Residuals:
    Min      1Q   Median      3Q      Max
-26.111  -4.328  -0.792   3.243   35.892


Coefficients:
              Estimate Std. Error t value Pr(>|t|)
(Intercept) -7.905243   0.607771  -13.01   <2e-16 ***
age          0.255101   0.008634   29.55   <2e-16 ***
sexMale      3.465251   0.208494   16.62   <2e-16 ***
```

```
education     0.918735    0.034514    26.62    <2e-16 ***
---
Signif. codes:  0 '***' 0.001 '**' 0.01 '*' 0.05 '.' 0.1 ' ' 1


(Dispersion parameter for Gaussian family taken to be 43.58492)


    Null deviance: 248686  on 4013   degrees of freedom
Residual deviance: 174776  on 4010   degrees of freedom
    (3411 observations deleted due to missingness)
AIC: 26549


Number of Fisher Scoring iterations: 2
```

2. Fit the independent variables, age, sex, and education, and the dependent variable wages to lm:

```
> lmfit2 = lm(wages ~ age + sex + education, data = SLID)
> summary(lmfit2)

Call:
lm(formula = wages ~ age + sex + education, data = SLID)

Residuals:
    Min      1Q  Median      3Q     Max
-26.111  -4.328  -0.792   3.243  35.892

Coefficients:
             Estimate Std. Error t value Pr(>|t|)
(Intercept) -7.905243   0.607771  -13.01   <2e-16 ***
age          0.255101   0.008634   29.55   <2e-16 ***
sexMale      3.465251   0.208494   16.62   <2e-16 ***
education    0.918735   0.034514   26.62   <2e-16 ***
---
Signif. codes:  0 '***' 0.001 '**' 0.01 '*' 0.05 '.' 0.1 ' ' 1


Residual standard error: 6.602 on 4010 degrees of freedom
    (3411 observations deleted due to missingness)
Multiple R-squared:  0.2972,     Adjusted R-squared:  0.2967
F-statistic: 565.3 on 3 and 4010 DF,  p-value: < 2.2e-16
```

3. Use `anova` to compare the two fitted models:

```
> anova(lmfit1, lmfit2)
Analysis of Deviance Table

Model: gaussian, link: identity

Response: wages

Terms added sequentially (first to last)
```

	Df	Deviance	Resid. Df	Resid. Dev
NULL			4013	248686
age	1	31953	4012	216733
sex	1	11074	4011	205659
education	1	30883	4010	174776

How it works...

The `glm` function fits a model to the data in a similar fashion to the `lm` function. The only difference is that you can specify a different link function in the parameter, `family` (you may use `?family` in the console to find different types of link functions). In this recipe, we first input the independent variables, `age`, `sex`, and `education`, and the dependent `wages` variable to the `glm` function, and assign the built model to `lmfit1`. You can use the built model for further prediction.

Next, to determine whether `glm` with a Gaussian model is exactly the same as `lm`, we fit the independent variables, `age`, `sex`, and `education`, and the dependent variable, `wages`, to the `lm` model. By applying the `summary` function to the two different models, it reveals that the residuals and coefficients of the two output summaries are exactly the same.

Finally, we further compare the two fitted models with the `anova` function. The result of the `anova` function shows that the two models are similar, with the same **residual degrees of freedom** (**Res.DF**) and **residual sum of squares** (**RSS Df**).

See also

► For a comparison of generalized linear models with linear models, you can refer to *Venables, W. N., & Ripley, B. D. (2002). Modern applied statistics with S. Springer.*

Applying the Poisson model for generalized linear regression

Generalized linear models allow response variables that have error distribution models other than a normal distribution (Gaussian). In this recipe, we demonstrate how to apply Poisson as a family object within `glm` with regard to count data.

Getting ready

The prerequisite of this task is to prepare the count data, with all the input data values as integers.

How to do it...

Perform the following steps to fit the generalized linear regression model with the Poisson model:

1. Load the `warpbreaks` data, and use `head` to view the first few lines:

   ```
   > data(warpbreaks)
   > head(warpbreaks)
     breaks wool tension
   1     26    A       L
   2     30    A       L
   3     54    A       L
   4     25    A       L
   5     70    A       L
   6     52    A       L
   ```

2. We apply Poisson as a family object for the independent variable, `tension`, and the dependent variable, `breaks`:

   ```
   > rs1 = glm(breaks ~ tension, data=warpbreaks, family="poisson")
   > summary(rs1)


   Call:
   glm(formula = breaks ~ tension, family = "poisson", data =
   warpbreaks)


   Deviance Residuals:
       Min        1Q    Median        3Q       Max
   ```

```
     -4.2464   -1.6031   -0.5872    1.2813    4.9366


  Coefficients:
                Estimate Std. Error z value Pr(>|z|)
  (Intercept)   3.59426    0.03907  91.988  < 2e-16 ***
  tensionM     -0.32132    0.06027  -5.332 9.73e-08 ***
  tensionH     -0.51849    0.06396  -8.107 5.21e-16 ***
  ---
  Signif. codes:  0 '***' 0.001 '**' 0.01 '*' 0.05 '.' 0.1 ' ' 1


  (Dispersion parameter for Poisson family taken to be 1)


      Null deviance: 297.37  on 53  degrees of freedom
  Residual deviance: 226.43  on 51  degrees of freedom
  AIC: 507.09


  Number of Fisher Scoring iterations: 4
```

How it works...

Under the assumption of a Poisson distribution, the count data can be fitted to a log-linear model. In this recipe, we first loaded a sample count data from the `warpbreaks` dataset, which contained data regarding the number of warp breaks per loom. Next, we applied the `glm` function with breaks as a dependent variable, `tension` as an independent variable, and Poisson as a family object. Finally, we viewed the fitted log-linear model with the summary function.

See also

▸ To understand more on how a Poisson model is related to count data, you can refer to *Cameron, A. C., & Trivedi, P. K. (2013). Regression analysis of count data (No. 53). Cambridge university press.*

Applying the Binomial model for generalized linear regression

For a binary dependent variable, one may apply a binomial model as the family object in the `glm` function.

Getting ready

The prerequisite of this task is to prepare a binary dependent variable. Here, we use the vs variable (V engine or straight engine) as the dependent variable.

How to do it...

Perform the following steps to fit a generalized linear regression model with the Binomial model:

1. First, we examine the first six elements of vs within mtcars:

   ```
   > head(mtcars$vs)
   [1] 0 0 1 1 0 1
   ```

2. We apply the glm function with binomial as the family object:

   ```
   > lm1 = glm(vs ~ hp+mpg+gear,data=mtcars, family=binomial)
   > summary(lm1)


   Call:
   glm(formula = vs ~ hp + mpg + gear, family = binomial, data =
   mtcars)


   Deviance Residuals:
       Min       1Q     Median       3Q       Max
   -1.68166  -0.23743  -0.00945   0.30884   1.55688


   Coefficients:
               Estimate Std. Error z value Pr(>|z|)
   (Intercept) 11.95183    8.00322   1.493   0.1353
   hp          -0.07322    0.03440  -2.129   0.0333 *
   mpg          0.16051    0.27538   0.583   0.5600
   gear        -1.66526    1.76407  -0.944   0.3452
   ---
   Signif. codes:  0 '***' 0.001 '**' 0.01 '*' 0.05 '.' 0.1 ' ' 1


   (Dispersion parameter for binomial family taken to be 1)
   ```

```
       Null deviance: 43.860   on 31   degrees of freedom
   Residual deviance: 15.651   on 28   degrees of freedom
   AIC: 23.651


   Number of Fisher Scoring iterations: 7
```

How it works...

Within the binary data, each observation of the response value is coded as either 0 or 1. Fitting into the regression model of the binary data requires a binomial distribution function. In this example, we first load the binary dependent variable, vs, from the mtcars dataset. The vs is suitable for the binomial model as it contains binary data. Next, we fit the model into the binary data using the glm function by specifying binomial as the family object. Last, by referring to the summary, we can obtain the description of the fitted model.

See also

▸ If you specify the family object in parameters only, you will use the default link to fit the model. However, to use an alternative link function, you can add a link argument. For example:

```
> lm1 = glm(vs ~ hp+mpg+gear,data=mtcars,
family=binomial(link="probit"))
```

▸ If you would like to know how many alternative links you can use, please refer to the family document via the help function:

```
> ?family
```

Fitting a generalized additive model to data

Generalized additive model (**GAM**), which is used to fit generalized additive models, can be viewed as a semiparametric extension of GLM. While GLM holds the assumption that there is a linear relationship between dependent and independent variables, GAM fits the model on account of the local behavior of data. As a result, GAM has the ability to deal with highly nonlinear relationships between dependent and independent variables. In the following recipe, we introduce how to fit regression using a generalized additive model.

Getting ready

We need to prepare a data frame containing variables, where one of the variables is a response variable and the others may be predictor variables.

How to do it...

Perform the following steps to fit a generalized additive model into data:

1. First, load the mgcv package, which contains the gam function:

   ```
   > install.packages("mgcv")
   > library(mgcv)
   ```

2. Then, install the MASS package and load the Boston dataset:

   ```
   > install.packages("MASS")
   > library(MASS)
   > attach(Boston)
   > str(Boston)
   ```

3. Fit the regression using gam:

   ```
   > fit = gam(dis ~ s(nox))
   ```

4. Get the summary information of the fitted model:

   ```
   > summary(fit)
   Family: gaussian
   Link function: identity

   Formula:
   dis ~ s(nox)

   Parametric coefficients:
               Estimate Std. Error t value Pr(>|t|)
   (Intercept)  3.79504    0.04507   84.21   <2e-16 ***
   ---
   Signif. codes:  0 '***' 0.001 '**' 0.01 '*' 0.05 '.' 0.1 ' ' 1

   Approximate significance of smooth terms:
            edf Ref.df    F p-value
   s(nox) 8.434  8.893  189  <2e-16 ***
   ---
   Signif. codes:  0 '***' 0.001 '**' 0.01 '*' 0.05 '.' 0.1 ' ' 1

   R-sq.(adj) =  0.768   Deviance explained = 77.2%
   GCV = 1.0472  Scale est. = 1.0277    n = 506
   ```

How it works

GAM is designed to maximize the prediction of a dependent variable, y, from various distributions by estimating the nonparametric functions of the predictors that link to the dependent variable through a link function. The notion of GAM is $g(E(y)) = \beta + f_1(x_1) + f_2(x_2) + \cdots f_n(x_n)$, where an exponential family, *E*, is specified for *y*, along with the g link function; f denotes the link function of predictors.

The gam function is contained in the mgcv package, so, install this package first and load it into an R session. Next, load the Boston dataset (*Housing Values in the Suburbs of Boston*) from the MASS package. From the dataset, we use dis (the weighted mean of the distance to five Boston employment centers) as the dependent variable, and nox (nitrogen oxide concentration) as the independent variable, and then input them into the gam function to generate a fitted model.

Similar to glm, gam allows users to summarize the gam fit. From the summary, one can find the parametric parameter, significance of smoothed terms, and other useful information.

See also

▸ Apart from gam, the mgcv package provides another generalized additive model, bam, for large datasets. The bam package is very similar to gam, but uses less memory and is relatively more efficient. Please use the help function for more information on this model:

```
> ? bam
```

▸ For more information about generalized additive models in R, please refer to *Wood, S. (2006). Generalized additive models: an introduction with R. CRC press.*

Visualizing a generalized additive model

In this recipe, we demonstrate how to add a gam fitted regression line to a scatter plot. In addition, we visualize the gam fit using the plot function.

Getting ready

Complete the previous recipe by assigning a gam fitted model to the fit variable.

How to do it...

Perform the following steps to visualize the generalized additive model:

1. Generate a scatter plot using the `nox` and `dis` variables:

```
> plot(nox, dis)
```

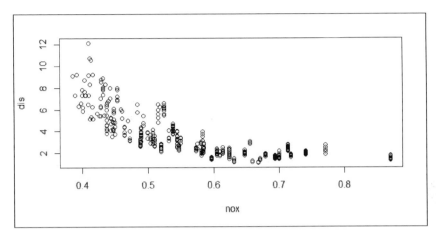

Scatter plot of variable nox against dis

2. Add the regression to the scatter plot:

```
> x = seq(0, 1, length = 500)
> y = predict(fit, data.frame(nox = x))
> lines(x, y, col = "red", lwd = 2)
```

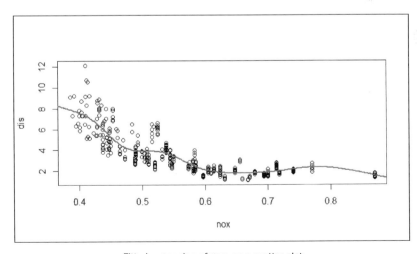

Fitted regression of gam on a scatter plot

3. Alternatively, you can plot the fitted model using the `plot` function:

```
> plot(fit)
```

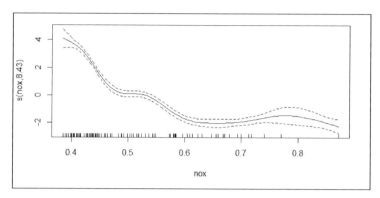

Plot of fitted gam

How it works...

To visualize the fitted regression, we first generate a scatter plot using the `dis` and `nox` variables. Then, we generate the sequence of x-axis, and respond y through the use of the `predict` function on the fitted model, `fit`. Finally, we use the `lines` function to add the regression line to the scatter plot.

Besides using the lines to add fitted regression lines on the scatter plot, `gam` has a `plot` function to visualize the fitted regression lines containing the confidence region. To shade the confidence region, we assign `shade = TRUE` within the function.

There's more...

The `vis.gam` function is used to produce perspective or contour plot views of the `gam` model predictions. It is helpful to observe how response variables interact with two predictor variables. The following is an example of a contour plot on the `Boston` dataset:

```
> fit2=gam(medv~crim+zn+crim:zn, data=Boston)
> vis.gam(fit2)
```

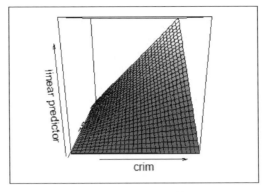

A sample contour plot produced by vis.gam

Diagnosing a generalized additive model

GAM also provides diagnostic information about the fitting procedure and results of the generalized additive model. In this recipe, we demonstrate how to plot diagnostic plots through the gam.check function.

Getting ready

Ensure that the previous recipe is completed with the gam fitted model assigned to the fit variable.

How to do it...

Perform the following step to diagnose the generalized additive model:

1. Generate the diagnostic plot using gam.check on the fitted model:

```
> gam.check(fit)

Method: GCV   Optimizer: magic
Smoothing parameter selection converged after 7 iterations.
The RMS GCV score gradient at convergence was 8.79622e-06 .
The Hessian was positive definite.
The estimated model rank was 10 (maximum possible: 10)
Model rank =  10 / 10
```

```
Basis dimension (k) checking results. Low p-value (k-index<1) may
indicate that k is too low, especially if edf is close to k'.

         k'    edf  k-index  p-value
s(nox) 9.000  8.434   0.397       0
```

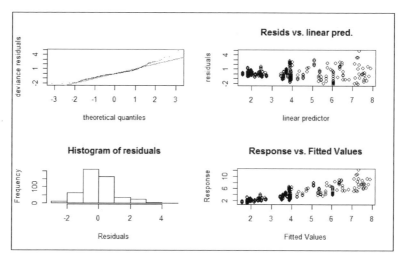

Diagnostic plot of fitted gam

How it works...

The gam.check function first produces the smoothing parameter estimation convergence information. In this example, the smoothing parameter, **GCV/UBRE (Generalized Cross Validation/ Unbiased Risk Estimator)** score converges after seven iterations. The mean absolute gradient of the GCV/UBRE function at the minimum is 8.79622e-06 and the estimated rank is 10. The dimension check is to test whether the basis dimension for a smooth function is adequate. From this example, the low p-value indicates that the k is set too low. One may adjust the dimension choice for smooth by specifying the argument, k, by fitting gam to the data.

In addition to providing information regarding smoothing parameter estimation convergence, the function returns four diagnostic plots. The upper-left section of the plot in the screenshot shows a **quantile-comparison** plot. This plot is useful to identify outliers and heavy tails. The upper-right section of the plot shows residuals versus linear predictors, which are useful in finding nonconstant error variances. The bottom-left section of the plot shows a histogram of the residuals, which is helpful in detecting non-normality. The bottom-right section shows response versus the fitted value.

There's more...

You can access the `help` function for more information on `gam.check`. In particular, this includes a detailed illustration of smoothing parameter estimation convergence and four returned plots:

```
> ?gam.check
```

In addition, more information for `choose.k` can be accessed by the following command:

```
> ?choose.k
```

5
Classification (I) – Tree, Lazy, and Probabilistic

In this chapter, we will cover the following recipes:

- ▶ Preparing the training and testing datasets
- ▶ Building a classification model with recursive partitioning trees
- ▶ Visualizing a recursive partitioning tree
- ▶ Measuring the prediction performance of a recursive partitioning tree
- ▶ Pruning a recursive partitioning tree
- ▶ Building a classification model with a conditional inference tree
- ▶ Visualizing a conditional inference tree
- ▶ Measuring the prediction performance of a conditional inference tree
- ▶ Classifying data with a k-nearest neighbor classifier
- ▶ Classifying data with logistic regression
- ▶ Classifying data with the Naïve Bayes classifier

Introduction

Classification is used to identify a category of new observations (testing datasets) based on a classification model built from the training dataset, of which the categories are already known. Similar to regression, classification is categorized as a supervised learning method as it employs known answers (label) of a training dataset to predict the answer (label) of the testing dataset. The main difference between regression and classification is that regression is used to predict continuous values.

In contrast to this, classification is used to identify the category of a given observation. For example, one may use regression to predict the future price of a given stock based on historical prices. However, one should use the classification method to predict whether the stock price will rise or fall.

In this chapter, we will illustrate how to use R to perform classification. We first build a training dataset and a testing dataset from the churn dataset, and then apply different classification methods to classify the churn dataset. In the following recipes, we will introduce the tree-based classification method using a traditional classification tree and a conditional inference tree, lazy-based algorithm, and a probabilistic-based method using the training dataset to build up a classification model, and then use the model to predict the category (class label) of the testing dataset. We will also use a confusion matrix to measure the performance.

Preparing the training and testing datasets

Building a classification model requires a training dataset to train the classification model, and testing data is needed to then validate the prediction performance. In the following recipe, we will demonstrate how to split the telecom churn dataset into training and testing datasets, respectively.

Getting ready

In this recipe, we will use the telecom churn dataset as the input data source, and split the data into training and testing datasets.

How to do it...

Perform the following steps to split the churn dataset into training and testing datasets:

1. You can retrieve the churn dataset from the C50 package:

    ```
    > install.packages("C50")
    > library(C50)
    > data(churn)
    ```

2. Use str to read the structure of the dataset:

    ```
    > str(churnTrain)
    ```

3. We can remove the state, area_code, and account_length attributes, which are not appropriate for classification features:

    ```
    > churnTrain = churnTrain[,! names(churnTrain) %in% c("state",
    "area_code", "account_length") ]
    ```

4. Then, split 70 percent of the data into the training dataset and 30 percent of the data into the testing dataset:

```
> set.seed(2)
> ind = sample(2, nrow(churnTrain), replace = TRUE, prob=c(0.7,
0.3))
> trainset = churnTrain[ind == 1,]
> testset = churnTrain[ind == 2,]
```

5. Lastly, use `dim` to explore the dimensions of both the training and testing datasets:

```
> dim(trainset)
[1] 2315    17
> dim(testset)
[1] 1018    17
```

How it works...

In this recipe, we use the telecom churn dataset as our example data source. The dataset contains 20 variables with 3,333 observations. We would like to build a classification model to predict whether a customer will churn, which is very important to the telecom company as the cost of acquiring a new customer is significantly more than retaining one.

Before building the classification model, we need to preprocess the data first. Thus, we load the churn data from the C50 package into the R session with the variable name as `churn`. As we determined that attributes such as `state`, `area_code`, and `account_length` are not useful features for building the classification model, we remove these attributes.

After preprocessing the data, we split it into training and testing datasets, respectively. We then use a sample function to randomly generate a sequence containing 70 percent of the training dataset and 30 percent of the testing dataset with a size equal to the number of observations. Then, we use a generated sequence to split the churn dataset into the training dataset, `trainset`, and the testing dataset, `testset`. Lastly, by using the `dim` function, we found that 2,315 out of the 3,333 observations are categorized into the training dataset, `trainset`, while the other 1,018 are categorized into the testing dataset, `testset`.

There's more...

You can combine the split process of the training and testing datasets into the `split.data` function. Therefore, you can easily split the data into the two datasets by calling this function and specifying the proportion and seed in the parameters:

```
> split.data = function(data, p = 0.7, s = 666){
+    set.seed(s)
+    index = sample(1:dim(data)[1])
```

```
+    train = data[index[1:floor(dim(data)[1] * p)], ]
+    test = data[index[((ceiling(dim(data)[1] * p)) + 1):dim(data)[1]], ]
+    return(list(train = train, test = test))
+ }
```

Building a classification model with recursive partitioning trees

A classification tree uses a split condition to predict class labels based on one or multiple input variables. The classification process starts from the root node of the tree; at each node, the process will check whether the input value should recursively continue to the right or left sub-branch according to the split condition, and stops when meeting any leaf (terminal) nodes of the decision tree. In this recipe, we will introduce how to apply a recursive partitioning tree on the customer churn dataset.

Getting ready

You need to have completed the previous recipe by splitting the churn dataset into the training dataset (`trainset`) and testing dataset (`testset`), and each dataset should contain exactly 17 variables.

How to do it...

Perform the following steps to split the churn dataset into training and testing datasets:

1. Load the rpart package:

    ```
    > library(rpart)
    ```

2. Use the rpart function to build a classification tree model:

    ```
    > churn.rp = rpart(churn ~ ., data=trainset)
    ```

3. Type churn.rp to retrieve the node detail of the classification tree:

    ```
    > churn.rp
    ```

4. Next, use the printcp function to examine the complexity parameter:

    ```
    > printcp(churn.rp)

    Classification tree:
    rpart(formula = churn ~ ., data = trainset)

    Variables actually used in tree construction:
    ```

```
[1] international_plan          number_customer_service_calls
[3] total_day_minutes          total_eve_minutes
[5] total_intl_calls           total_intl_minutes
[7] voice_mail_plan
```

Root node error: 342/2315 = 0.14773

n= 2315

	CP	nsplit	rel error	xerror	xstd
1	0.076023	0	1.00000	1.00000	0.049920
2	0.074561	2	0.84795	0.99708	0.049860
3	0.055556	4	0.69883	0.76023	0.044421
4	0.026316	7	0.49415	0.52632	0.037673
5	0.023392	8	0.46784	0.52047	0.037481
6	0.020468	10	0.42105	0.50877	0.037092
7	0.017544	11	0.40058	0.47076	0.035788
8	0.010000	12	0.38304	0.47661	0.035993

5. Next, use the `plotcp` function to plot the cost complexity parameters:

    ```
    > plotcp(churn.rp)
    ```

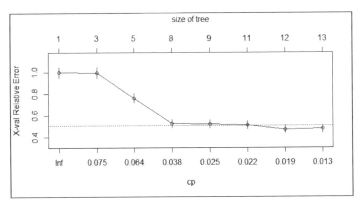

Figure 1: The cost complexity parameter plot

6. Lastly, use the `summary` function to examine the built model:

    ```
    > summary(churn.rp)
    ```

How it works...

In this recipe, we use a recursive partitioning tree from the `rpart` package to build a tree-based classification model. The recursive portioning tree includes two processes: recursion and partitioning. During the process of decision induction, we have to consider a statistic evaluation question (or simply a yes/no question) to partition the data into different partitions in accordance with the assessment result. Then, as we have determined the child node, we can repeatedly perform the splitting until the stop criteria is satisfied.

For example, the data (shown in the following figure) in the root node can be partitioned into two groups with regard to the question of whether **f1** is smaller than **X**. If so, the data is divided into the left-hand side. Otherwise, it is split into the right-hand side. Then, we can continue to partition the left-hand side data with the question of whether **f2** is smaller than **Y**:

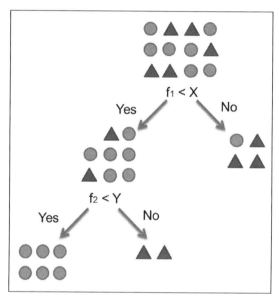

Figure 2: Recursive partioning tree

In the first step, we load the `rpart` package with the `library` function. Next, we build a classification model using the `churn` variable as a classification category (class label) and the remaining variables as input features.

After the model is built, you can type the variable name of the built model, `churn.rp`, to display the tree node details. In the printed node detail, `n` indicates the sample size, `loss` indicates the misclassification cost, `yval` stands for the classified membership (no or yes, in this case), and `yprob` stands for the probabilities of two classes (the left value refers to the probability reaching label `no`, and the right value refers to the probability reaching label, `yes`).

Then, we use the `printcp` function to print the complexity parameters of the built tree model. From the output of `printcp`, one should find the value of CP, a complexity parameter, which serves as a penalty to control the size of the tree. In short, the greater the CP value, the fewer the number of splits there are (`nsplit`). The output value (the `rel` error) represents the average deviance of the current tree divided by the average deviance of the null tree. A `xerror` value represents the relative error estimated by a 10-fold classification. `xstd` stands for the standard error of the relative error.

To make the **CP** (**cost complexity parameter**) table more readable, we use `plotcp` to generate an information graphic of the CP table. As per the screenshot (step 5), the x-axis at the bottom illustrates the `cp` value, the y-axis illustrates the relative error, and the upper x-axis displays the size of the tree. The dotted line indicates the upper limit of a standard deviation. From the screenshot, we can determine that minimum cross-validation error occurs when the tree is at a size of 12.

We can also use the `summary` function to display the function call, complexity parameter table for the fitted tree model, variable importance, which helps identify the most important variable for the tree classification (summing up to 100), and detailed information of each node.

The advantage of using the decision tree is that it is very flexible and easy to interpret. It works on both classification and regression problems, and more; it is nonparametric. Therefore, one does not have to worry about whether the data is linear separable. As for the disadvantage of using the decision tree, it is that it tends to be biased and over-fitted. However, you can conquer the bias problem through the use of a conditional inference tree, and solve the problem of over-fitting through a random forest method or tree pruning.

See also

▸ For more information about the `rpart`, `printcp`, and `summary` functions, please use the `help` function:

```
> ?rpart
> ?printcp
> ?summary.rpart
```

▸ C50 is another package that provides a decision tree and a rule-based model. If you are interested in the package, you may refer to the document at `http://cran.r-project.org/web/packages/C50/C50.pdf`.

Visualizing a recursive partitioning tree

From the last recipe, we learned how to print the classification tree in a text format. To make the tree more readable, we can use the `plot` function to obtain the graphical display of a built classification tree.

Getting ready

One needs to have the previous recipe completed by generating a classification model, and assign the model into the `churn.rp` variable.

How to do it...

Perform the following steps to visualize the classification tree:

1. Use the `plot` function and the `text` function to plot the classification tree:

```
> plot(churn.rp, margin= 0.1)
> text(churn.rp, all=TRUE, use.n = TRUE)
```

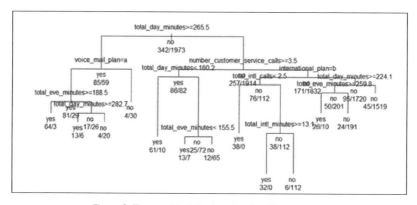

Figure 3: The graphical display of a classification tree

2. You can also specify the `uniform`, `branch`, and `margin` parameter to adjust the layout:

```
> plot(churn.rp, uniform=TRUE, branch=0.6, margin=0.1)
> text(churn.rp, all=TRUE, use.n = TRUE)
```

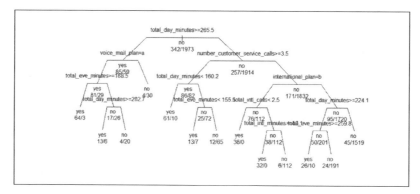

Figure 4: Adjust the layout of the classification tree

How it works...

Here, we demonstrate how to use the `plot` function to graphically display a classification tree. The `plot` function can simply visualize the classification tree, and you can then use the `text` function to add text to the plot.

In *Figure 3*, we assign margin = 0.1 as a parameter to add extra white space around the border to prevent the displayed text being truncated by the margin. It shows that the length of the branches displays the relative magnitude of the drop in deviance. We then use the text function to add labels for the nodes and branches. By default, the text function will add a split condition on each split, and add a category label in each terminal node. In order to add extra information on the tree plot, we set the parameter as all equal to TRUE to add a label to all the nodes. In addition to this, we add a parameter by specifying `use.n = TRUE` to add extra information, which shows that the actual number of observations fall into two different categories (no and yes).

In *Figure 4*, we set the option branch to 0.6 to add a shoulder to each plotted branch. In addition to this, in order to display branches of an equal length rather than relative magnitude of the drop in deviance, we set the option uniform to TRUE. As a result, *Figure 4* shows a classification tree with short shoulders and branches of equal length.

See also

▶ You may use `?plot.rpart` to read more about the plotting of the classification tree. This document also includes information on how to specify the parameters, `uniform`, `branch`, `compress`, `nspace`, `margin`, and `minbranch`, to adjust the layout of the classification tree.

Measuring the prediction performance of a recursive partitioning tree

Since we have built a classification tree in the previous recipes, we can use it to predict the category (class label) of new observations. Before making a prediction, we first validate the prediction power of the classification tree, which can be done by generating a classification table on the testing dataset. In this recipe, we will introduce how to generate a predicted label versus a real label table with the `predict` function and the `table` function, and explain how to generate a confusion matrix to measure the performance.

Getting ready

You need to have the previous recipe completed by generating the classification model, `churn.rp`. In addition to this, you have to prepare the training dataset, `trainset`, and the testing dataset, `testset`, generated in the first recipe of this chapter.

How to do it...

Perform the following steps to validate the prediction performance of a classification tree:

1. You can use the `predict` function to generate a predicted label of testing the dataset:

   ```
   > predictions = predict(churn.rp, testset, type="class")
   ```

2. Use the `table` function to generate a classification table for the testing dataset:

   ```
   > table(testset$churn, predictions)
         predictions
          yes   no
     yes 100    41
     no   18   859
   ```

3. One can further generate a confusion matrix using the `confusionMatrix` function provided in the `caret` package:

   ```
   > library(caret)
   > confusionMatrix(table(predictions, testset$churn))
   Confusion Matrix and Statistics


   predictions yes   no
           yes 100   18
           no   41  859


                  Accuracy : 0.942
                    95% CI : (0.9259, 0.9556)
       No Information Rate : 0.8615
       P-Value [Acc > NIR] : < 2.2e-16


                     Kappa : 0.7393
    Mcnemar's Test P-Value : 0.004181


               Sensitivity : 0.70922
               Specificity : 0.97948
            Pos Pred Value : 0.84746
            Neg Pred Value : 0.95444
                Prevalence : 0.13851
   ```

```
        Detection Rate : 0.09823
  Detection Prevalence : 0.11591
     Balanced Accuracy : 0.84435


        'Positive' Class : yes
```

How it works...

In this recipe, we use a `predict` function and built up classification model, `churn.rp`, to predict the possible class labels of the testing dataset, `testset`. The predicted categories (class labels) are coded as either no or yes. Then, we use the `table` function to generate a classification table on the testing dataset. From the table, we discover that there are 859 correctly predicted as no, while 18 are misclassified as yes. 100 of the yes predictions are correctly predicted, but 41 observations are misclassified into no. Further, we use the `confusionMatrix` function from the `caret` package to produce a measurement of the classification model.

See also

▶ You may use `?confusionMatrix` to read more about the performance measurement using the confusion matrix

▶ For those who are interested in the definition output by the confusion matrix, please refer to the Wikipedia entry, **Confusion_matrix** (`http://en.wikipedia.org/wiki/Confusion_matrix`)

Pruning a recursive partitioning tree

In previous recipes, we have built a complex decision tree for the churn dataset. However, sometimes we have to remove sections that are not powerful in classifying instances to avoid over-fitting, and to improve the prediction accuracy. Therefore, in this recipe, we introduce the cost complexity pruning method to prune the classification tree.

Getting ready

You need to have the previous recipe completed by generating a classification model, and assign the model into the `churn.rp` variable.

How to do it...

Perform the following steps to prune the classification tree:

1. Find the minimum cross-validation error of the classification tree model:

```
> min(churn.rp$cptable[,"xerror"])
[1] 0.4707602
```

2. Locate the record with the minimum cross-validation errors:

```
> which.min(churn.rp$cptable[,"xerror"])
7
```

3. Get the cost complexity parameter of the record with the minimum cross-validation errors:

```
> churn.cp = churn.rp$cptable[7,"CP"]
> churn.cp
[1] 0.01754386
```

4. Prune the tree by setting the `cp` parameter to the CP value of the record with minimum cross-validation errors:

```
> prune.tree = prune(churn.rp, cp= churn.cp)
```

5. Visualize the classification tree by using the `plot` and `text` function:

```
> plot(prune.tree, margin= 0.1)
> text(prune.tree, all=TRUE , use.n=TRUE)
```

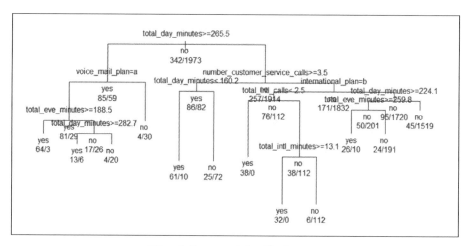

Figure 5: The pruned classification tree

6. Next, you can generate a classification table based on the pruned classification tree model:

```
> predictions = predict(prune.tree, testset, type="class")
> table(testset$churn, predictions)
     predictions
     yes  no
yes  95  46
no   14 863
```

7. Lastly, you can generate a confusion matrix based on the classification table:

```
> confusionMatrix(table(predictions, testset$churn))
Confusion Matrix and Statistics


predictions yes   no
        yes  95   14
        no   46  863


               Accuracy : 0.9411
                 95% CI : (0.9248, 0.9547)
    No Information Rate : 0.8615
    P-Value [Acc > NIR] : 2.786e-16

                  Kappa : 0.727
 Mcnemar's Test P-Value : 6.279e-05

            Sensitivity : 0.67376
            Specificity : 0.98404
         Pos Pred Value : 0.87156
         Neg Pred Value : 0.94939
             Prevalence : 0.13851
         Detection Rate : 0.09332
   Detection Prevalence : 0.10707
      Balanced Accuracy : 0.82890

       'Positive' Class : yes
```

How it works...

In this recipe, we discussed pruning a classification tree to avoid over-fitting and producing a more robust classification model. We first located the record with the minimum cross-validation errors within the `cptable`, and we then extracted the CP of the record and assigned the value to `churn.cp`. Next, we used the `prune` function to prune the classification tree with `churn.cp` as the parameter. Then, by using the `plot` function, we graphically displayed the pruned classification tree. From *Figure 5*, it is clear that the split of the tree is less than the original classification tree (*Figure 3*). Lastly, we produced a classification table and used the confusion matrix to validate the performance of the pruned tree. The result shows that the accuracy (0.9411) is slightly lower than the original model (0.942), and also suggests that the pruned tree may not perform better than the original classification tree as we have pruned some split conditions (Still, one should examine the change in sensitivity and specificity). However, the pruned tree model is more robust as it removes some split conditions that may lead to over-fitting.

See also

▶   For those who would like to know more about cost complexity pruning, please refer to the Wikipedia article for **Pruning (decision_trees)**: `http://en.wikipedia.org/wiki/Pruning_(decision_trees`

Building a classification model with a conditional inference tree

In addition to traditional decision trees (`rpart`), conditional inference trees (`ctree`) are another popular tree-based classification method. Similar to traditional decision trees, conditional inference trees also recursively partition the data by performing a univariate split on the dependent variable. However, what makes conditional inference trees different from traditional decision trees is that conditional inference trees adapt the significance test procedures to select variables rather than selecting variables by maximizing information measures (`rpart` employs a Gini coefficient). In this recipe, we will introduce how to adapt a conditional inference tree to build a classification model.

Getting ready

You need to have the first recipe completed by generating the training dataset, `trainset`, and the testing dataset, `testset`.

How to do it...

Perform the following steps to build the conditional inference tree:

1. First, we use `ctree` from the `party` package to build the classification model:

```
> library(party)
> ctree.model = ctree(churn ~ . , data = trainset)
```

2. Then, we examine the built tree model:

```
> ctree.model
```

How it works...

In this recipe, we used a conditional inference tree to build a classification tree. The use of `ctree` is similar to `rpart`. Therefore, you can easily test the classification power using either a traditional decision tree or a conditional inference tree while confronting classification problems. Next, we obtain the node details of the classification tree by examining the built model. Within the model, we discover that `ctree` provides information similar to a split condition, criterion (1 – p-value), statistics (test statistics), and weight (the case weight corresponding to the node). However, it does not offer as much information as `rpart` does through the use of the `summary` function.

See also

▶ You may use the `help` function to refer to the definition of **Binary Tree Class** and read more about the properties of binary trees:

```
> help("BinaryTree-class")
```

Visualizing a conditional inference tree

Similar to `rpart`, the `party` package also provides a visualization method for users to plot conditional inference trees. In the following recipe, we will introduce how to use the `plot` function to visualize conditional inference trees.

Getting ready

You need to have the first recipe completed by generating the conditional inference tree model, `ctree.model`. In addition to this, you need to have both, `trainset` and `testset`, loaded in an R session.

How to do it...

Perform the following steps to visualize the conditional inference tree:

1. Use the `plot` function to plot `ctree.model` built in the last recipe:

    ```
    > plot(ctree.model)
    ```

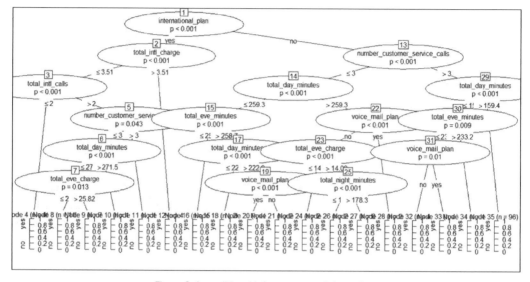

Figure 6: A conditional inference tree of churn data

2. To obtain a simple conditional inference tree, one can reduce the built model with less input features, and redraw the classification tree:

    ```
    > daycharge.model = ctree(churn ~ total_day_charge, data =
    trainset)
    ```

    ```
    > plot(daycharge.model)
    ```

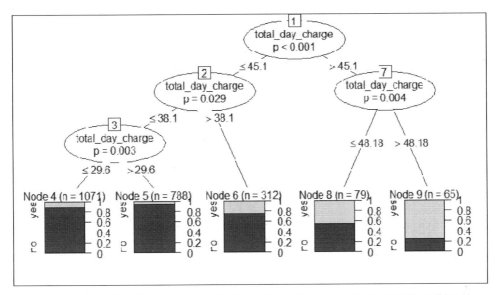

Figure 7: A conditional inference tree using the total_day_charge variable as only split condition

How it works...

To visualize the node detail of the conditional inference tree, we can apply the plot function on a built classification model. The output figure reveals that every intermediate node shows the dependent variable name and the p-value. The split condition is displayed on the left and right branches. The terminal nodes show the number of categorized observations, *n*, and the probability of a class label of either 0 or 1.

Taking *Figure 7* as an example, we first build a classification model using total_day_charge as the only feature and churn as the class label. The built classification tree shows that when total_day_charge is above 48.18, the lighter gray area is greater than the darker gray in node 9, which indicates that the customer with a day charge of over 48.18 has a greater likelihood to churn (label = yes).

See also

▸ The visualization of the conditional inference tree comes from the plot. BinaryTree function. If you are interested in adjusting the layout of the classification tree, you may use the help function to read the following document:

```
> ?plot.BinaryTree
```

Measuring the prediction performance of a conditional inference tree

After building a conditional inference tree as a classification model, we can use the `treeresponse` and `predict` functions to predict categories of the testing dataset, `testset`, and further validate the prediction power with a classification table and a confusion matrix.

Getting ready

You need to have the previous recipe completed by generating the conditional inference tree model, `ctree.model`. In addition to this, you need to have both `trainset` and `testset` loaded in an R session.

How to do it...

Perform the following steps to measure the prediction performance of a conditional inference tree:

1. You can use the `predict` function to predict the category of the testing dataset, `testset`:

    ```
    > ctree.predict = predict(ctree.model ,testset)
    > table(ctree.predict, testset$churn)
    ```

    ```
    ctree.predict yes   no
             yes   99   15
             no    42  862
    ```

2. Furthermore, you can use `confusionMatrix` from the caret package to generate the performance measurements of the prediction result:

    ```
    > confusionMatrix(table(ctree.predict, testset$churn))
    Confusion Matrix and Statistics
    ```

    ```
    ctree.predict yes   no
             yes   99   15
             no    42  862
    ```

    ```
              Accuracy : 0.944
                95% CI : (0.9281, 0.9573)
    ```

```
             No Information Rate : 0.8615
           P-Value [Acc > NIR] : < 2.2e-16


                        Kappa : 0.7449
      Mcnemar's Test P-Value : 0.0005736


                  Sensitivity : 0.70213
                  Specificity : 0.98290
               Pos Pred Value : 0.86842
               Neg Pred Value : 0.95354
                   Prevalence : 0.13851
               Detection Rate : 0.09725
         Detection Prevalence : 0.11198
            Balanced Accuracy : 0.84251


              'Positive' Class : yes
```

3. You can also use the `treeresponse` function, which will tell you the list of class probabilities:

```
> tr = treeresponse(ctree.model, newdata = testset[1:5,])
> tr
[[1]]
[1] 0.03497409 0.96502591

[[2]]
[1] 0.02586207 0.97413793

[[3]]
[1] 0.02586207 0.97413793

[[4]]
[1] 0.02586207 0.97413793

[[5]]
[1] 0.03497409 0.96502591
```

How it works...

In this recipe, we first demonstrate that one can use the `prediction` function to predict the category (class label) of the testing dataset, `testset`, and then employ a `table` function to generate a classification table. Next, you can use the `confusionMatrix` function built into the caret package to determine the performance measurements.

In addition to the `predict` function, `treeresponse` is also capable of estimating the class probability, which will often classify labels with a higher probability. In this example, we demonstrated how to obtain the estimated class probability using the top five records of the testing dataset, `testset`. The `treeresponse` function returns a list of five probabilities. You can use the list to determine the label of instance.

See also

  ▸ For the `predict` function, you can specify the type as `response`, `prob`, or `node`. If you specify the type as `prob` when using the `predict` function (for example, `predict(... type="prob")`), you will get exactly the same result as what `treeresponse` returns.

Classifying data with the k-nearest neighbor classifier

K-nearest neighbor (**knn**) is a nonparametric lazy learning method. From a nonparametric view, it does not make any assumptions about data distribution. In terms of lazy learning, it does not require an explicit learning phase for generalization. The following recipe will introduce how to apply the k-nearest neighbor algorithm on the churn dataset.

Getting ready

You need to have the previous recipe completed by generating the training and testing datasets.

How to do it...

Perform the following steps to classify the churn data with the k-nearest neighbor algorithm:

1. First, one has to install the `class` package and have it loaded in an R session:

```
> install.packages("class")
> library(class)
```

2. Replace `yes` and `no` of the `voice_mail_plan` and `international_plan` attributes in both the training dataset and testing dataset to 1 and 0:

```
> levels(trainset$international_plan) = list("0"="no", "1"="yes")
> levels(trainset$voice_mail_plan) = list("0"="no", "1"="yes")
> levels(testset$international_plan) = list("0"="no", "1"="yes")
> levels(testset$voice_mail_plan) = list("0"="no", "1"="yes")
```

3. Use the `knn` classification method on the training dataset and the testing dataset:

```
> churn.knn  = knn(trainset[,! names(trainset) %in% c("churn")],
testset[,! names(testset) %in% c("churn")], trainset$churn, k=3)
```

4. Then, you can use the `summary` function to retrieve the number of predicted labels:

```
> summary(churn.knn)
```

```
yes  no
 77 941
```

5. Next, you can generate the classification matrix using the `table` function:

```
> table(testset$churn, churn.knn)
```

```
       churn.knn

       yes   no
yes    44   97
no     33  844
```

6. Lastly, you can generate a confusion matrix by using the `confusionMatrix` function:

```
> confusionMatrix(table(testset$churn, churn.knn))
Confusion Matrix and Statistics
```

```
       churn.knn

       yes   no
yes    44   97
no     33  844
```

```
              Accuracy : 0.8723
                95% CI : (0.8502, 0.8922)
    No Information Rate : 0.9244
    P-Value [Acc > NIR] : 1


                 Kappa : 0.339
```

```
Mcnemar's Test P-Value : 3.286e-08

          Sensitivity : 0.57143
          Specificity : 0.89692
       Pos Pred Value : 0.31206
       Neg Pred Value : 0.96237
           Prevalence : 0.07564
       Detection Rate : 0.04322
 Detection Prevalence : 0.13851
    Balanced Accuracy : 0.73417


     'Positive' Class : yes
```

How it works...

knn trains all samples and classifies new instances based on a similarity (distance) measure. For example, the similarity measure can be formulated as follows:

▸ **Euclidian Distance:** $\sqrt{\sum_{i=1}^{k}\left(x_i - y_i\right)^2}$

▸ **Manhattan Distance:** $\sum_{i=1}^{k}\left|\left(x_i - y_i\right)\right|$

In knn, a new instance is classified to a label (class) that is common among the k-nearest neighbors. If *k = 1*, then the new instance is assigned to the class where its nearest neighbor belongs. The only required input for the algorithm is k. If we give a small k input, it may lead to over-fitting. On the other hand, if we give a large k input, it may result in under-fitting. To choose a proper k-value, one can count on cross-validation.

The advantages of knn are:

▸ The cost of the learning process is zero

▸ It is nonparametric, which means that you do not have to make the assumption of data distribution

▸ You can classify any data whenever you can find similarity measures of given instances

The main disadvantages of knn are:

▸ It is hard to interpret the classified result.

▸ It is an expensive computation for a large dataset.

▸ The performance relies on the number of dimensions. Therefore, for a high dimension problem, you should reduce the dimension first to increase the process performance.

The use of knn does not vary significantly from applying a tree-based algorithm mentioned in the previous recipes. However, while a tree-based algorithm may show you the decision tree model, the output produced by knn only reveals classification category factors. However, before building a classification model, one should replace the attribute with a string type to an integer since the k-nearest neighbor algorithm needs to calculate the distance between observations. Then, we build up a classification model by specifying *k=3*, which means choosing the three nearest neighbors. After the classification model is built, we can generate a classification table using predicted factors and the testing dataset label as the input. Lastly, we can generate a confusion matrix from the classification table. The confusion matrix output reveals an accuracy result of (0.8723), which suggests that both the tree-based methods mentioned in previous recipes outperform the accuracy of the k-nearest neighbor classification method in this case. Still, we cannot determine which model is better depending merely on accuracy, one should also examine the specificity and sensitivity from the output.

See also

▸ There is another package named `kknn`, which provides a weighted k-nearest neighbor classification, regression, and clustering. You can learn more about the package by reading this document: `http://cran.r-project.org/web/packages/kknn/kknn.pdf`.

Classifying data with logistic regression

Logistic regression is a form of probabilistic statistical classification model, which can be used to predict class labels based on one or more features. The classification is done by using the `logit` function to estimate the outcome probability. One can use logistic regression by specifying the family as a binomial while using the `glm` function. In this recipe, we will introduce how to classify data using logistic regression.

Getting ready

You need to have completed the first recipe by generating training and testing datasets.

How to do it...

Perform the following steps to classify the churn data with logistic regression:

1. With the specification of family as a binomial, we apply the `glm` function on the dataset, `trainset`, by using churn as a class label and the rest of the variables as input features:

   ```
   > fit = glm(churn ~ ., data = trainset, family=binomial)
   ```

2. Use the `summary` function to obtain summary information of the built logistic regression model:

   ```
   > summary(fit)
   ```

   ```
   Call:

   glm(formula = churn ~ ., family = binomial, data = trainset)


   Deviance Residuals:
        Min        1Q    Median        3Q       Max
    -3.1519    0.1983    0.3460    0.5186    2.1284


   Coefficients:
   ```

	Estimate	Std. Error	z value	Pr(>|z|)
(Intercept)	8.3462866	0.8364914	9.978	< 2e-16
international_planyes	-2.0534243	0.1726694	-11.892	< 2e-16
voice_mail_planyes	1.3445887	0.6618905	2.031	0.042211
number_vmail_messages	-0.0155101	0.0209220	-0.741	0.458496
total_day_minutes	0.2398946	3.9168466	0.061	0.951163
total_day_calls	-0.0014003	0.0032769	-0.427	0.669141
total_day_charge	-1.4855284	23.0402950	-0.064	0.948592
total_eve_minutes	0.3600678	1.9349825	0.186	0.852379

total_eve_calls 0.388928	-0.0028484	0.0033061	-0.862	
total_eve_charge 0.849475	-4.3204432	22.7644698	-0.190	
total_night_minutes 0.672367	0.4431210	1.0478105	0.423	
total_night_calls 0.904588	0.0003978	0.0033188	0.120	
total_night_charge 0.670188	-9.9162795	23.2836376	-0.426	
total_intl_minutes 0.942435	0.4587114	6.3524560	0.072	
total_intl_calls 0.000464	0.1065264	0.0304318	3.500	
total_intl_charge 0.929538	-2.0803428	23.5262100	-0.088	
number_customer_service_calls 16	-0.5109077	0.0476289	-10.727	< 2e-

(Intercept)	***
international_planyes	***
voice_mail_planyes	*
number_vmail_messages	
total_day_minutes	
total_day_calls	
total_day_charge	
total_eve_minutes	
total_eve_calls	
total_eve_charge	
total_night_minutes	
total_night_calls	
total_night_charge	
total_intl_minutes	
total_intl_calls	***
total_intl_charge	
number_customer_service_calls	***

```
Signif. codes:   0 '***' 0.001 '**' 0.01 '*' 0.05 '.' 0.1 ' ' 1


(Dispersion parameter for binomial family taken to be 1)


    Null deviance: 1938.8  on 2314  degrees of freedom
Residual deviance: 1515.3  on 2298  degrees of freedom
AIC: 1549.3


Number of Fisher Scoring iterations: 6
```

3. Then, we find that the built model contains insignificant variables, which would lead to misclassification. Therefore, we use significant variables only to train the classification model:

```
> fit = glm(churn ~ international_plan + voice_mail_plan+total_
intl_calls+number_customer_service_calls, data = trainset,
family=binomial)
> summary(fit)


Call:
glm(formula = churn ~ international_plan + voice_mail_plan +
    total_intl_calls + number_customer_service_calls, family =
binomial,
    data = trainset)


Deviance Residuals:
    Min       1Q    Median       3Q       Max
-2.7308   0.3103   0.4196   0.5381   1.6716
```

Coefficients:

	Estimate	Std. Error	z value
(Intercept)	2.32304	0.16770	13.852
international_planyes	-2.00346	0.16096	-12.447
voice_mail_planyes	0.79228	0.16380	4.837
total_intl_calls	0.08414	0.02862	2.939
number_customer_service_calls	-0.44227	0.04451	-9.937

$$Pr(>|z|)$$

```
(Intercept)                          < 2e-16 ***
international_planyes                 < 2e-16 ***
voice_mail_planyes                   1.32e-06 ***
total_intl_calls                     0.00329 **
number_customer_service_calls        < 2e-16 ***
---
Signif. codes:
0  es:    des:   **rvice_calls < '.  es:    de


(Dispersion parameter for binomial family taken to be 1)


    Null deviance: 1938.8  on 2314  degrees of freedom
Residual deviance: 1669.4  on 2310  degrees of freedom
AIC: 1679.4


Number of Fisher Scoring iterations: 5
```

4. Then, you can then use a fitted model, `fit`, to predict the outcome of `testset`. You can also determine the class by judging whether the probability is above 0.5:

```
> pred = predict(fit,testset, type="response")
> Class = pred >.5
```

5. Next, the use of the `summary` function will show you the binary outcome count, and reveal whether the probability is above 0.5:

```
> summary(Class)
   Mode    FALSE    TRUE    NA's
logical       29     989       0
```

6. You can generate the counting statistics based on the testing dataset label and predicted result:

```
> tb = table(testset$churn,Class)
> tb
      Class
      FALSE TRUE
  yes    18  123
  no     11  866
```

7. You can turn the statistics of the previous step into a classification table, and then generate the confusion matrix:

```
> churn.mod = ifelse(testset$churn == "yes", 1, 0)
> pred_class = churn.mod
> pred_class[pred<=.5] = 1- pred_class[pred<=.5]
> ctb = table(churn.mod, pred_class)
> ctb
          pred_class
churn.mod   0    1
        0 866   11
        1  18  123
> confusionMatrix(ctb)
Confusion Matrix and Statistics

          pred_class
churn.mod   0    1
        0 866   11
        1  18  123

               Accuracy : 0.9715
                 95% CI : (0.9593, 0.9808)
    No Information Rate : 0.8684
    P-Value [Acc > NIR] : <2e-16

                  Kappa : 0.8781
 Mcnemar's Test P-Value : 0.2652

            Sensitivity : 0.9796
            Specificity : 0.9179
         Pos Pred Value : 0.9875
         Neg Pred Value : 0.8723
             Prevalence : 0.8684
         Detection Rate : 0.8507
   Detection Prevalence : 0.8615
      Balanced Accuracy : 0.9488

       'Positive' Class : 0
```

How it works...

Logistic regression is very similar to linear regression; the main difference is that the dependent variable in linear regression is continuous, but the dependent variable in logistic regression is dichotomous (or nominal). The primary goal of logistic regression is to use logit to yield the probability of a nominal variable is related to the measurement variable. We can formulate logit in following equation: $\ln(P/(1-P))$, where P is the probability that certain event occurs.

The advantage of logistic regression is that it is easy to interpret, it directs model logistic probability, and provides a confidence interval for the result. Unlike the decision tree, which is hard to update the model, you can quickly update the classification model to incorporate new data in logistic regression. The main drawback of the algorithm is that it suffers from multicollinearity and, therefore, the explanatory variables must be linear independent. `glm` provides a generalized linear regression model, which enables specifying the model in the option family. If the family is specified to a binomial logistic, you can set the family as a binomial to classify the dependent variable of the category.

The classification process begins by generating a logistic regression model with the use of the training dataset by specifying `Churn` as the class label, the other variables as training features, and family set as binomial. We then use the `summary` function to generate the model's summary information. From the summary information, we may find some insignificant variables (p-values > 0.05), which may lead to misclassification. Therefore, we should consider only significant variables for the model.

Next, we use the `fit` function to predict the categorical dependent variable of the testing dataset, `testset`. The `fit` function outputs the probability of a class label, with a result equal to 0.5 and below, suggesting that the predicted label does not match the label of the testing dataset, and a probability above 0.5 indicates that the predicted label matches the label of the testing dataset. Further, we can use the `summary` function to obtain the statistics of whether the predicted label matches the label of the testing dataset. Lastly, in order to generate a confusion matrix, we first generate a classification table, and then use `confusionMatrix` to generate the performance measurement.

See also

- For more information of how to use the `glm` function, please refer to *Chapter 4, Understanding Regression Analysis*, which covers how to interpret the output of the `glm` function

Classifying data with the Naïve Bayes classifier

The Naïve Bayes classifier is also a probability-based classifier, which is based on applying the Bayes theorem with a strong independent assumption. In this recipe, we will introduce how to classify data with the Naïve Bayes classifier.

Getting ready

You need to have the first recipe completed by generating training and testing datasets.

How to do it...

Perform the following steps to classify the churn data with the Naïve Bayes classifier:

1. Load the `e1071` library and employ the `naiveBayes` function to build the classifier:

   ```
   > library(e1071)
   > classifier=naiveBayes(trainset[, !names(trainset) %in%
   c("churn")], trainset$churn)
   ```

2. Type `classifier` to examine the function call, a-priori probability, and conditional probability:

   ```
   > classifier


   Naive Bayes Classifier for Discrete Predictors


   Call:
   naiveBayes.default(x = trainset[, !names(trainset) %in%
   c("churn")],
       y = trainset$churn)


   A-priori probabilities:
   trainset$churn
         yes         no
   0.1477322 0.8522678


   Conditional probabilities:
                   international_plan
   ```

```
trainset$churn          no          yes
        yes 0.70467836 0.29532164
        no  0.93512418 0.06487582
```

3. Next, you can generate a classification table for the testing dataset:

```
> bayes.table = table(predict(classifier, testset[,
!names(testset) %in% c("churn")]), testset$churn)
> bayes.table
```

```
       yes  no
 yes   68   45
 no    73  832
```

4. Lastly, you can generate a confusion matrix from the classification table:

```
> confusionMatrix(bayes.table)
Confusion Matrix and Statistics
```

```
       yes  no
 yes   68   45
 no    73  832
```

```
                  Accuracy : 0.8841
                    95% CI : (0.8628, 0.9031)
       No Information Rate : 0.8615
       P-Value [Acc > NIR] : 0.01880

                     Kappa : 0.4701
   Mcnemar's Test P-Value : 0.01294

               Sensitivity : 0.4823
               Specificity : 0.9487
            Pos Pred Value : 0.6018
            Neg Pred Value : 0.9193
                Prevalence : 0.1385
            Detection Rate : 0.0668
      Detection Prevalence : 0.1110
         Balanced Accuracy : 0.7155

          'Positive' Class : yes
```

How it works...

Naive Bayes assumes that features are conditionally independent, which the effect of a predictor(x) to class (c) is independent of the effect of other predictors to class(c). It computes the posterior probability, $P(c|x)$, as the following formula:

$$P(c|x) = \frac{P(x|c)P(c)}{P(x)}$$

Where $P(x|c)$ is called likelihood, $p(x)$ is called the marginal likelihood, and $p(c)$ is called the prior probability. If there are many predictors, we can formulate the posterior probability as follows:

$$P(c|x) = P(x_1|c) \times P(x_2|c) \times \dots P(x_n|c) \times P(c)$$

The advantage of Naïve Bayes is that it is relatively simple and straightforward to use. It is suitable when the training set is relative small, and may contain some noisy and missing data. Moreover, you can easily obtain the probability for a prediction. The drawbacks of Naïve Bayes are that it assumes that all features are independent and equally important, which is very unlikely in real-world cases.

In this recipe, we use the Naïve Bayes classifier from the `e1071` package to build a classification model. First, we specify all the variables (excluding the `churn` class label) as the first input parameters, and specify the `churn` class label as the second parameter in the `naiveBayes` function call. Next, we assign the classification model into the variable classifier. Then, we print the variable classifier to obtain information, such as function call, A-priori probabilities, and conditional probabilities. We can also use the `predict` function to obtain the predicted outcome and the `table` function to retrieve the classification table of the testing dataset. Finally, we use a confusion matrix to calculate the performance measurement of the classification model.

At last, we list a comparison table of all the mentioned algorithms in this chapter:

Algorithm	Advantage	Disadvantage
Recursive partitioning tree	► Very flexible and easy to interpret ► Works on both classification and regression problems ► Nonparametric	► Prone to bias and over-fitting
Conditional inference tree	► Very flexible and easy to interpret ► Works on both classification and regression problems ► Nonparametric ► Less prone to bias than a recursive partitioning tree	► Prone to over-fitting
K-nearest neighbor classifier	► The cost of the learning process is zero ► Nonparametric ► You can classify any data whenever you can find similarity measures of any given instances	► Hard to interpret the classified result ► Computation is expensive for a large dataset ► The performance relies on the number of dimensions
Logistic regression	► Easy to interpret ► Provides model logistic probability ► Provides confidence interval ► You can quickly update the classification model to incorporate new data	► Suffers multicollinearity ► Does not handle the missing value of continuous variables ► Sensitive to extreme values of continuous variables
Naïve Bayes	► Relatively simple and straightforward to use ► Suitable when the training set is relative small ► Can deal with some noisy and missing data ► Can easily obtain the probability for a prediction	► Assumes all features are independent and equally important, which is very unlikely in real-world cases ► Prone to bias when the number of training sets increase

See also

▶   To learn more about the Bayes theorem, you can refer to the following Wikipedia article: `http://en.wikipedia.org/wiki/Bayes'_theorem`

6

Classification (II) – Neural Network and SVM

In this chapter, we will cover the following recipes:

- ▶ Classifying data with a support vector machine
- ▶ Choosing the cost of a support vector machine
- ▶ Visualizing an SVM fit
- ▶ Predicting labels based on a model trained by a support vector machine
- ▶ Tuning a support vector machine
- ▶ Training a neural network with neuralnet
- ▶ Visualizing a neural network trained by neuralnet
- ▶ Predicting labels based on a model trained by neuralnet
- ▶ Training a neural network with nnet
- ▶ Predicting labels based on a model trained by nnet

Introduction

Most research has shown that **support vector machines** (**SVM**) and **neural networks** (**NN**) are powerful classification tools, which can be applied to several different areas. Unlike tree-based or probabilistic-based methods that were mentioned in the previous chapter, the process of how support vector machines and neural networks transform from input to output is less clear and can be hard to interpret. As a result, both support vector machines and neural networks are referred to as black box methods.

The development of a neural network is inspired by human brain activities. As such, this type of network is a computational model that mimics the pattern of the human mind. In contrast to this, support vector machines first map input data into a high dimension feature space defined by the kernel function, and find the optimum hyperplane that separates the training data by the maximum margin. In short, we can think of support vector machines as a linear algorithm in a high dimensional space.

Both these methods have advantages and disadvantages in solving classification problems. For example, support vector machine solutions are the global optimum, while neural networks may suffer from multiple local optimums. Thus, choosing between either depends on the characteristics of the dataset source. In this chapter, we will illustrate the following:

- ▶ How to train a support vector machine
- ▶ Observing how the choice of cost can affect the SVM classifier
- ▶ Visualizing the SVM fit
- ▶ Predicting the labels of a testing dataset based on the model trained by SVM
- ▶ Tuning the SVM

In the neural network section, we will cover:

- ▶ How to train a neural network
- ▶ How to visualize a neural network model
- ▶ Predicting the labels of a testing dataset based on a model trained by `neuralnet`
- ▶ Finally, we will show how to train a neural network with `nnet`, and how to use it to predict the labels of a testing dataset

Classifying data with a support vector machine

The two most well known and popular support vector machine tools are `libsvm` and `SVMLite`. For R users, you can find the implementation of `libsvm` in the `e1071` package and `SVMLite` in the `klaR` package. Therefore, you can use the implemented function of these two packages to train support vector machines. In this recipe, we will focus on using the `svm` function (the `libsvm` implemented version) from the `e1071` package to train a support vector machine based on the telecom customer churn data training dataset.

Getting ready

In this recipe, we will continue to use the telecom churn dataset as the input data source to train the support vector machine. For those who have not prepared the dataset, please refer to *Chapter 5, Classification (I) – Tree, Lazy, and Probabilistic*, for details.

How to do it...

Perform the following steps to train the SVM:

1. Load the `e1071` package:

   ```
   > library(e1071)
   ```

2. Train the support vector machine using the `svm` function with `trainset` as the input dataset, and use `churn` as the classification category:

   ```
   > model   = svm(churn~., data = trainset, kernel="radial", cost=1,
   gamma = 1/ncol(trainset))
   ```

3. Finally, you can obtain overall information about the built model with `summary`:

   ```
   > summary(model)


   Call:
   svm(formula = churn ~ ., data = trainset, kernel = "radial", cost
   = 1, gamma = 1/ncol(trainset))



   Parameters:
      SVM-Type:  C-classification
    SVM-Kernel:  radial
          cost:  1
         gamma:  0.05882353


   Number of Support Vectors:  691


    ( 394 297 )



   Number of Classes:  2


   Levels:
    yes no
   ```

How it works...

The support vector machine constructs a hyperplane (or set of hyperplanes) that maximize the margin width between two classes in a high dimensional space. In these, the cases that define the hyperplane are support vectors, as shown in the following figure:

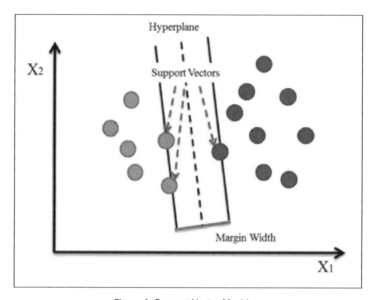

Figure 1: Support Vector Machine

Support vector machine starts from constructing a hyperplane that maximizes the margin width. Then, it extends the definition to a nonlinear separable problem. Lastly, it maps the data to a high dimensional space where the data can be more easily separated with a linear boundary.

The advantage of using SVM is that it builds a highly accurate model through an engineering problem-oriented kernel. Also, it makes use of the regularization term to avoid over-fitting. It also does not suffer from local optimal and multicollinearity. The main limitation of SVM is its speed and size in the training and testing time. Therefore, it is not suitable or efficient enough to construct classification models for data that is large in size. Also, since it is hard to interpret SVM, how does the determination of the kernel take place? Regularization is another problem that we need tackle.

In this recipe, we continue to use the telecom `churn` dataset as our example data source. We begin training a support vector machine using `libsvm` provided in the `e1071` package. Within the training function, `svm`, one can specify the `kernel` function, cost, and the `gamma` function. For the `kernel` argument, the default value is radial, and one can specify the kernel to a linear, polynomial, radial basis, and sigmoid. As for the `gamma` argument, the default value is equal to (1/data dimension), and it controls the shape of the separating hyperplane. Increasing the `gamma` argument usually increases the number of support vectors.

As for the cost, the default value is set to 1, which indicates that the regularization term is constant, and the larger the value, the smaller the margin is. We will discuss more on how the cost can affect the SVM classifier in the next recipe. Once the support vector machine is built, the summary function can be used to obtain information, such as calls, parameters, number of classes, and the types of label.

See also

Another popular support vector machine tool is SVMLight. Unlike the e1071 package, which provides the full implementation of libsvm, the klaR package simply provides an interface to SVMLight only. To use SVMLight, one can perform the following steps:

1. Install the klaR package:

   ```
   > install.packages("klaR")
   > library(klaR)
   ```

2. Download the SVMLight source code and binary for your platform from http://svmlight.joachims.org/. For example, if your guest OS is Windows 64-bit, you should download the file from http://download.joachims.org/svm_light/current/svm_light_windows64.zip.

3. Then, you should unzip the file and put the workable binary in the working directory; you may check your working directory by using the getwd function:

   ```
   > getwd()
   ```

4. Train the support vector machine using the svmlight function:

   ```
   > model.light  = svmlight(churn~., data = trainset,
   kernel="radial", cost=1, gamma = 1/ncol(trainset))
   ```

Choosing the cost of a support vector machine

The support vector machines create an optimum hyperplane that separates the training data by the maximum margin. However, sometimes we would like to allow some misclassifications while separating categories. The SVM model has a cost function, which controls training errors and margins. For example, a small cost creates a large margin (a soft margin) and allows more misclassifications. On the other hand, a large cost creates a narrow margin (a hard margin) and permits fewer misclassifications. In this recipe, we will illustrate how the large and small cost will affect the SVM classifier.

Getting ready

In this recipe, we will use the `iris` dataset as our example data source.

How to do it...

Perform the following steps to generate two different classification examples with different costs:

1. Subset the `iris` dataset with columns named as `Sepal.Length`, `Sepal.Width`, `Species`, with species in `setosa` and `virginica`:

   ```
   > iris.subset = subset(iris, select=c("Sepal.Length", "Sepal.
   Width", "Species"), Species %in% c("setosa","virginica"))
   ```

2. Then, you can generate a scatter plot with `Sepal.Length` as the x-axis and the `Sepal.Width` as the y-axis:

   ```
   > plot(x=iris.subset$Sepal.Length,y=iris.subset$Sepal.Width,
   col=iris.subset$Species, pch=19)
   ```

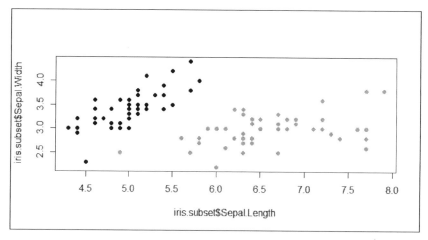

Figure 2: Scatter plot of Sepal.Length and Sepal.Width with subset of iris dataset

3. Next, you can train SVM based on `iris.subset` with the cost equal to 1:

   ```
   > svm.model = svm(Species ~ ., data=iris.subset, kernel='linear',
   cost=1, scale=FALSE)
   ```

4. Then, we can circle the support vector with blue circles:

```
> points(iris.subset[svm.model$index,c(1,2)],col="blue",cex=2)
```

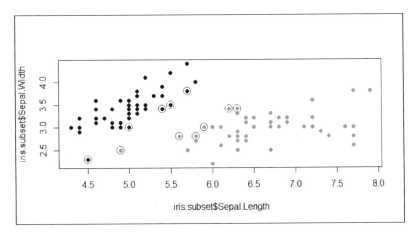

Figure 3: Circling support vectors with blue ring

5. Lastly, we can add a separation line on the plot:

```
> w = t(svm.model$coefs) %*% svm.model$SV

> b = -svm.model$rho

> abline(a=-b/w[1,2], b=-w[1,1]/w[1,2], col="red", lty=5)
```

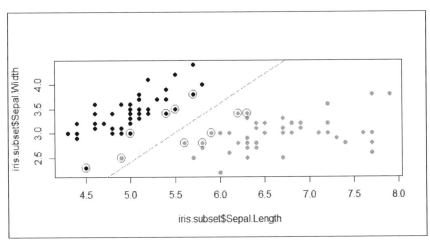

Figure 4: Add separation line to scatter plot

6. In addition to this, we create another SVM classifier where `cost = 10,000`:

```
> plot(x=iris.subset$Sepal.Length,y=iris.subset$Sepal.Width,
col=iris.subset$Species, pch=19)

> svm.model = svm(Species ~ ., data=iris.subset, type='C-
classification', kernel='linear', cost=10000, scale=FALSE)

> points(iris.subset[svm.model$index,c(1,2)],col="blue",cex=2)

> w = t(svm.model$coefs) %*% svm.model$SV

> b = -svm.model$rho

> abline(a=-b/w[1,2], b=-w[1,1]/w[1,2], col="red", lty=5)
```

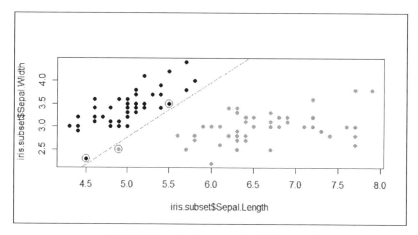

Figure 5: A classification example with large cost

How it works...

In this recipe, we demonstrate how different costs can affect the SVM classifier. First, we create an iris subset with the columns, `Sepal.Length`, `Sepal.Width`, and `Species` containing the species, `setosa` and `virginica`. Then, in order to create a soft margin and allow some misclassification, we use an SVM with small cost (where `cost = 1`) to train the support of the vector machine. Next, we circle the support vectors with blue circles and add the separation line. As per *Figure 5*, one of the green points (`virginica`) is misclassified (it is classified to `setosa`) to the other side of the separation line due to the choice of the small cost.

In addition to this, we would like to determine how a large cost can affect the SVM classifier. Therefore, we choose a large cost (where `cost = 10,000`). From Figure 5, we can see that the margin created is narrow (a hard margin) and no misclassification cases are present. As a result, the two examples show that the choice of different costs may affect the margin created and also affect the possibilities of misclassification.

See also

▶ The idea of soft margin, which allows misclassified examples, was suggested by Corinna Cortes and Vladimir N. Vapnik in 1995 in the following paper: Cortes, C., and Vapnik, V. (1995). *Support-vector networks. Machine learning*, 20(3), 273-297.

Visualizing an SVM fit

To visualize the built model, one can first use the plot function to generate a scatter plot of data input and the SVM fit. In this plot, support vectors and classes are highlighted through the color symbol. In addition to this, one can draw a contour filled plot of the class regions to easily identify misclassified samples from the plot.

Getting ready

In this recipe, we will use two datasets: the `iris` dataset and the telecom `churn` dataset. For the telecom `churn` dataset, one needs to have completed the previous recipe by training a support vector machine with SVM, and to have saved the SVM fit model.

How to do it...

Perform the following steps to visualize the SVM fit object:

1. Use SVM to train the support vector machine based on the iris dataset, and use the `plot` function to visualize the fitted model:

```
> data(iris)

> model.iris  = svm(Species~., iris)

> plot(model.iris, iris, Petal.Width ~ Petal.Length, slice =
list(Sepal.Width = 3, Sepal.Length = 4))
```

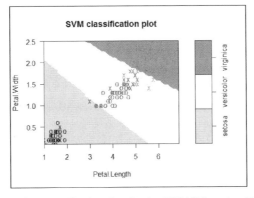

Figure 6: The SVM classification plot of trained SVM fit based on iris dataset

2. Visualize the SVM fit object, `model`, using the `plot` function with the dimensions of `total_day_minutes` and `total_intl_charge`:

```
> plot(model, trainset, total_day_minutes ~ total_intl_charge)
```

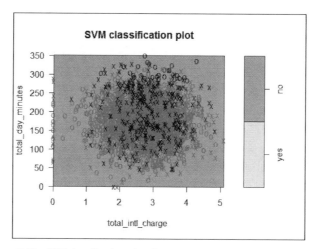

Figure 7: The SVM classification plot of trained SVM fit based on churn dataset

How it works...

In this recipe, we demonstrate how to use the `plot` function to visualize the SVM fit. In the first plot, we train a support vector machine using the `iris` dataset. Then, we use the `plot` function to visualize the fitted SVM.

In the argument list, we specify the fitted model in the first argument and the dataset (this should be the same data used to build the model) as the second parameter. The third parameter indicates the dimension used to generate the classification plot. By default, the `plot` function can only generate a scatter plot based on two dimensions (for the x-axis and y-axis). Therefore, we select the variables, `Petal.Length` and `Petal.Width` as the two dimensions to generate the scatter plot.

From *Figure 6*, we find `Petal.Length` assigned to the x-axis, `Petal.Width` assigned to the y-axis, and data points with x and o symbols scattered on the plot. Within the scatter plot, the X symbol shows the support vector and the o symbol represents the data points. These two symbols can be altered through the configuration of the `svSymbol` and `dataSymbol` options. Both the support vectors and true classes are highlighted and colored depending on their label (green refers to viginica, red refers to versicolor, and black refers to setosa). The last argument, `slice`, is set when there are more than two variables. Therefore, in this example, we use the additional variables, `Sepal.width` and `Sepal.length`, by assigning a constant of 3 and 4.

Next, we take the same approach to draw the SVM fit based on customer churn data. In this example, we use `total_day_minutes` and `total_intl_charge` as the two dimensions used to plot the scatterplot. As per *Figure 7*, the support vectors and data points in red and black are scattered closely together in the central region of the plot, and there is no simple way to separate them.

See also

▶ There are other **parameters**, such as `fill`, `grid`, `symbolPalette`, and so on, that can be configured to change the layout of the plot. You can use the `help` function to view the following document for further information:

```
> ?svm.plot
```

Predicting labels based on a model trained by a support vector machine

In the previous recipe, we trained an SVM based on the training dataset. The training process finds the optimum hyperplane that separates the training data by the maximum margin. We can then utilize the SVM fit to predict the label (category) of new observations. In this recipe, we will demonstrate how to use the `predict` function to predict values based on a model trained by SVM.

Getting ready

You need to have completed the previous recipe by generating a fitted SVM, and save the fitted model in model.

How to do it...

Perform the following steps to predict the labels of the testing dataset:

1. Predict the label of the testing dataset based on the fitted SVM and attributes of the testing dataset:

```
> svm.pred = predict(model, testset[, !names(testset) %in%
c("churn")])
```

2. Then, you can use the `table` function to generate a classification table with the prediction result and labels of the testing dataset:

```
> svm.table=table(svm.pred, testset$churn)
> svm.table
```

```
svm.pred yes   no
    yes   70  12
    no    71 865
```

3. Next, you can use `classAgreement` to calculate coefficients compared to the classification agreement:

```
> classAgreement(svm.table)
$diag
[1] 0.9184676

$kappa
[1] 0.5855903

$rand
[1] 0.850083

$crand
[1] 0.5260472
```

4. Now, you can use `confusionMatrix` to measure the prediction performance based on the classification table:

```
> library(caret)
> confusionMatrix(svm.table)
Confusion Matrix and Statistics


svm.pred yes   no
    yes   70  12
    no    71 865


               Accuracy : 0.9185
                 95% CI : (0.8999, 0.9345)
    No Information Rate : 0.8615
    P-Value [Acc > NIR] : 1.251e-08

                  Kappa : 0.5856
 Mcnemar's Test P-Value : 1.936e-10
```

```
            Sensitivity : 0.49645
            Specificity : 0.98632
         Pos Pred Value : 0.85366
         Neg Pred Value : 0.92415
             Prevalence : 0.13851
         Detection Rate : 0.06876
   Detection Prevalence : 0.08055
      Balanced Accuracy : 0.74139


        'Positive' Class : yes
```

How it works...

In this recipe, we first used the `predict` function to obtain the predicted labels of the testing dataset. Next, we used the `table` function to generate the classification table based on the predicted labels of the testing dataset. So far, the evaluation procedure is very similar to the evaluation process mentioned in the previous chapter.

We then introduced a new function, `classAgreement`, which computes several coefficients of agreement between the columns and rows of a two-way contingency table. The coefficients include diag, kappa, rand, and crand. The `diag` coefficient represents the percentage of data points in the main diagonal of the classification table, `kappa` refers to `diag`, which is corrected for an agreement by a change (the probability of random agreements), `rand` represents the Rand index, which measures the similarity between two data clusters, and `crand` indicates the Rand index, which is adjusted for the chance grouping of elements.

Finally, we used `confusionMatrix` from the `caret` package to measure the performance of the classification model. The accuracy of 0.9185 shows that the trained support vector machine can correctly classify most of the observations. However, accuracy alone is not a good measurement of a classification model. One should also reference sensitivity and specificity.

There's more...

Besides using SVM to predict the category of new observations, you can use SVM to predict continuous values. In other words, one can use SVM to perform regression analysis.

In the following example, we will show how to perform a simple regression prediction based on a fitted SVM with the type specified as `eps-regression`.

Perform the following steps to train a regression model with SVM:

1. Train a support vector machine based on a `Quartet` dataset:

    ```
    > library(car)
    > data(Quartet)
    > model.regression = svm(Quartet$y1~Quartet$x,type="eps-
    regression")
    ```

2. Use the `predict` function to obtain prediction results:

    ```
    > predict.y = predict(model.regression, Quartet$x)
    > predict.y
            1         2         3         4         5         6         7
    8
    8.196894 7.152946 8.807471 7.713099 8.533578 8.774046 6.186349
    5.763689
            9        10        11
    8.726925 6.621373 5.882946
    ```

3. Plot the predicted points as squares and the training data points as circles on the same plot:

    ```
    > plot(Quartet$x, Quartet$y1, pch=19)
    > points(Quartet$x, predict.y, pch=15, col="red")
    ```

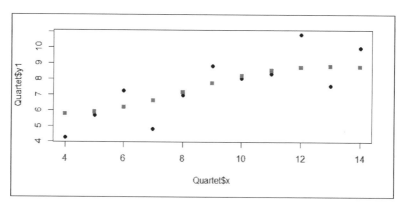

Figure 8: The scatter plot contains predicted data points and training data points

Tuning a support vector machine

Besides using different feature sets and the `kernel` function in support vector machines, one trick that you can use to tune its performance is to adjust the gamma and cost configured in the argument. One possible approach to test the performance of different gamma and cost combination values is to write a `for` loop to generate all the combinations of gamma and cost as inputs to train different support vector machines. Fortunately, SVM provides a tuning function, `tune.svm`, which makes the tuning much easier. In this recipe, we will demonstrate how to tune a support vector machine through the use of `tune.svm`.

Getting ready

You need to have completed the previous recipe by preparing a training dataset, `trainset`.

How to do it...

Perform the following steps to tune the support vector machine:

1. First, tune the support vector machine using `tune.svm`:

    ```
    > tuned = tune.svm(churn~., data = trainset, gamma = 10^(-6:-1),
    cost = 10^(1:2))
    ```

2. Next, you can use the `summary` function to obtain the tuning result:

    ```
    > summary(tuned)


    Parameter tuning of 'svm':


    - sampling method: 10-fold cross validation


    - best parameters:
     gamma cost
      0.01   100


    - best performance: 0.08077885


    - Detailed performance results:
        gamma cost       error dispersion
    1   1e-06   10 0.14774780 0.02399512
    2   1e-05   10 0.14774780 0.02399512
    ```

```
3   1e-04    10 0.14774780 0.02399512
4   1e-03    10 0.14774780 0.02399512
5   1e-02    10 0.09245223 0.02046032
6   1e-01    10 0.09202306 0.01938475
7   1e-06   100 0.14774780 0.02399512
8   1e-05   100 0.14774780 0.02399512
9   1e-04   100 0.14774780 0.02399512
10 1e-03   100 0.11794484 0.02368343
11 1e-02   100 0.08077885 0.01858195
12 1e-01   100 0.12356135 0.01661508
```

3. After retrieving the best performance parameter from tuning the result, you can retrain the support vector machine with the best performance parameter:

```
> model.tuned = svm(churn~., data = trainset, gamma = tuned$best.
parameters$gamma, cost = tuned$best.parameters$cost)
> summary(model.tuned)
```

```
Call:
svm(formula = churn ~ ., data = trainset, gamma = 10^-2, cost =
100)


Parameters:
    SVM-Type:  C-classification
  SVM-Kernel:  radial
        cost:  100
       gamma:  0.01


Number of Support Vectors:   547


( 304 243 )


Number of Classes:  2


Levels:
 yes no
```

4. Then, you can use the `predict` function to predict labels based on the fitted SVM:

```
> svm.tuned.pred = predict(model.tuned, testset[, !names(testset)
%in% c("churn")])
```

5. Next, generate a classification table based on the predicted and original labels of the testing dataset:

```
> svm.tuned.table=table(svm.tuned.pred, testset$churn)
> svm.tuned.table


svm.tuned.pred yes   no
          yes   95   24
          no    46  853
```

6. Also, generate a class agreement to measure the performance:

```
> classAgreement(svm.tuned.table)
$diag
[1] 0.9312377


$kappa
[1] 0.691678


$rand
[1] 0.871806


$crand
[1] 0.6303615
```

7. Finally, you can use a confusion matrix to measure the performance of the retrained model:

```
> confusionMatrix(svm.tuned.table)
Confusion Matrix and Statistics


svm.tuned.pred yes   no
          yes   95   24
          no    46  853


          Accuracy : 0.9312
```

```
               95% CI  :  (0.9139, 0.946)
   No Information Rate  :  0.8615
  P-Value [Acc > NIR]  :  1.56e-12

                 Kappa  :  0.6917
 Mcnemar's Test P-Value :  0.01207

           Sensitivity  :  0.67376
           Specificity  :  0.97263
        Pos Pred Value  :  0.79832
        Neg Pred Value  :  0.94883
            Prevalence  :  0.13851
        Detection Rate  :  0.09332
  Detection Prevalence  :  0.11690
     Balanced Accuracy  :  0.82320

       'Positive' Class :  yes
```

How it works...

To tune the support vector machine, you can use a trial and error method to find the best gamma and cost parameters. In other words, one has to generate a variety of combinations of gamma and cost for the purpose of training different support vector machines.

In this example, we generate different gamma values from *10^-6* to *10^-1*, and cost with a value of either 10 or 100. Therefore, you can use the tuning function, svm.tune, to generate 12 sets of parameters. The function then makes 10 cross-validations and outputs the error dispersion of each combination. As a result, the combination with the least error dispersion is regarded as the best parameter set. From the summary table, we found that gamma with a value of 0.01 and cost with a value of 100 are the best parameters for the SVM fit.

After obtaining the best parameters, we can then train a new support vector machine with gamma equal to 0.01 and cost equal to 100. Additionally, we can obtain a classification table based on the predicted labels and labels of the testing dataset. We can also obtain a confusion matrix from the classification table. From the output of the confusion matrix, you can determine the accuracy of the newly trained model in comparison to the original model.

▶ For more information about how to tune SVM with `svm.tune`, you can use the `help` function to access this document:

```
> ?svm.tune
```

Training a neural network with neuralnet

The neural network is constructed with an interconnected group of nodes, which involves the input, connected weights, processing element, and output. Neural networks can be applied to many areas, such as classification, clustering, and prediction. To train a neural network in R, you can use neuralnet, which is built to train multilayer perceptron in the context of regression analysis, and contains many flexible functions to train forward neural networks. In this recipe, we will introduce how to use neuralnet to train a neural network.

Getting ready

In this recipe, we will use an `iris` dataset as our example dataset. We will first split the `iris` dataset into a training and testing datasets, respectively.

How to do it...

Perform the following steps to train a neural network with neuralnet:

1. First load the `iris` dataset and split the data into training and testing datasets:

```
> data(iris)
> ind = sample(2, nrow(iris), replace = TRUE, prob=c(0.7, 0.3))
> trainset = iris[ind == 1,]
> testset = iris[ind == 2,]
```

2. Then, install and load the `neuralnet` package:

```
> install.packages("neuralnet")
> library(neuralnet)
```

3. Add the columns versicolor, setosa, and virginica based on the name matched value in the `Species` column:

```
> trainset$setosa = trainset$Species == "setosa"
> trainset$virginica = trainset$Species == "virginica"
> trainset$versicolor = trainset$Species == "versicolor"
```

4. Next, train the neural network with the `neuralnet` function with three hidden neurons in each layer. Notice that the results may vary with each training, so you might not get the same result. However, you can use set.seed at the beginning, so you can get the same result in every training process

```
> network = neuralnet(versicolor + virginica + setosa~ Sepal.
Length + Sepal.Width + Petal.Length + Petal.Width, trainset,
hidden=3)
```

```
> network
```

```
Call: neuralnet(formula = versicolor + virginica + setosa ~ Sepal.
Length +     Sepal.Width + Petal.Length + Petal.Width, data =
trainset,      hidden = 3)
```

```
1 repetition was calculated.
```

```
        Error Reached Threshold Steps
1 0.8156100175     0.009994274769 11063
```

5. Now, you can view the `summary` information by accessing the `result.matrix` attribute of the built neural network model:

```
> network$result.matrix
```

```
                                        1
error                        0.815610017474
reached.threshold            0.009994274769
steps                     11063.000000000000
Intercept.to.1layhid1          1.686593311644
Sepal.Length.to.1layhid1       0.947415215237
Sepal.Width.to.1layhid1       -7.220058260187
Petal.Length.to.1layhid1       1.790333443486
Petal.Width.to.1layhid1        9.943109233330
Intercept.to.1layhid2          1.411026063895
Sepal.Length.to.1layhid2       0.240309549505
Sepal.Width.to.1layhid2        0.480654059973
Petal.Length.to.1layhid2       2.221435192437
Petal.Width.to.1layhid2        0.154879347818
Intercept.to.1layhid3         24.399329878242
Sepal.Length.to.1layhid3       3.313958088512
Sepal.Width.to.1layhid3        5.845670010464
Petal.Length.to.1layhid3      -6.337082722485
Petal.Width.to.1layhid3      -17.990352566695
Intercept.to.versicolor       -1.959842102421
1layhid.1.to.versicolor        1.010292389835
```

```
1layhid.2.to.versicolor          0.936519720978
1layhid.3.to.versicolor          1.023305801833
Intercept.to.virginica          -0.908909982893
1layhid.1.to.virginica          -0.009904635231
1layhid.2.to.virginica           1.931747950462
1layhid.3.to.virginica          -1.021438938226
Intercept.to.setosa              1.500533827729
1layhid.1.to.setosa             -1.001683936613
1layhid.2.to.setosa             -0.498758815934
1layhid.3.to.setosa             -0.001881935696
```

6. Lastly, you can view the generalized weight by accessing it in the network:

```
> head(network$generalized.weights[[1]])
```

How it works...

The neural network is a network made up of artificial neurons (or nodes). There are three types of neurons within the network: input neurons, hidden neurons, and output neurons. In the network, neurons are connected; the connection strength between neurons is called weights. If the weight is greater than zero, it is in an excitation status. Otherwise, it is in an inhibition status. Input neurons receive the input information; the higher the input value, the greater the activation. Then, the activation value is passed through the network in regard to weights and transfer functions in the graph. The hidden neurons (or output neurons) then sum up the activation values and modify the summed values with the transfer function. The activation value then flows through hidden neurons and stops when it reaches the output nodes. As a result, one can use the output value from the output neurons to classify the data.

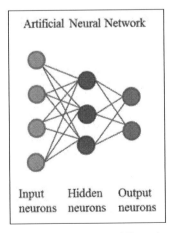

Artificial Neural Network

Input neurons   Hidden neurons   Output neurons

Figure 9: Artificial Neural Network

The advantages of a neural network are: first, it can detect nonlinear relationships between the dependent and independent variable. Second, one can efficiently train large datasets using the parallel architecture. Third, it is a nonparametric model so that one can eliminate errors in the estimation of parameters. The main disadvantages of a neural network are that it often converges to the local minimum rather than the global minimum. Also, it might over-fit when the training process goes on for too long.

In this recipe, we demonstrate how to train a neural network. First, we split the `iris` dataset into training and testing datasets, and then install the `neuralnet` package and load the library into an R session. Next, we add the columns `versicolor`, `setosa`, and `virginica` based on the name matched value in the `Species` column, respectively. We then use the `neuralnet` function to train the network model. Besides specifying the label (the column where the name equals to versicolor, virginica, and setosa) and training attributes in the function, we also configure the number of hidden neurons (vertices) as three in each layer.

Then, we examine the basic information about the training process and the trained network saved in the network. From the output message, it shows the training process needed 11,063 steps until all the absolute partial derivatives of the error function were lower than 0.01 (specified in the threshold). The error refers to the likelihood of calculating **Akaike Information Criterion** (**AIC**). To see detailed information on this, you can access the `result.matrix` of the built neural network to see the estimated weight. The output reveals that the estimated weight ranges from -18 to 24.40; the intercepts of the first hidden layer are 1.69, 1.41 and 24.40, and the two weights leading to the first hidden neuron are estimated as 0.95 (`Sepal.Length`), -7.22 (`Sepal.Width`), 1.79 (`Petal.Length`), and 9.94 (`Petal.Width`). We can lastly determine that the trained neural network information includes generalized weights, which express the effect of each covariate. In this recipe, the model generates 12 generalized weights, which are the combination of four covariates (`Sepal.Length`, `Sepal.Width`, `Petal.Length`, `Petal.Width`) to three responses (`setosa`, `virginica`, `versicolor`).

See also

▸ For a more detailed introduction on neuralnet, one can refer to the following paper: Günther, F., and Fritsch, S. (2010). *neuralnet: Training of neural networks. The R journal*, 2(1), 30-38.

Visualizing a neural network trained by neuralnet

The package, `neuralnet`, provides the `plot` function to visualize a built neural network and the `gwplot` function to visualize generalized weights. In following recipe, we will cover how to use these two functions.

Getting ready

You need to have completed the previous recipe by training a neural network and have all basic information saved in the network.

How to do it...

Perform the following steps to visualize the neural network and the generalized weights:

1. You can visualize the trained neural network with the `plot` function:

    ```
    > plot(network)
    ```

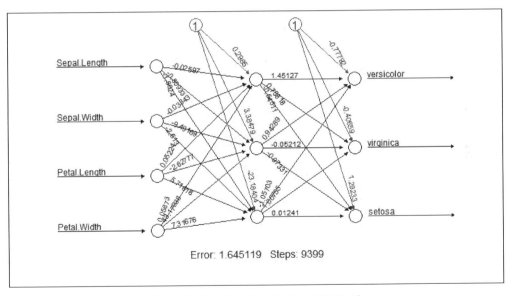

Figure 10: The plot of the trained neural network

2. Furthermore, you can use `gwplot` to visualize the generalized weights:

```
> par(mfrow=c(2,2))
> gwplot(network,selected.covariate="Petal.Width")
> gwplot(network,selected.covariate="Sepal.Width")
> gwplot(network,selected.covariate="Petal.Length")
> gwplot(network,selected.covariate="Petal.Width")
```

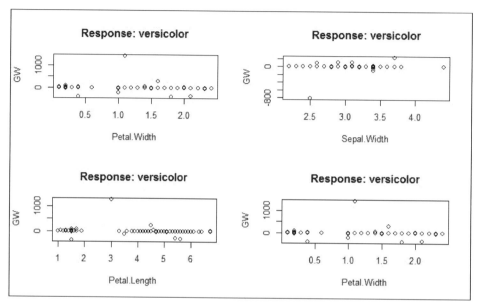

Figure 11: The plot of generalized weights

How it works...

In this recipe, we demonstrate how to visualize the trained neural network and the generalized weights of each trained attribute. As per *Figure 10*, the plot displays the network topology of the trained neural network. Also, the plot includes the estimated weight, intercepts and basic information about the training process. At the bottom of the figure, one can find the overall error and number of steps required to converge.

Figure 11 presents the generalized weight plot in regard to `network$generalized.weights`. The four plots in *Figure 11* display the four covariates: `Petal.Width`, `Sepal.Width`, `Petal.Length`, and `Petal.Width`, in regard to the versicolor response. If all the generalized weights are close to zero on the plot, it means the covariate has little effect. However, if the overall variance is greater than one, it means the covariate has a nonlinear effect.

See also

▸ For more information about `gwplot`, one can use the `help` function to access the following document:

```
> ?gwplot
```

Predicting labels based on a model trained by neuralnet

Similar to other classification methods, we can predict the labels of new observations based on trained neural networks. Furthermore, we can validate the performance of these networks through the use of a confusion matrix. In the following recipe, we will introduce how to use the `compute` function in a neural network to obtain a probability matrix of the testing dataset labels, and use a table and confusion matrix to measure the prediction performance.

Getting ready

You need to have completed the previous recipe by generating the training dataset, `trainset`, and the testing dataset, `testset`. The trained neural network needs to be saved in the network.

How to do it...

Perform the following steps to measure the prediction performance of the trained neural network:

1. First, generate a prediction probability matrix based on a trained neural network and the testing dataset, `testset`:

```
> net.predict = compute(network, testset[-5])$net.result
```

2. Then, obtain other possible labels by finding the column with the greatest probability:

```
> net.prediction = c("versicolor", "virginica", "setosa")
[apply(net.predict, 1, which.max)]
```

3. Generate a classification table based on the predicted labels and the labels of the testing dataset:

```
> predict.table = table(testset$Species, net.prediction)

> predict.table

            prediction

            setosa versicolor virginica
```

setosa	20	0	0
versicolor	0	19	1
virginica	0	2	16

4. Next, generate `classAgreement` from the classification table:

```
> classAgreement(predict.table)
$diag
[1] 0.9444444444


$kappa
[1] 0.9154488518


$rand
[1] 0.9224318658


$crand
[1] 0.8248251737
```

5. Finally, use `confusionMatrix` to measure the prediction performance:

```
> confusionMatrix(predict.table)
Confusion Matrix and Statistics

            prediction
            setosa versicolor virginica
  setosa       20         0         0
  versicolor    0        19         1
  virginica     0         2        16


Overall Statistics

               Accuracy : 0.9482759
                 95% CI : (0.8561954, 0.9892035)
    No Information Rate : 0.362069
    P-Value [Acc > NIR] : < 0.00000000000000022204

                  Kappa : 0.922252
 Mcnemar's Test P-Value : NA
```

```
Statistics by Class:
```

	Class: setosa	Class: versicolor	Class: virginica
Sensitivity	1.0000000	0.9047619	0.9411765
Specificity	1.0000000	0.9729730	0.9512195
Pos Pred Value	1.0000000	0.9500000	0.8888889
Neg Pred Value	1.0000000	0.9473684	0.9750000
Prevalence	0.3448276	0.3620690	0.2931034
Detection Rate	0.3448276	0.3275862	0.2758621
Detection Prevalence	0.3448276	0.3448276	0.3103448
Balanced Accuracy	1.0000000	0.9388674	0.9461980

How it works...

In this recipe, we demonstrate how to predict labels based on a model trained by neuralnet. Initially, we use the `compute` function to create an output probability matrix based on the trained neural network and the testing dataset. Then, to convert the probability matrix to class labels, we use the `which.max` function to determine the class label by selecting the column with the maximum probability within the row. Next, we use a table to generate a classification matrix based on the labels of the testing dataset and the predicted labels. As we have created the classification table, we can employ a confusion matrix to measure the prediction performance of the built neural network.

See also

▸ In this recipe, we use the `net.result` function, which is the overall result of the neural network, used to predict the labels of the testing dataset. Apart from examining the overall result by accessing `net.result`, the `compute` function also generates the output from neurons in each layer. You can examine the output of neurons to get a better understanding of how `compute` works:

```
> compute(network, testset[-5])
```

Training a neural network with nnet

The nnet package is another package that can deal with artificial neural networks. This package provides the functionality to train feed-forward neural networks with traditional back propagation. As you can find most of the neural network function implemented in the neuralnet package, in this recipe we provide a short overview of how to train neural networks with nnet.

Getting ready

In this recipe, we do not use the trainset and trainset generated from the previous step; please reload the iris dataset again.

How to do it...

Perform the following steps to train the neural network with nnet:

1. First, install and load the nnet package:

    ```
    > install.packages("nnet")
    > library(nnet)
    ```

2. Next, split the dataset into training and testing datasets:

    ```
    > data(iris)
    > set.seed(2)
    > ind = sample(2, nrow(iris), replace = TRUE, prob=c(0.7, 0.3))
    > trainset = iris[ind == 1,]
    > testset = iris[ind == 2,]
    ```

3. Then, train the neural network with nnet:

    ```
    > iris.nn = nnet(Species ~ ., data = trainset, size = 2, rang =
    0.1, decay = 5e-4, maxit = 200)
    # weights:  19
    initial  value 165.086674
    iter  10 value 70.447976
    iter  20 value 69.667465
    iter  30 value 69.505739
    iter  40 value 21.588943
    iter  50 value 8.691760
    iter  60 value 8.521214
    iter  70 value 8.138961
    ```

```
iter   80 value 7.291365
iter   90 value 7.039209
iter  100 value 6.570987
iter  110 value 6.355346
iter  120 value 6.345511
iter  130 value 6.340208
iter  140 value 6.337271
iter  150 value 6.334285
iter  160 value 6.333792
iter  170 value 6.333578
iter  180 value 6.333498
final    value 6.333471
converged
```

4. Use the `summary` to obtain information about the trained neural network:

```
> summary(iris.nn)
a 4-2-3 network with 19 weights
options were - softmax modelling  decay=0.0005
 b->h1 i1->h1 i2->h1 i3->h1 i4->h1
 -0.38  -0.63  -1.96   3.13   1.53
 b->h2 i1->h2 i2->h2 i3->h2 i4->h2
  8.95   0.52   1.42  -1.98  -3.85
 b->o1 h1->o1 h2->o1
  3.08 -10.78   4.99
 b->o2 h1->o2 h2->o2
 -7.41   6.37   7.18
 b->o3 h1->o3 h2->o3
  4.33   4.42 -12.16
```

How it works...

In this recipe, we demonstrate steps to train a neural network model with the `nnet` package. We first use `nnet` to train the neural network. With this function, we can set the classification formula, source of data, number of hidden units in the `size` parameter, initial random weight in the `rang` parameter, parameter for weight decay in the `decay` parameter, and the maximum iteration in the `maxit` parameter. As we set `maxit` to 200, the training process repeatedly runs till the value of the fitting criterion plus the decay term converge. Finally, we use the `summary` function to obtain information about the built neural network, which reveals that the model is built with 4-2-3 networks with 19 weights. Also, the model shows a list of weight transitions from one node to another at the bottom of the printed message.

See also

For those who are interested in the background theory of `nnet` and how it is made, please refer to the following articles:

- Ripley, B. D. (1996) *Pattern Recognition and Neural Networks*. Cambridge
- Venables, W. N., and Ripley, B. D. (2002). *Modern applied statistics with S. Fourth edition*. Springer

Predicting labels based on a model trained by nnet

As we have trained a neural network with `nnet` in the previous recipe, we can now predict the labels of the testing dataset based on the trained neural network. Furthermore, we can assess the model with a confusion matrix adapted from the `caret` package.

Getting ready

You need to have completed the previous recipe by generating the training dataset, `trainset`, and the testing dataset, `testset`, from the `iris` dataset. The trained neural network also needs to be saved as `iris.nn`.

How to do it...

Perform the following steps to predict labels based on the trained neural network:

1. Generate the predictions of the testing dataset based on the model, `iris.nn`:

   ```
   > iris.predict = predict(iris.nn, testset, type="class")
   ```

2. Generate a classification table based on the predicted labels and labels of the testing dataset:

   ```
   > nn.table = table(testset$Species, iris.predict)
             iris.predict
             setosa versicolor virginica
   setosa        17          0         0
   versicolor     0         14         0
   virginica      0          1        14
   ```

3. Lastly, generate a confusion matrix based on the classification table:

```
> confusionMatrix(nn.table)
Confusion Matrix and Statistics

             iris.predict
             setosa versicolor virginica
  setosa        17         0         0
  versicolor     0        14         0
  virginica      0         1        14


Overall Statistics

               Accuracy : 0.9782609
                 95% CI : (0.8847282, 0.9994498)
    No Information Rate : 0.3695652
    P-Value [Acc > NIR] : < 0.00000000000000022204


                  Kappa : 0.9673063
 Mcnemar's Test P-Value : NA


Statistics by Class:

                     Class: setosa Class: versicolor
Sensitivity              1.0000000         0.9333333
Specificity              1.0000000         1.0000000
Pos Pred Value           1.0000000         1.0000000
Neg Pred Value           1.0000000         0.9687500
Prevalence               0.3695652         0.3260870
Detection Rate           0.3695652         0.3043478
Detection Prevalence     0.3695652         0.3043478
Balanced Accuracy        1.0000000         0.9666667
                     Class: virginica
Sensitivity                  1.0000000
Specificity                  0.9687500
Pos Pred Value               0.9333333
```

`Neg Pred Value`	1.0000000
`Prevalence`	0.3043478
`Detection Rate`	0.3043478
`Detection Prevalence`	0.3260870
`Balanced Accuracy`	0.9843750

How it works...

Similar to other classification methods, one can also predict labels based on the neural networks trained by `nnet`. First, we use the `predict` function to generate the predicted labels based on a testing dataset, `testset`. Within the `predict` function, we specify the `type` argument to the class, so the output will be class labels instead of a probability matrix. Next, we use the `table` function to generate a classification table based on predicted labels and labels written in the testing dataset. Finally, as we have created the classification table, we can employ a confusion matrix from the `caret` package to measure the prediction performance of the trained neural network.

See also

▶ For the `predict` function, if the `type` argument to `class` is not specified, by default, it will generate a probability matrix as a prediction result, which is very similar to `net.result` generated from the `compute` function within the `neuralnet` package:

```
> head(predict(iris.nn, testset))
```

7

Model Evaluation

In this chapter, we will cover the following topics:

- ▶ Estimating model performance with k-fold cross-validation
- ▶ Performing cross-validation with the e1071 package
- ▶ Performing cross-validation with the caret package
- ▶ Ranking the variable importance with the caret package
- ▶ Ranking the variable importance with the rminer package
- ▶ Finding highly correlated features with the caret package
- ▶ Selecting features using the caret package
- ▶ Measuring the performance of a regression model
- ▶ Measuring the prediction performance with the confusion matrix
- ▶ Measuring the prediction performance using ROCR
- ▶ Comparing an ROC curve using the caret package
- ▶ Measuring performance differences between models with the caret package

Introduction

Model evaluation is performed to ensure that a fitted model can accurately predict responses for future or unknown subjects. Without model evaluation, we might train models that over-fit in the training data. To prevent overfitting, we can employ packages, such as caret, rminer, and rocr to evaluate the performance of the fitted model. Furthermore, model evaluation can help select the optimum model, which is more robust and can accurately predict responses for future subjects.

In the following chapter, we will discuss how one can implement a simple R script or use one of the packages (for example, `caret` or `rminer`) to evaluate the performance of a fitted model.

Estimating model performance with k-fold cross-validation

The k-fold cross-validation technique is a common technique used to estimate the performance of a classifier as it overcomes the problem of over-fitting. For k-fold cross-validation, the method does not use the entire dataset to build the model, instead it splits the data into a training dataset and a testing dataset. Therefore, the model built with a training dataset can then be used to assess the performance of the model on the testing dataset. By performing n repeats of the k-fold validation, we can then use the average of *n* accuracies to truly assess the performance of the built model. In this recipe, we will illustrate how to perform a k-fold cross-validation.

Getting ready

In this recipe, we will continue to use the telecom `churn` dataset as the input data source to train the support vector machine. For those who have not prepared the dataset, please refer to *Chapter 5, Classification (I) – Tree, Lazy, and Probabilistic*, for detailed information.

How to do it...

Perform the following steps to cross-validate the telecom `churn` dataset:

1. Split the index into `10` fold using the cut function:

    ```
    > ind = cut(1:nrow(churnTrain), breaks=10, labels=F)
    ```

2. Next, use `for` loop to perform a 10 fold cross-validation, repeated `10` times:

    ```
    > accuracies = c()
    > for (i in 1:10) {
    +    fit = svm(churn ~., churnTrain[ind != i,])
    +    predictions = predict(fit, churnTrain[ind == i, !
    names(churnTrain) %in% c("churn")])
    +    correct_count = sum(predictions == churnTrain[ind ==
    i,c("churn")])
    +    accuracies = append(correct_count / nrow(churnTrain[ind ==
    i,]), accuracies)
    + }
    ```

3. You can then print the accuracies:

```
> accuracies
 [1] 0.9341317 0.8948949 0.8978979 0.9459459 0.9219219 0.9281437
 0.9219219 0.9249249 0.9189189 0.9251497
```

4. Lastly, you can generate average accuracies with the `mean` function:

```
> mean(accuracies)
 [1] 0.9213852
```

How it works...

In this recipe, we implement a simple script performing 10-fold cross-validations. We first generate an index with 10 fold with the `cut` function. Then, we implement a `for` loop to perform a 10-fold cross-validation 10 times. Within the loop, we first apply `svm` on 9 folds of data as the training set. We then use the fitted model to predict the label of the rest of the data (the testing dataset). Next, we use the sum of the correctly predicted labels to generate the accuracy. As a result of this, the loop stores 10 generated accuracies. Finally, we use the `mean` function to retrieve the average of the accuracies.

There's more...

If you wish to perform the k-fold validation with the use of other models, simply replace the line to generate the variable fit to whatever classifier you prefer. For example, if you would like to assess the Naïve Bayes model with a 10-fold cross-validation, you just need to replace the calling function from `svm` to `naiveBayes`:

```
> for (i in 1:10) {
+    fit = naiveBayes(churn ~., churnTrain[ind != i,])
+    predictions = predict(fit, churnTrain[ind == i, ! names(churnTrain)
%in% c("churn")])
+    correct_count = sum(predictions == churnTrain[ind == i,c("churn")])
+    accuracies = append(correct_count / nrow(churnTrain[ind == i,]),
accuracies)
+ }
```

Performing cross-validation with the e1071 package

Besides implementing a `loop` function to perform the k-fold cross-validation, you can use the `tuning` function (for example, `tune.nnet`, `tune.randomForest`, `tune.rpart`, `tune.svm`, and `tune.knn`.) within the `e1071` package to obtain the minimum error value. In this recipe, we will illustrate how to use `tune.svm` to perform the 10-fold cross-validation and obtain the optimum classification model.

Getting ready

In this recipe, we continue to use the telecom `churn` dataset as the input data source to perform 10-fold cross-validation.

How to do it...

Perform the following steps to retrieve the minimum estimation error using cross-validation:

1. Apply `tune.svm` on the training dataset, `trainset`, with the 10-fold cross-validation as the tuning control. (If you find an error message, such as `could not find function predict.func`, please clear the workspace, restart the R session and reload the `e1071` library again):

   ```
   > tuned = tune.svm(churn~., data = trainset, gamma = 10^-2, cost = 10^2, tunecontrol=tune.control(cross=10))
   ```

2. Next, you can obtain the summary information of the model, tuned:

   ```
   > summary(tuned)

   Error estimation of 'svm' using 10-fold cross validation:
   0.08164651
   ```

3. Then, you can access the performance details of the tuned model:

   ```
   > tuned$performances
     gamma cost      error dispersion
   1  0.01  100 0.08164651 0.02437228
   ```

4. Lastly, you can use the optimum model to generate a classification table:

   ```
   > svmfit = tuned$best.model
   > table(trainset[,c("churn")], predict(svmfit))

         yes   no
   yes   234  108
   no     13 1960
   ```

How it works...

The `e1071` package provides miscellaneous functions to build and assess models, therefore, you do not need to reinvent the wheel to evaluate a fitted model. In this recipe, we use the `tune.svm` function to tune the svm model with the given formula, dataset, gamma, cost, and control functions. Within the `tune.control` options, we configure the option as `cross=10`, which performs a 10-fold cross validation during the tuning process. The tuning process will eventually return the minimum estimation error, performance detail, and the best model during the tuning process. Therefore, we can obtain the performance measures of the tuning and further use the optimum model to generate a classification table.

See also

▶   In the `e1071` package, the `tune` function uses a grid search to tune parameters. For those interested in other tuning functions, use the help function to view the `tune` document:

```
> ?e1071::tune
```

Performing cross-validation with the caret package

The `Caret` (classification and regression training) package contains many functions in regard to the training process for regression and classification problems. Similar to the `e1071` package, it also contains a function to perform the k-fold cross validation. In this recipe, we will demonstrate how to the perform k-fold cross validation using the `caret` package.

Getting ready

In this recipe, we will continue to use the telecom `churn` dataset as the input data source to perform the k-fold cross validation.

How to do it...

Perform the following steps to perform the k-fold cross-validation with the `caret` package:

1.   First, set up the control parameter to train with the 10-fold cross validation in 3 repetitions:

```
> control = trainControl(method="repeatedcv", number=10,
repeats=3)
```

2. Then, you can train the classification model on telecom churn data with `rpart`:

```
> model = train(churn~., data=trainset, method="rpart",
preProcess="scale", trControl=control)
```

3. Finally, you can examine the output of the generated model:

```
> model
CART


2315 samples
  16 predictor
   2 classes: 'yes', 'no'


Pre-processing: scaled
Resampling: Cross-Validated (10 fold, repeated 3 times)


Summary of sample sizes: 2084, 2083, 2082, 2084, 2083, 2084, ...


Resampling results across tuning parameters:
```

cp	Accuracy	Kappa	Accuracy SD	Kappa SD
0.0556	0.904	0.531	0.0236	0.155
0.0746	0.867	0.269	0.0153	0.153
0.0760	0.860	0.212	0.0107	0.141

```
Accuracy was used to select the optimal model using the largest
value.
The final value used for the model was cp = 0.05555556.
```

How it works...

In this recipe, we demonstrate how convenient it is to conduct the k-fold cross-validation using the `caret` package. In the first step, we set up the training control and select the option to perform the 10-fold cross-validation in three repetitions. The process of repeating the k-fold validation is called repeated k-fold validation, which is used to test the stability of the model. If the model is stable, one should get a similar test result. Then, we apply `rpart` on the training dataset with the option to scale the data and to train the model with the options configured in the previous step.

After the training process is complete, the model outputs three resampling results. Of these results, the model with `cp=0.05555556` has the largest accuracy value (`0.904`), and is therefore selected as the optimal model for classification.

See also

▶ You can configure the `resampling` function in `trainControl`, in which you can specify `boot`, `boot632`, `cv`, `repeatedcv`, `LOOCV`, `LGOCV`, `none`, `oob`, `adaptive_cv`, `adaptive_boot`, or `adaptive_LGOCV`. To view more detailed information of how to choose the resampling method, view the `trainControl` document:

```
> ?trainControl
```

Ranking the variable importance with the caret package

After building a supervised learning model, we can estimate the importance of features. This estimation employs a sensitivity analysis to measure the effect on the output of a given model when the inputs are varied. In this recipe, we will show you how to rank the variable importance with the `caret` package.

Getting ready

You need to have completed the previous recipe by storing the fitted `rpart` object in the `model` variable.

How to do it...

Perform the following steps to rank the variable importance with the `caret` package:

1. First, you can estimate the variable importance with the `varImp` function:

```
> importance = varImp(model, scale=FALSE)
> importance
rpart variable importance
```

```
                              Overall
number_customer_service_calls 116.015
total_day_minutes             106.988
total_day_charge              100.648
international_planyes           86.789
```

```
voice_mail_planyes              25.974
total_eve_charge                23.097
total_eve_minutes               23.097
number_vmail_messages           19.885
total_intl_minutes               6.347
total_eve_calls                  0.000
total_day_calls                  0.000
total_night_charge               0.000
total_intl_calls                 0.000
total_intl_charge                0.000
total_night_minutes              0.000
total_night_calls                0.000
```

2. Then, you can generate the variable importance plot with the `plot` function:

```
> plot(importance)
```

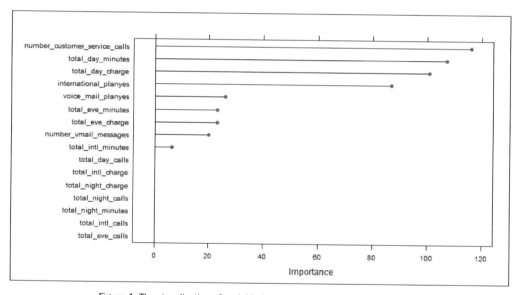

Figure 1: The visualization of variable importance using the caret package

How it works...

In this recipe, we first use the `varImp` function to retrieve the variable importance and obtain the summary. The overall results show the sensitivity measure of each attribute. Next, we plot the variable importance in terms of rank, which shows that the `number_customer_service_calls` attribute is the most important variable in the sensitivity measure.

There's more...

In some classification packages, such as `rpart`, the object generated from the training model contains the variable importance. We can examine the variable importance by accessing the output object:

```
> library(rpart)
> model.rp = rpart(churn~., data=trainset)
> model.rp$variable.importance
```

total_day_minutes	total_day_charge
111.645286	110.881583
number_customer_service_calls	total_intl_minutes
58.486651	48.283228
total_intl_charge	total_eve_charge
47.698379	47.166646
total_eve_minutes	international_plan
47.166646	42.194508
total_intl_calls	number_vmail_messages
36.730344	19.884863
voice_mail_plan	total_night_calls
19.884863	7.195828
total_eve_calls	total_night_charge
3.553423	1.754547
total_night_minutes	total_day_calls
1.754547	1.494986

Ranking the variable importance with the rminer package

Besides using the `caret` package to generate variable importance, you can use the `rminer` package to generate the variable importance of a classification model. In the following recipe, we will illustrate how to use `rminer` to obtain the variable importance of a fitted model.

Getting ready

In this recipe, we will continue to use the telecom `churn` dataset as the input data source to rank the variable importance.

How to do it...

Perform the following steps to rank the variable importance with `rminer`:

1. Install and load the package, `rminer`:

    ```
    > install.packages("rminer")
    > library(rminer)
    ```

2. Fit the svm model with the training set:

    ```
    > model=fit(churn~.,trainset,model="svm")
    ```

3. Use the `Importance` function to obtain the variable importance:

    ```
    > VariableImportance=Importance(model,trainset,method="sensv")
    ```

4. Plot the variable importance ranked by the variance:

    ```
    > L=list(runs=1,sen=t(VariableImportance$imp),sresponses=VariableI
    mportance$sresponses)
    > mgraph(L,graph="IMP",leg=names(trainset),col="gray",Grid=10)
    ```

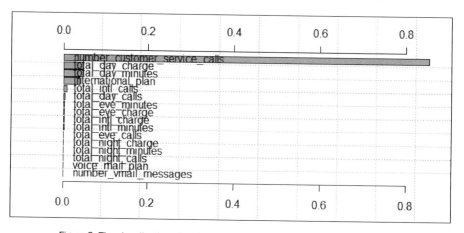

Figure 2: The visualization of variable importance using the `rminer` package

How it works...

Similar to the `caret` package, the `rminer` package can also generate the variable importance of a classification model. In this recipe, we first train the svm model on the training dataset, `trainset`, with the `fit` function. Then, we use the `Importance` function to rank the variable importance with a sensitivity measure. Finally, we use `mgraph` to plot the rank of the variable importance. Similar to the result obtained from using the `caret` package, `number_customer_service_calls` is the most important variable in the measure of sensitivity.

- ▸ The `rminer` package provides many classification models for one to choose from. If you are interested in using models other than svm, you can view these options with the following command:

```
> ?rminer::fit
```

Finding highly correlated features with the caret package

When performing regression or classification, some models perform better if highly correlated attributes are removed. The `caret` package provides the `findCorrelation` function, which can be used to find attributes that are highly correlated to each other. In this recipe, we will demonstrate how to find highly correlated features using the `caret` package.

Getting ready

In this recipe, we will continue to use the telecom `churn` dataset as the input data source to find highly correlated features.

How to do it...

Perform the following steps to find highly correlated attributes:

1. Remove the features that are not coded in numeric characters:

```
> new_train = trainset[,! names(churnTrain) %in% c("churn",
"international_plan", "voice_mail_plan")]
```

2. Then, you can obtain the correlation of each attribute:

```
>cor_mat = cor(new_train)
```

3. Next, we use `findCorrelation` to search for highly correlated attributes with a cut off equal to 0.75:

```
> highlyCorrelated = findCorrelation(cor_mat, cutoff=0.75)
```

4. We then obtain the name of highly correlated attributes:

```
> names(new_train)[highlyCorrelated]
[1] "total_intl_minutes"  "total_day_charge"     "total_eve_
minutes"    "total_night_minutes"
```

How it works...

In this recipe, we search for highly correlated attributes using the `caret` package. In order to retrieve the correlation of each attribute, one should first remove nonnumeric attributes. Then, we perform correlation to obtain a correlation matrix. Next, we use `findCorrelation` to find highly correlated attributes with the cut off set to 0.75. We finally obtain the names of highly correlated (with a correlation coefficient over 0.75) attributes, which are `total_intl_minutes`, `total_day_charge`, `total_eve_minutes`, and `total_night_minutes`. You can consider removing some highly correlated attributes and keep one or two attributes for better accuracy.

See also

▸ In addition to the `caret` package, you can use the `leaps`, `genetic`, and `anneal` functions in the `subselect` package to achieve the same goal

Selecting features using the caret package

The feature selection method searches the subset of features with minimized predictive errors. We can apply feature selection to identify which attributes are required to build an accurate model. The `caret` package provides a recursive feature elimination function, `rfe`, which can help automatically select the required features. In the following recipe, we will demonstrate how to use the `caret` package to perform feature selection.

Getting ready

In this recipe, we will continue to use the telecom `churn` dataset as the input data source for feature selection.

How to do it...

Perform the following steps to select features:

1. Transform the feature named as `international_plan` of the training dataset, `trainset`, to `intl_yes` and `intl_no`:

```
> intl_plan = model.matrix(~ trainset.international_plan - 1,
data=data.frame(trainset$international_plan))

> colnames(intl_plan) = c("trainset.international_planno"="intl_no", "trainset.international_planyes"= "intl_yes")
```

2. Transform the feature named as `voice_mail_plan` of the training dataset, `trainset`, to `voice_yes` and `voice_no`:

```
> voice_plan = model.matrix(~ trainset.voice_mail_plan - 1,
data=data.frame(trainset$voice_mail_plan))
```
```
> colnames(voice_plan) = c("trainset.voice_mail_planno" ="voice_
no", "trainset.voice_mail_planyes"="voidce_yes")
```

3. Remove the `international_plan` and `voice_mail_plan` attributes and combine the training dataset, `trainset` with the data frames, `intl_plan` and `voice_plan`:

```
> trainset$international_plan = NULL
```
```
> trainset$voice_mail_plan = NULL
```
```
> trainset = cbind(intl_plan,voice_plan, trainset)
```

4. Transform the feature named as `international_plan` of the testing dataset, `testset`, to `intl_yes` and `intl_no`:

```
> intl_plan = model.matrix(~ testset.international_plan - 1,
data=data.frame(testset$international_plan))
```
```
> colnames(intl_plan) = c("testset.international_planno"="intl_
no", "testset.international_planyes"= "intl_yes")
```

5. Transform the feature named as `voice_mail_plan` of the training dataset, `trainset`, to `voice_yes` and `voice_no`:

```
> voice_plan = model.matrix(~ testset.voice_mail_plan - 1,
data=data.frame(testset$voice_mail_plan))
```
```
> colnames(voice_plan) = c("testset.voice_mail_planno" ="voice_
no", "testset.voice_mail_planyes"="voidce_yes")
```

6. Remove the `international_plan` and `voice_mail_plan` attributes and combine the testing dataset, `testset` with the data frames, `intl_plan` and `voice_plan`:

```
> testset$international_plan = NULL
```
```
> testset$voice_mail_plan = NULL
```
```
> testset = cbind(intl_plan,voice_plan, testset)
```

7. We then create a feature selection algorithm using linear discriminant analysis:

```
> ldaControl = rfeControl(functions = ldaFuncs, method = "cv")
```

8. Next, we perform a backward feature selection on the training dataset, `trainset` using subsets from 1 to 18:

```
> ldaProfile = rfe(trainset[, !names(trainset) %in% c("churn")],
trainset[,c("churn")],sizes = c(1:18), rfeControl = ldaControl)
> ldaProfile
```

```
Recursive feature selection


Outer resampling method: Cross-Validated (10 fold)


Resampling performance over subset size:
```

Variables	Accuracy	Kappa	AccuracySD	KappaSD	Selected
1	0.8523	0.0000	0.001325	0.00000	
2	0.8523	0.0000	0.001325	0.00000	
3	0.8423	0.1877	0.015468	0.09787	
4	0.8462	0.2285	0.016593	0.09610	
5	0.8466	0.2384	0.020710	0.09970	
6	0.8466	0.2364	0.019612	0.09387	
7	0.8458	0.2315	0.017551	0.08670	
8	0.8458	0.2284	0.016608	0.09536	
9	0.8475	0.2430	0.016882	0.10147	
10	0.8514	0.2577	0.014281	0.08076	
11	0.8518	0.2587	0.014124	0.08075	
12	0.8544	0.2702	0.015078	0.09208	*
13	0.8544	0.2721	0.015352	0.09421	
14	0.8531	0.2663	0.018428	0.11022	
15	0.8527	0.2652	0.017958	0.10850	
16	0.8531	0.2684	0.017897	0.10884	
17	0.8531	0.2684	0.017897	0.10884	
18	0.8531	0.2684	0.017897	0.10884	

```
The top 5 variables (out of 12):
    total_day_charge, total_day_minutes, intl_no, number_customer_
service_calls, total_eve_charge
```

9. Next, we can plot the selection result:

```
> plot(ldaProfile, type = c("o", "g"))
```

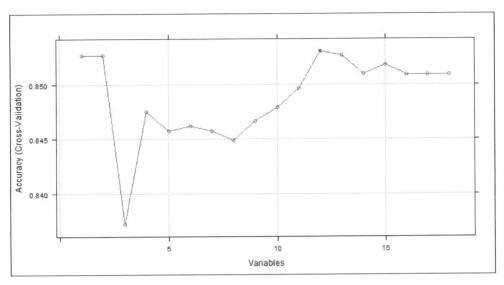

Figure 3: The feature selection result

10. We can then examine the best subset of the variables:

```
> ldaProfile$optVariables
 [1] "total_day_charge"
 [2] "total_day_minutes"
 [3] "intl_no"
 [4] "number_customer_service_calls"
 [5] "total_eve_charge"
 [6] "total_eve_minutes"
 [7] "voidce_yes"
 [8] "total_intl_calls"
 [9] "number_vmail_messages"
[10] "total_intl_charge"
[11] "total_intl_minutes"
[12] "total_night_minutes"
```

11. Now, we can examine the fitted model:

```
> ldaProfile$fit
Call:
lda(x, y)
```

```
Prior probabilities of groups:
     yes          no
0.1477322 0.8522678


Group means:
    total_day_charge total_day_minutes    intl_no
yes          35.00143           205.8877 0.7046784
no           29.62402           174.2555 0.9351242
    number_customer_service_calls total_eve_charge
yes                      2.204678         18.16702
no                       1.441460         16.96789
    total_eve_minutes voidce_yes total_intl_calls
yes          213.7269  0.1666667         4.134503
no           199.6197  0.2954891         4.514445
    number_vmail_messages total_intl_charge
yes              5.099415          2.899386
no               8.674607          2.741343
    total_intl_minutes total_night_minutes
yes           10.73684             205.4640
no            10.15119             201.4184


Coefficients of linear discriminants:
                                       LD1
total_day_charge                0.715025524
total_day_minutes              -0.130486470
intl_no                         2.259889324
number_customer_service_calls  -0.421997335
total_eve_charge               -2.390372793
total_eve_minutes               0.198406977
voidce_yes                      0.660927935
total_intl_calls                0.066240268
number_vmail_messages          -0.003529233
total_intl_charge               2.315069869
total_intl_minutes             -0.693504606
total_night_minutes            -0.002127471
```

12. Finally, we can calculate the performance across resamples:

```
> postResample(predict(ldaProfile, testset[, !names(testset) %in%
c("churn")]), testset[,c("churn")])

Accuracy     Kappa

0.8605108 0.2672027
```

How it works...

In this recipe, we perform feature selection using the `caret` package. As there are factor-coded attributes within the dataset, we first use a function called `model.matrix` to transform the factor-coded attributes into multiple binary attributes. Therefore, we transform the `international_plan` attribute to `intl_yes` and `intl_no`. Additionally, we transform the `voice_mail_plan` attribute to `voice_yes` and `voice_no`.

Next, we set up control parameters for training using the cross-validation method, `cv`, with the linear discriminant function, `ldaFuncs`. Then, we use the recursive feature elimination, `rfe`, to perform feature selection with the use of the `control` function, `ldaFuncs`. The `rfe` function generates the summary of feature selection, which contains resampling a performance over the subset size and top variables.

We can then use the obtained model information to plot the number of variables against accuracy. From Figure 3, it is obvious that using 12 features can obtain the best accuracy. In addition to this, we can retrieve the best subset of the variables in (12 variables in total) the fitted model. Lastly, we can calculate the performance across resamples, which yields an accuracy of 0.86 and a kappa of 0.27.

See also

▶ In order to specify the algorithm used to control feature selection, one can change the control function specified in `rfeControl`. Here are some of the options you can use:

```
caretFuncs       SVM (caret)
lmFuncs          lm (base)
rfFuncs          RF(randomForest)
treebagFuncs     DT (ipred)
ldaFuncs         lda(base)
nbFuncs          NB(klaR)
gamFuncs         gam(gam)
```

Measuring the performance of the regression model

To measure the performance of a regression model, we can calculate the distance from predicted output and the actual output as a quantifier of the performance of the model. Here, we often use the **root mean square error** (**RMSE**), **relative square error** (**RSE**) and R-Square as common measurements. In the following recipe, we will illustrate how to compute these measurements from a built regression model.

Getting ready

In this recipe, we will use the `Quartet` dataset, which contains four regression datasets, as our input data source.

How to do it...

Perform the following steps to measure the performance of the regression model:

1. Load the `Quartet` dataset from the `car` package:

   ```
   > library(car)
   > data(Quartet)
   ```

2. Plot the attribute, `y3`, against x using the `lm` function:

   ```
   > plot(Quartet$x, Quartet$y3)
   > lmfit = lm(Quartet$y3~Quartet$x)
   > abline(lmfit, col="red")
   ```

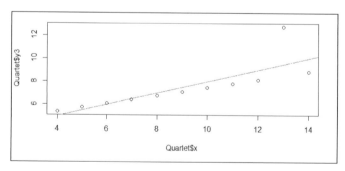

Figure 4: The linear regression plot

3. You can retrieve predicted values by using the `predict` function:

   ```
   > predicted= predict(lmfit, newdata=Quartet[c("x")])
   ```

4. Now, you can calculate the root mean square error:

```
> actual = Quartet$y3
> rmse = (mean((predicted - actual)^2))^0.5
> rmse
[1] 1.118286
```

5. You can calculate the relative square error:

```
> mu = mean(actual)
> rse = mean((predicted - actual)^2) / mean((mu - actual)^2)
> rse
[1] 0.333676
```

6. Also, you can use R-Square as a measurement:

```
> rsquare = 1 - rse
> rsquare
[1] 0.666324
```

7. Then, you can plot attribute, y3, against x using the `rlm` function from the MASS package:

```
> library(MASS)
> plot(Quartet$x, Quartet$y3)
> rlmfit = rlm(Quartet$y3~Quartet$x)
> abline(rlmfit, col="red")
```

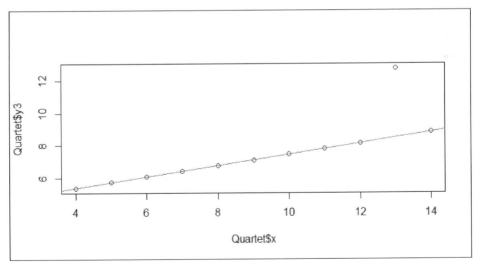

Figure 5: The robust linear regression plot on the Quartet dataset

8. You can then retrieve the predicted value using the `predict` function:

```
> predicted = predict(rlmfit, newdata=Quartet[c("x")])
```

9. Next, you can calculate the root mean square error using the distance of the predicted and actual value:

```
> actual = Quartet$y3
> rmse = (mean((predicted - actual)^2))^0.5
> rmse
[1] 1.279045
```

10. Calculate the relative square error between the predicted and actual labels:

```
> mu = mean(actual)
> rse =mean((predicted - actual)^2) / mean((mu - actual)^2)
> rse
[1] 0.4365067
```

11. Now, you can calculate the R-Square value:

```
> rsquare = 1 - rse
> rsquare
[1] 0.5634933
```

How it works...

The measurement of the performance of the regression model employs the distance between the predicted value and the actual value. We often use these three measurements, root mean square error, relative square error, and R-Square, as the quantifier of the performance of regression models. In this recipe, we first load the Quartet data from the car package. We then use the lm function to fit the linear model, and add the regression line on a scatter plot of the x variable against the y3 variable. Next, we compute the predicted value using the predict function, and begin to compute the **root mean square error** (**RMSE**), **relative square error** (**RSE**), and R-Square for the built model.

As this dataset has an outlier at x=13, we would like to quantify how the outlier affects the performance measurement. To achieve this, we first train a regression model using the rlm function from the MASS package. Similar to the previous step, we then generate a performance measurement of the root square mean error, relative error and R-Square. From the output measurement, it is obvious that the mean square error and the relative square errors of the lm model are smaller than the model built by rlm, and the score of R-Square shows that the model built with lm has a greater prediction power. However, for the actual scenario, we should remove the outlier at x=13. This comparison shows that the outlier may be biased toward the performance measure and may lead us to choose the wrong model.

There's more...

If you would like to perform cross-validation on a linear regression model, you can use the `tune` function within the `e1071` package:

```
> tune(lm, y3~x, data = Quartet)
Error estimation of 'lm' using 10-fold cross validation: 2.33754
```

Other than the `e1071` package, you can use the `train` function from the `caret` package to perform cross-validation. In addition to this, you can also use `cv.lm` from the DAAG package to achieve the same goal.

Measuring prediction performance with a confusion matrix

To measure the performance of a classification model, we can first generate a classification table based on our predicted label and actual label. Then, we can use a confusion matrix to obtain performance measures such as precision, recall, specificity, and accuracy. In this recipe, we will demonstrate how to retrieve a confusion matrix using the `caret` package.

Getting ready

In this recipe, we will continue to use the telecom `churn` dataset as our example dataset.

How to do it...

Perform the following steps to generate a classification measurement:

1. Train an svm model using the training dataset:

    ```
    > svm.model= train(churn ~ .,
    +                   data = trainset,
    +                   method = "svmRadial")
    ```

2. You can then predict labels using the fitted model, `svm.model`:

    ```
    > svm.pred = predict(svm.model, testset[,! names(testset) %in%
    c("churn")])
    ```

3. Next, you can generate a classification table:

    ```
    > table(svm.pred, testset[,c("churn")])

    svm.pred yes   no
         yes  73   16
         no   68  861
    ```

4. Lastly, you can generate a confusion matrix using the prediction results and the actual labels from the testing dataset:

```
> confusionMatrix(svm.pred, testset[,c("churn")])
Confusion Matrix and Statistics

          Reference
Prediction yes  no
       yes  73  16
       no   68 861

               Accuracy : 0.9175
                 95% CI : (0.8989, 0.9337)
    No Information Rate : 0.8615
    P-Value [Acc > NIR] : 2.273e-08

                  Kappa : 0.5909
 Mcnemar's Test P-Value : 2.628e-08

            Sensitivity : 0.51773
            Specificity : 0.98176
         Pos Pred Value : 0.82022
         Neg Pred Value : 0.92680
             Prevalence : 0.13851
         Detection Rate : 0.07171
   Detection Prevalence : 0.08743
      Balanced Accuracy : 0.74974

       'Positive' Class : yes
```

How it works...

In this recipe, we demonstrate how to obtain a confusion matrix to measure the performance of a classification model. First, we use the `train` function from the `caret` package to train an svm model. Next, we use the `predict` function to extract the predicted labels of the svm model using the testing dataset. Then, we perform the `table` function to obtain the classification table based on the predicted and actual labels. Finally, we use the `confusionMatrix` function from the `caret` package to a generate a confusion matrix to measure the performance of the classification model.

▶ If you are interested in the available methods that can be used in the `train` function, you can refer to this website: `http://topepo.github.io/caret/modelList.html`

Measuring prediction performance using ROCR

A **receiver operating characteristic** (**ROC**) curve is a plot that illustrates the performance of a binary classifier system, and plots the true positive rate against the false positive rate for different cut points. We most commonly use this plot to calculate the **area under curve** (**AUC**) to measure the performance of a classification model. In this recipe, we will demonstrate how to illustrate an ROC curve and calculate the AUC to measure the performance of a classification model.

Getting ready

In this recipe, we will continue using the telecom `churn` dataset as our example dataset.

How to do it...

Perform the following steps to generate two different classification examples with different costs:

1. First, you should install and load the ROCR package:

   ```
   > install.packages("ROCR")
   > library(ROCR)
   ```

2. Train the svm model using the training dataset with a probability equal to TRUE:

   ```
   > svmfit=svm(churn~ ., data=trainset, prob=TRUE)
   ```

3. Make predictions based on the trained model on the testing dataset with the probability set as TRUE:

   ```
   >pred=predict(svmfit,testset[, !names(testset) %in% c("churn")],
   probability=TRUE)
   ```

4. Obtain the probability of labels with yes:

   ```
   > pred.prob = attr(pred, "probabilities")
   > pred.to.roc = pred.prob[, 2]
   ```

5. Use the `prediction` function to generate a prediction result:

   ```
   > pred.rocr = prediction(pred.to.roc, testset$churn)
   ```

6. Use the `performance` function to obtain the performance measurement:

   ```
   > perf.rocr = performance(pred.rocr, measure = "auc", x.measure =
   "cutoff")

   > perf.tpr.rocr = performance(pred.rocr, "tpr","fpr")
   ```

7. Visualize the ROC curve using the `plot` function:

   ```
   > plot(perf.tpr.rocr, colorize=T,main=paste("AUC:", (perf.rocr@y.
   values)))
   ```

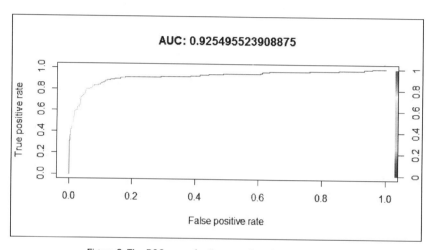

Figure 6: The ROC curve for the svm classifier performance

How it works...

In this recipe, we demonstrated how to generate an ROC curve to illustrate the performance of a binary classifier. First, we should install and load the library, ROCR. Then, we use svm, from the `e1071` package, to train a classification model, and then use the model to predict labels for the testing dataset. Next, we use the prediction function (from the package, ROCR) to generate prediction results. We then adapt the performance function to obtain the performance measurement of the true positive rate against the false positive rate. Finally, we use the `plot` function to visualize the ROC plot, and add the value of AUC on the title. In this example, the AUC value is 0.92, which indicates that the svm classifier performs well in classifying telecom user churn datasets.

See also

▸ For those interested in the concept and terminology of ROC, you can refer to
http://en.wikipedia.org/wiki/Receiver_operating_characteristic

Comparing an ROC curve using the caret package

In previous chapters, we introduced many classification methods; each method has its own advantages and disadvantages. However, when it comes to the problem of how to choose the best fitted model, you need to compare all the performance measures generated from different prediction models. To make the comparison easy, the caret package allows us to generate and compare the performance of models. In this recipe, we will use the function provided by the `caret` package to compare different algorithm trained models on the same dataset.

Getting ready

Here, we will continue to use telecom dataset as our input data source.

How to do it...

Perform the following steps to generate an ROC curve of each fitted model:

1. Install and load the library, pROC:

   ```
   > install.packages("pROC")
   > library("pROC")
   ```

2. Set up the training control with a 10-fold cross-validation in 3 repetitions:

   ```
   > control = trainControl(method = "repeatedcv",
   +                        number = 10,
   +                        repeats = 3,
   +                        classProbs = TRUE,
   +                        summaryFunction = twoClassSummary)
   ```

3. Then, you can train a classifier on the training dataset using glm:

   ```
   > glm.model= train(churn ~ .,
   +                  data = trainset,
   +                  method = "glm",
   +                  metric = "ROC",
   +                  trControl = control)
   ```

4. Also, you can train a classifier on the training dataset using svm:

   ```
   > svm.model= train(churn ~ .,
   +                  data = trainset,
   ```

```
+                     method = "svmRadial",
+                     metric = "ROC",
+                     trControl = control)
```

5. To see how `rpart` performs on the training data, we use the `rpart` function:

```
> rpart.model= train(churn ~ .,
+                     data = trainset,
+                     method = "rpart",
+                     metric = "ROC",
+                     trControl = control)
```

6. You can make predictions separately based on different trained models:

```
> glm.probs = predict(glm.model, testset[,! names(testset) %in%
c("churn")], type = "prob")

> svm.probs = predict(svm.model, testset[,! names(testset) %in%
c("churn")], type = "prob")

> rpart.probs = predict(rpart.model, testset[,! names(testset)
%in% c("churn")], type = "prob")
```

7. You can generate the ROC curve of each model, and plot the curve on the same figure:

```
> glm.ROC = roc(response = testset[,c("churn")],
+                     predictor =glm.probs$yes,
+                     levels = levels(testset[,c("churn")]))
> plot(glm.ROC, type="S", col="red")


Call:
roc.default(response = testset[, c("churn")], predictor = glm.
probs$yes,      levels = levels(testset[, c("churn")]))


Data: glm.probs$yes in 141 controls (testset[, c("churn")] yes) >
877 cases (testset[, c("churn")] no).
Area under the curve: 0.82


> svm.ROC = roc(response = testset[,c("churn")],
+                     predictor =svm.probs$yes,
+                     levels = levels(testset[,c("churn")]))
> plot(svm.ROC, add=TRUE, col="green")
```

```
Call:
roc.default(response = testset[, c("churn")], predictor = svm.
probs$yes,    levels = levels(testset[, c("churn")]))


Data: svm.probs$yes in 141 controls (testset[, c("churn")] yes) >
877 cases (testset[, c("churn")] no).
Area under the curve: 0.9233


> rpart.ROC = roc(response = testset[,c("churn")],
+               predictor =rpart.probs$yes,
+               levels = levels(testset[,c("churn")]))
> plot(rpart.ROC, add=TRUE, col="blue")


Call:
roc.default(response = testset[, c("churn")], predictor = rpart.
probs$yes,    levels = levels(testset[, c("churn")]))


Data: rpart.probs$yes in 141 controls (testset[, c("churn")] yes)
> 877 cases (testset[, c("churn")] no).
Area under the curve: 0.7581
```

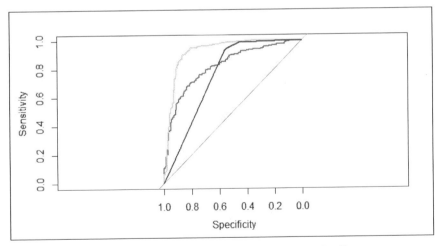

Figure 7: The ROC curve for the performance of three classifiers

How it works...

Here, we demonstrate how we can compare fitted models by illustrating their ROC curve in one figure. First, we set up the control of the training process with a 10-fold cross validation in 3 repetitions with the performance evaluation in `twoClassSummary`. After setting up control of the training process, we then apply `glm`, `svm`, and `rpart` algorithms on the training dataset to fit the classification models. Next, we can make a prediction based on each generated model and plot the ROC curve, respectively. Within the generated figure, we find that the model trained by svm has the largest area under curve, which is 0.9233 (plotted in green), the AUC of the `glm` model (red) is 0.82, and the AUC of the `rpart` model (blue) is 0.7581. From *Figure 7*, it is obvious that `svm` performs the best among all the fitted models on this training dataset (without requiring tuning).

See also

▶   We use another ROC visualization package, pROC, which can be employed to display and analyze ROC curves. If you would like to know more about the package, please use the `help` function:

```
> help(package="pROC")
```

Measuring performance differences between models with the caret package

In the previous recipe, we introduced how to generate ROC curves for each generated model, and have the curve plotted on the same figure. Apart from using an ROC curve, one can use the resampling method to generate statistics of each fitted model in ROC, sensitivity and specificity metrics. Therefore, we can use these statistics to compare the performance differences between each model. In the following recipe, we will introduce how to measure performance differences between fitted models with the `caret` package.

Getting ready

One needs to have completed the previous recipe by storing the `glm` fitted model, `svm` fitted model, and the `rpart` fitted model into `glm.model`, `svm.model`, and `rpart.model`, respectively.

How to do it...

Perform the following steps to measure performance differences between each fitted model:

1. Resample the three generated models:

    ```
    > cv.values = resamples(list(glm = glm.model, svm=svm.model, rpart
    = rpart.model))
    ```

2. Then, you can obtain a summary of the resampling result:

    ```
    > summary(cv.values)
    ```

    ```
    Call:
    summary.resamples(object = cv.values)


    Models: glm, svm, rpart
    Number of resamples: 30


    ROC
              Min. 1st Qu. Median   Mean 3rd Qu.   Max. NA's
    glm    0.7206  0.7847 0.8126 0.8116  0.8371 0.8877    0
    svm    0.8337  0.8673 0.8946 0.8929  0.9194 0.9458    0
    rpart  0.2802  0.7159 0.7413 0.6769  0.8105 0.8821    0


    Sens
               Min. 1st Qu. Median   Mean 3rd Qu.   Max. NA's
    glm    0.08824  0.2000 0.2286 0.2194  0.2517 0.3529    0
    svm    0.44120  0.5368 0.5714 0.5866  0.6424 0.7143    0
    rpart  0.20590  0.3742 0.4706 0.4745  0.5929 0.6471    0


    Spec
              Min. 1st Qu. Median   Mean 3rd Qu.   Max. NA's
    glm    0.9442  0.9608 0.9746 0.9701  0.9797 0.9949    0
    svm    0.9442  0.9646 0.9746 0.9740  0.9835 0.9949    0
    rpart  0.9492  0.9709 0.9797 0.9780  0.9848 0.9949    0
    ```

3. Use `dotplot` to plot the resampling result in the ROC metric:

    ```
    > dotplot(cv.values, metric = "ROC")
    ```

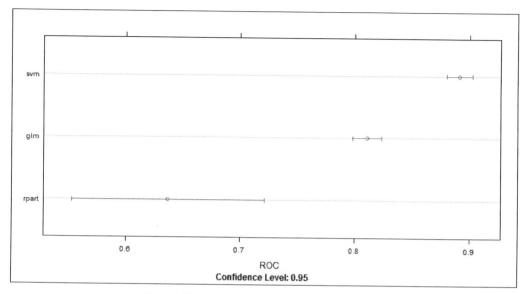

Figure 8: The dotplot of resampling result in ROC metric

4. Also, you can use a box-whisker plot to plot the resampling result:

    ```
    > bwplot(cv.values, layout = c(3, 1))
    ```

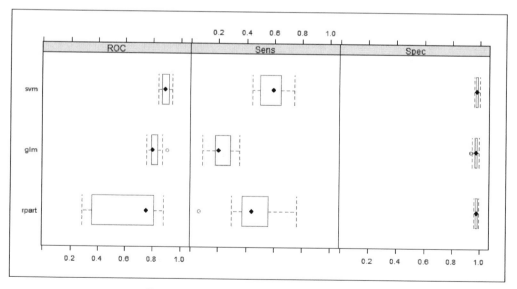

Figure 9: The box-whisker plot of resampling result

How it works...

In this recipe, we demonstrate how to measure the performance differences among three fitted models using the resampling method. First, we use the `resample` function to generate the statistics of each fitted model (`svm.model`, `glm.model`, and `rpart.model`). Then, we can use the `summary` function to obtain the statistics of these three models in the ROC, sensitivity and specificity metrics. Next, we can apply a `dotplot` on the resampling result to see how ROC varied between each model. Last, we use a box-whisker plot on the resampling results to show the box-whisker plot of different models in the ROC, sensitivity and specificity metrics on a single plot.

See also

- Besides using `dotplot` and `bwplot` to measure performance differences, one can use `densityplot`, `splom`, and `xyplot` to visualize the performance differences of each fitted model in the ROC, sensitivity, and specificity metrics.

8
Ensemble Learning

In this chapter, we will cover the following topics:

- ▶ Classifying data with the bagging method
- ▶ Performing cross-validation with the bagging method
- ▶ Classifying data with the boosting method
- ▶ Performing cross-validation with the boosting method
- ▶ Classifying data with gradient boosting
- ▶ Calculating the margins of a classifier
- ▶ Calculating the error evolution of the ensemble method
- ▶ Classifying the data with random forest
- ▶ Estimating the prediction errors of different classifiers

Introduction

Ensemble learning is a method to combine results produced by different learners into one format, with the aim of producing better classification results and regression results. In previous chapters, we discussed several classification methods. These methods take different approaches but they all have the same goal, that is, finding an optimum classification model. However, a single classifier may be imperfect, which may misclassify data in certain categories. As not all classifiers are imperfect, a better approach is to average the results by voting. In other words, if we average the prediction results of every classifier with the same input, we may create a superior model compared to using an individual method.

In ensemble learning, bagging, boosting, and random forest are the three most common methods:

▸ Bagging is a voting method, which first uses Bootstrap to generate a different training set, and then uses the training set to make different base learners. The bagging method employs a combination of base learners to make a better prediction.

▸ Boosting is similar to the bagging method. However, what makes boosting different is that it first constructs the base learning in sequence, where each successive learner is built for the prediction residuals of the preceding learner. With the means to create a complementary learner, it uses the mistakes made by previous learners to train the next base learner.

▸ Random forest uses the classification results voted from many classification trees. The idea is simple; a single classification tree will obtain a single classification result with a single input vector. However, a random forest grows many classification trees, obtaining multiple results from a single input. Therefore, a random forest will use the majority of votes from all the decision trees to classify data or use an average output for regression.

In the following recipes, we will discuss how to use bagging and boosting to classify data. We can then perform cross-validation to estimate the error rate of each classifier. In addition to this, we'll introduce the use of a margin to measure the certainty of a model. Next, we cover random forests, similar to the bagging and boosting methods, and introduce how to train the model to classify data and use margins to estimate the model certainty. Lastly, we'll demonstrate how to estimate the error rate of each classifier, and use the error rate to compare the performance of different classifiers.

Classifying data with the bagging method

The `adabag` package implements both boosting and bagging methods. For the bagging method, the package implements Breiman's Bagging algorithm, which first generates multiple versions of classifiers, and then obtains an aggregated classifier. In this recipe, we will illustrate how to use the bagging method from `adabag` to generate a classification model using the telecom `churn` dataset.

Getting ready

In this recipe, we continue to use the telecom `churn` dataset as the input data source for the bagging method. For those who have not prepared the dataset, please refer to *Chapter 5, Classification (I) – Tree, Lazy, and Probabilistic*, for detailed information.

How to do it...

Perform the following steps to generate a classification model for the telecom `churn` dataset:

1. First, you need to install and load the `adabag` package (it might take a while to install adabag):

```
> install.packages("adabag")
> library(adabag)
```

2. Next, you can use the `bagging` function to train a training dataset (the result may vary during the training process):

```
> set.seed(2)
> churn.bagging = bagging(churn ~ ., data=trainset, mfinal=10)
```

3. Access the variable importance from the bagging result:

```
> churn.bagging$importance
```

international_plan	number_customer_service_calls
10.4948380	16.4260510
number_vmail_messages	total_day_calls
0.5319143	0.3774190
total_day_charge	total_day_minutes
0.0000000	28.7545042
total_eve_calls	total_eve_charge
0.1463585	0.0000000
total_eve_minutes	total_intl_calls
14.2366754	8.7733895
total_intl_charge	total_intl_minutes
0.0000000	9.7838256
total_night_calls	total_night_charge
0.4349952	0.0000000
total_night_minutes	voice_mail_plan
2.3379622	7.7020671

4. After generating the classification model, you can use the predicted results from the testing dataset:

```
> churn.predbagging= predict.bagging(churn.bagging,
newdata=testset)
```

5. From the predicted results, you can obtain a classification table:

```
> churn.predbagging$confusion
                Observed Class
Predicted Class yes   no
            no   35  866
            yes 106   11
```

6. Finally, you can retrieve the average error of the bagging result:

```
> churn.predbagging$error
[1]  0.0451866
```

How it works...

Bagging is derived from the name Bootstrap aggregating, which is a stable, accurate, and easy to implement model for data classification and regression. The definition of bagging is as follows: given a training dataset of size n, bagging performs Bootstrap sampling and generates m new training sets, Di, each of size n. Finally, we can fit m Bootstrap samples to m models and combine the result by averaging the output (for regression) or voting (for classification):

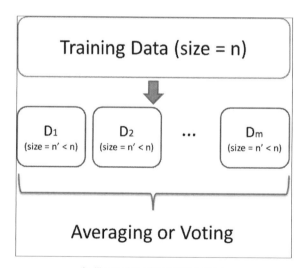

An illustration of bagging method

The advantage of using bagging is that it is a powerful learning method, which is easy to understand and implement. However, the main drawback of this technique is that it is hard to analyze the result.

In this recipe, we use the boosting method from adabag to classify the telecom churn data. Similar to other classification methods discussed in previous chapters, you can train a boosting classifier with a formula and a training dataset. Additionally, you can set the number of iterations to 10 in the `mfinal` argument. Once the classification model is built, you can examine the importance of each attribute. Ranking the attributes by importance reveals that the number of customer service calls play a crucial role in the classification model.

Next, with a fitted model, you can apply the `predict.bagging` function to predict the labels of the testing dataset. Therefore, you can use the labels of the testing dataset and predicted results to generate a classification table and obtain the average error, which is 0.045 in this example.

There's more...

Besides adabag, the ipred package provides a bagging method for a classification tree. We demonstrate here how to use the bagging method of the ipred package to train a classification model:

1. First, you need to install and load the `ipred` package:

   ```
   > install.packages("ipred")
   > library(ipred)
   ```

2. You can then use the `bagging` method to fit the classification method:

   ```
   > churn.bagging = bagging(churn ~ ., data = trainset, coob = T)
   > churn.bagging


   Bagging classification trees with 25 bootstrap replications


   Call: bagging.data.frame(formula = churn ~ ., data = trainset,
   coob = T)


   Out-of-bag estimate of misclassification error:  0.0605
   ```

3. Obtain an out of bag estimate of misclassification of the errors:

   ```
   > mean(predict(churn.bagging) != trainset$churn)
   [1] 0.06047516
   ```

4. You can then use the `predict` function to obtain the predicted labels of the testing dataset:

   ```
   > churn.prediction = predict(churn.bagging, newdata=testset,
   type="class")
   ```

5. Obtain the classification table from the labels of the testing dataset and prediction result:

```
> prediction.table = table(churn.prediction, testset$churn)


churn.prediction yes   no
            no    31  869
           yes  110    8
```

Performing cross-validation with the bagging method

To assess the prediction power of a classifier, you can run a cross-validation method to test the robustness of the classification model. In this recipe, we will introduce how to use `bagging.cv` to perform cross-validation with the bagging method.

Getting ready

In this recipe, we continue to use the telecom `churn` dataset as the input data source to perform a k-fold cross-validation with the bagging method.

How to do it...

Perform the following steps to retrieve the minimum estimation errors by performing cross-validation with the bagging method:

1. First, we use `bagging.cv` to make a 10-fold classification on the training dataset with 10 iterations:

```
> churn.baggingcv = bagging.cv(churn ~ ., v=10, data=trainset,
mfinal=10)
```

2. You can then obtain the confusion matrix from the cross-validation results:

```
> churn.baggingcv$confusion
                Observed Class
Predicted Class  yes    no
            no   100  1938
           yes   242    35
```

3. Lastly, you can retrieve the minimum estimation errors from the cross-validation results:

```
> churn.baggingcv$error
[1] 0.05831533
```

How it works...

The `adabag` package provides a function to perform the k-fold validation with either the bagging or boosting method. In this example, we use `bagging.cv` to make the k-fold cross-validation with the bagging method. We first perform a 10-fold cross validation with 10 iterations by specifying `v=10` and `mfinal=10`. Please note that this is quite time consuming due to the number of iterations. After the cross-validation process is complete, we can obtain the confusion matrix and average errors (0.058 in this case) from the cross-validation results.

See also

▶ For those interested in tuning the parameters of `bagging.cv`, please view the `bagging.cv` document by using the `help` function:

```
> help(bagging.cv)
```

Classifying data with the boosting method

Similar to the bagging method, boosting starts with a simple or weak classifier and gradually improves it by reweighting the misclassified samples. Thus, the new classifier can learn from previous classifiers. The `adabag` package provides implementation of the **AdaBoost.M1** and **SAMME** algorithms. Therefore, one can use the boosting method in `adabag` to perform ensemble learning. In this recipe, we will use the boosting method in `adabag` to classify the telecom `churn` dataset.

Getting ready

In this recipe, we will continue to use the telecom churn dataset as the input data source to perform classifications with the boosting method. Also, you need to have the `adabag` package loaded in R before commencing the recipe.

How to do it...

Perform the following steps to classify the telecom `churn` dataset with the boosting method:

1. You can use the boosting function from the `adabag` package to train the classification model:

```
> set.seed(2)
> churn.boost = boosting(churn ~.,data=trainset,mfinal=10,
coeflearn="Freund", boos=FALSE , control=rpart.
control(maxdepth=3))
```

2. You can then make a prediction based on the boosted model and testing dataset:

```
> churn.boost.pred = predict.boosting(churn.boost,newdata=testset)
```

3. Next, you can retrieve the classification table from the predicted results:

```
> churn.boost.pred$confusion
                Observed Class
Predicted Class yes   no
            no    41  858
           yes   100   19
```

4. Finally, you can obtain the average errors from the predicted results:

```
> churn.boost.pred$error
[1] 0.0589391
```

How it works...

The idea of boosting is to "boost" weak learners (for example, a single decision tree) into strong learners. Assuming that we have n points in our training dataset, we can assign a weight, Wi ($0 <= i < n$), for each point. Then, during the iterative learning process (we assume the number of iterations is m), we can reweigh each point in accordance with the classification result in each iteration. If the point is correctly classified, we should decrease the weight. Otherwise, we increase the weight of the point. When the iteration process is finished, we can then obtain the m fitted model, $f_i(x)$ ($0 <= i < n$). Finally, we can obtain the final prediction through the weighted average of each tree's prediction, where the weight, β, is based on the quality of each tree:

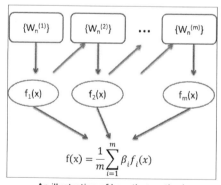

An illustration of boosting method

Both bagging and boosting are ensemble methods, which combine the prediction power of each single learner into a strong learner. The difference between bagging and boosting is that the bagging method combines independent models, but boosting performs an iterative process to reduce the errors of preceding models by predicting them with successive models.

In this recipe, we demonstrate how to fit a classification model within the boosting method. Similar to bagging, one has to specify the formula and the training dataset used to train the classification model. In addition, one can specify parameters, such as the number of iterations (mfinal), the weight update coefficient (coeflearn), the weight of how each observation is used (boos), and the control for rpart (a single decision tree). In this recipe, we set the iteration to 10, using Freund (the AdaBoost.M1 algorithm implemented method) as coeflearn, boos set to false and max depth set to 3 for rpart configuration.

We use the boosting method to fit the classification model and then save it in churn.boost. We can then obtain predicted labels using the prediction function. Furthermore, we can use the table function to retrieve a classification table based on the predicted labels and testing the dataset labels. Lastly, we can get the average errors of the predicted results.

There's more...

In addition to using the boosting function in the adabag package, one can also use the caret package to perform a classification with the boosting method:

1. First, load the mboost and pROC package:

```
> library(mboost)
> install.packages("pROC")
> library(pROC)
```

2. We can then set the training control with the trainControl function and use the train function to train the classification model with adaboost:

```
> set.seed(2)
> ctrl = trainControl(method = "repeatedcv", repeats = 1,
classProbs = TRUE, summaryFunction = twoClassSummary)
> ada.train = train(churn ~ ., data = trainset, method = "ada",
metric = "ROC", trControl = ctrl)
```

3. Use the summary function to obtain the details of the classification model:

```
> ada.train$result
```

	nu	maxdepth	iter	ROC	Sens	Spec	ROCSD	SensSD	SpecSD
1	0.1	1	50	0.8571988	0.9152941	0.012662155	0.03448418	0.04430519	0.007251045
4	0.1	2	50	0.8905514	0.7138655	0.006083679	0.03538445	0.10089887	0.006236741
7	0.1	3	50	0.9056456	0.4036134	0.007093780	0.03934631	0.09406015	0.006407402
2	0.1	1	100	0.8550789	0.8918487	0.015705276	0.03434382	0.06190546	0.006503191
5	0.1	2	100	0.8907720	0.6609244	0.009626724	0.03788941	0.11403364	0.006940001

```
8 0.1        3  100 0.9077750 0.3832773 0.005576065 0.03601187
0.09630026 0.003738978

3 0.1        1  150 0.8571743 0.8714286 0.016720505 0.03481526
0.06198773 0.006767313

6 0.1        2  150 0.8929524 0.6171429 0.011654617 0.03638272
0.11383803 0.006777465

9 0.1        3  150 0.9093921 0.3743697 0.007093780 0.03258220
0.09504202 0.005446136
```

4. Use the `plot` function to plot the ROC curve within different iterations:

```
> plot(ada.train)
```

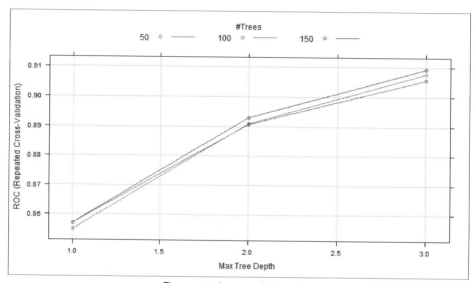

The repeated cross validation plot

5. Finally, we can make predictions using the `predict` function and view the classification table:

```
> ada.predict = predict(ada.train, testset, "prob")
> ada.predict.result = ifelse(ada.predict[1] > 0.5, "yes", "no")

> table(testset$churn, ada.predict.result)
    ada.predict.result
       no yes
  yes  40 101
  no  872   5
```

Performing cross-validation with the boosting method

Similar to the `bagging` function, `adabag` provides a cross-validation function for the boosting method, named `boosting.cv`. In this recipe, we will demonstrate how to perform cross-validation using `boosting.cv` from the package, `adabag`.

Getting ready

In this recipe, we continue to use the telecom `churn` dataset as the input data source to perform a k-fold cross-validation with the `boosting` method.

How to do it...

Perform the following steps to retrieve the minimum estimation errors via cross-validation with the `boosting` method:

1. First, you can use `boosting.cv` to cross-validate the training dataset:

   ```
   > churn.boostcv = boosting.cv(churn ~ ., v=10, data=trainset,
   mfinal=5,control=rpart.control(cp=0.01))
   ```

2. You can then obtain the confusion matrix from the boosting results:

   ```
   > churn.boostcv$confusion
                   Observed Class
   Predicted Class  yes    no
               no   119 1940
               yes  223    33
   ```

3. Finally, you can retrieve the average errors of the boosting method:

   ```
   > churn.boostcv$error
   [1] 0.06565875
   ```

How it works...

Similar to `bagging.cv`, we can perform cross-validation with the boosting method using `boosting.cv`. If `v` is set to `10` and `mfinal` is set to `5`, the `boosting` method will perform 10-fold cross-validations with five iterations. Also, one can set the control of the `rpart` fit within the parameter. We can set the complexity parameter to 0.01 in this example. Once the training is complete, the confusion matrix and average errors of the boosted results will be obtained.

See also

▸ For those who require more information on tuning the parameters of `boosting.cv`, please view the `boosting.cv` document by using the `help` function:

```
> help(boosting.cv)
```

Classifying data with gradient boosting

Gradient boosting ensembles weak learners and creates a new base learner that maximally correlates with the negative gradient of the loss function. One may apply this method on either regression or classification problems, and it will perform well in different datasets. In this recipe, we will introduce how to use `gbm` to classify a telecom `churn` dataset.

Getting ready

In this recipe, we continue to use the telecom `churn` dataset as the input data source for the `bagging` method. For those who have not prepared the dataset, please refer to *Chapter 5, Classification (I) – Tree, Lazy, and Probabilistic*, for detailed information.

How to do it...

Perform the following steps to calculate and classify data with the gradient boosting method:

1. First, install and load the package, `gbm`:

```
> install.packages("gbm")
> library(gbm)
```

2. The `gbm` function only uses responses ranging from 0 to 1; therefore, you should transform yes/no responses to numeric responses (0/1):

```
> trainset$churn = ifelse(trainset$churn == "yes", 1, 0)
```

3. Next, you can use the `gbm` function to train a training dataset:

```
> set.seed(2)
> churn.gbm = gbm(formula = churn ~ .,distribution =
"bernoulli",data = trainset,n.trees = 1000,interaction.depth =
7,shrinkage = 0.01, cv.folds=3)
```

4. Then, you can obtain the summary information from the fitted model:

```
> summary(churn.gbm)
```

	var	rel.inf
total_day_minutes	total_day_minutes	28.1217147
total_eve_minutes	total_eve_minutes	16.8097151
number_customer_service_calls	number_customer_service_calls	12.7894464
total_intl_minutes	total_intl_minutes	9.4515822
total_intl_calls	total_intl_calls	8.1379826
international_plan	international_plan	8.0703900
total_night_minutes	total_night_minutes	4.0805153
number_vmail_messages	number_vmail_messages	3.9173515
voice_mail_plan	voice_mail_plan	2.5501480
total_night_calls	total_night_calls	2.1357970
total_day_calls	total_day_calls	1.7367888
total_eve_calls	total_eve_calls	1.4398047
total_eve_charge	total_eve_charge	0.5457486
total_night_charge	total_night_charge	0.2130152
total_day_charge	total_day_charge	0.0000000
total_intl_charge	total_intl_charge	0.0000000

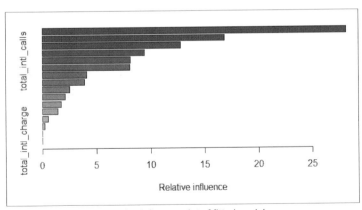

Relative influence plot of fitted model

5. You can obtain the best iteration using cross-validation:

```
> churn.iter = gbm.perf(churn.gbm,method="cv")
```

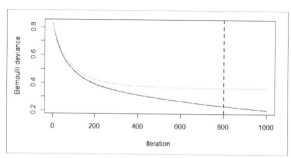

The performance measurement plot

6. Then, you can retrieve the odd value of the log returned from the Bernoulli loss function:

```
> churn.predict = predict(churn.gbm, testset, n.trees = churn.
iter)
```

```
> str(churn.predict)
```

```
 num [1:1018] -3.31 -2.91 -3.16 -3.47 -3.48 ...
```

7. Next, you can plot the ROC curve and get the best cut off that will have the maximum accuracy:

```
> churn.roc = roc(testset$churn, churn.predict)
```

```
> plot(churn.roc)
```

```
Call:
```

```
roc.default(response = testset$churn, predictor = churn.predict)
```

```
Data: churn.predict in 141 controls (testset$churn yes) > 877
cases (testset$churn no).
```

```
Area under the curve: 0.9393
```

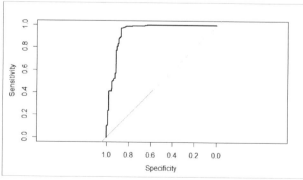

The ROC curve of fitted model

8. You can retrieve the best cut off with the `coords` function and use this cut off to obtain the predicted label:

```
> coords(churn.roc, "best")
  threshold specificity sensitivity
 -0.9495258   0.8723404   0.9703535
> churn.predict.class = ifelse(churn.predict > coords(churn.roc,
"best")["threshold"], "yes", "no")
```

9. Lastly, you can obtain the classification table from the predicted results:

```
> table( testset$churn,churn.predict.class)
       churn.predict.class
        no yes
   yes  18 123
   no  851  26
```

How it works...

The algorithm of gradient boosting involves, first, the process computes the deviation of residuals for each partition, and then, determines the best data partitioning in each stage. Next, the successive model will fit the residuals from the previous stage and build a new model to reduce the residual variance (an error). The reduction of the residual variance follows the functional gradient descent technique, in which it minimizes the residual variance by going down its derivative, as show here:

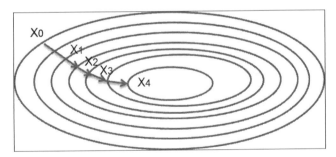

Gradient descent method

In this recipe, we use the gradient boosting method from `gbm` to classify the telecom churn dataset. To begin the classification, we first install and load the `gbm` package. Then, we use the `gbm` function to train the classification model. Here, as our prediction target is the `churn` attribute, which is a binary outcome, we therefore set the distribution as `bernoulli` in the `distribution` argument. Also, we set the 1000 trees to fit in the `n.tree` argument, the maximum depth of the variable interaction to 7 in `interaction.depth`, the learning rate of the step size reduction to 0.01 in `shrinkage`, and the number of cross-validations to 3 in `cv.folds`. After the model is fitted, we can use the summary function to obtain the relative influence information of each variable in the table and figure. The relative influence shows the reduction attributable to each variable in the sum of the square error. Here, we can find `total_day_minutes` is the most influential one in reducing the loss function.

Next, we use the `gbm.perf` function to find the optimum iteration. Here, we estimate the optimum number with cross-validation by specifying the `method` argument to `cv`. The function further generates two plots, where the black line plots the training error and the green one plots the validation error. The error measurement here is a `bernoulli` distribution, which we have defined earlier in the training stage. The blue dash line on the plot shows where the optimum iteration is.

Then, we use the `predict` function to obtain the odd value of a log in each testing case returned from the Bernoulli loss function. In order to get the best prediction result, one can set the `n.trees` argument to an optimum iteration number. However, as the returned value is an odd value log, we still have to determine the best cut off to determine the label. Therefore, we use the `roc` function to generate an ROC curve and get the cut off with the maximum accuracy.

Finally, we can use the function, `coords`, to retrieve the best cut off threshold and use the `ifelse` function to determine the class label from the odd value of the log. Now, we can use the `table` function to generate the classification table and see how accurate the classification model is.

There's more...

In addition to using the boosting function in the `gbm` package, one can also use the `mboost` package to perform classifications with the gradient boosting method:

1. First, install and load the `mboost` package:

   ```
   > install.packages("mboost")
   > library(mboost)
   ```

2. The `mboost` function only uses numeric responses; therefore, you should transform yes/no responses to numeric responses (0/1):

   ```
   > trainset$churn = ifelse(trainset$churn == "yes", 1, 0)
   ```

3. Also, you should remove nonnumerical attributes, such as `voice_mail_plan` and `international_plan`:

    ```
    > trainset$voice_mail_plan = NULL
    > trainset$international_plan = NULL
    ```

4. We can then use `mboost` to train the classification model:

    ```
    > churn.mboost = mboost(churn ~ ., data=trainset, control = boost_control(mstop = 10))
    ```

5. Use the `summary` function to obtain the details of the classification model:

    ```
    > summary(churn.mboost)


        Model-based Boosting


    Call:
    mboost(formula = churn ~ ., data = trainset, control = boost_control(mstop = 10))



        Squared Error (Regression)


    Loss function: (y - f)^2



    Number of boosting iterations: mstop = 10
    Step size:  0.1
    Offset:  1.147732
    Number of baselearners:  14


    Selection frequencies:
            bbs(total_day_minutes) bbs(number_customer_service_
    calls)
                0.6                             0.4
    ```

6. Lastly, use the `plot` function to draw a partial contribution plot of each attribute:

```
> par(mfrow=c(1,2))

> plot(churn.mboost)
```

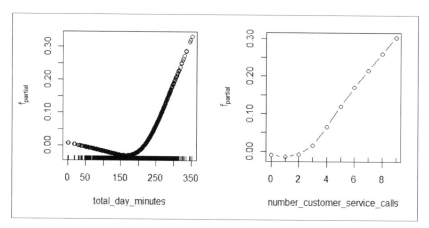

The partial contribution plot of important attributes

Calculating the margins of a classifier

A margin is a measure of the certainty of classification. This method calculates the difference between the support of a correct class and the maximum support of an incorrect class. In this recipe, we will demonstrate how to calculate the margins of the generated classifiers.

Getting ready

You need to have completed the previous recipe by storing a fitted bagging model in the variables, `churn.bagging` and `churn.predbagging`. Also, put the fitted boosting classifier in both `churn.boost` and `churn.boost.pred`.

How to do it...

Perform the following steps to calculate the margin of each ensemble learner:

1. First, use the `margins` function to calculate the margins of the boosting classifiers:

```
> boost.margins = margins(churn.boost, trainset)

> boost.pred.margins = margins(churn.boost.pred, testset)
```

2. You can then use the `plot` function to plot a marginal cumulative distribution graph of the boosting classifiers:

```
> plot(sort(boost.margins[[1]]), (1:length(boost.margins[[1]]))/
length(boost.margins[[1]]), type="l",xlim=c(-1,1),main="Boosting:
Margin cumulative distribution graph", xlab="margin", ylab="%
observations", col = "blue")
```

```
> lines(sort(boost.pred.margins[[1]]), (1:length(boost.pred.
margins[[1]]))/length(boost.pred.margins[[1]]), type="l", col =
"green")
```

```
> abline(v=0, col="red",lty=2)
```

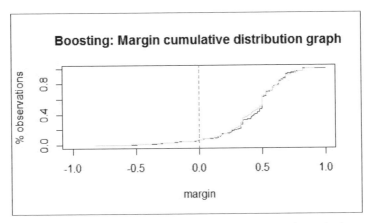

The margin cumulative distribution graph of using the boosting method

3. You can then calculate the percentage of negative margin matches training errors and the percentage of negative margin matches test errors:

```
> boosting.training.margin = table(boost.margins[[1]] > 0)
```

```
> boosting.negative.training = as.numeric(boosting.training.
margin[1]/boosting.training.margin[2])
```

```
> boosting.negative.training
```

```
[1] 0.06387868
```

```
> boosting.testing.margin = table(boost.pred.margins[[1]] > 0)
```

```
> boosting.negative.testing = as.numeric(boosting.testing.
margin[1]/boosting.testing.margin[2])
```

```
> boosting.negative.testing
```

```
[1] 0.06263048
```

4. Also, you can calculate the margins of the bagging classifiers. You might see the warning message showing "no non-missing argument to min". The message simply indicates that the min/max function is applied to the numeric of the 0 length argument:

```
> bagging.margins = margins(churn.bagging, trainset)

> bagging.pred.margins = margins(churn.predbagging, testset)
```

5. You can then use the `plot` function to plot a margin cumulative distribution graph of the bagging classifiers:

```
> plot(sort(bagging.margins[[1]]), (1:length(bagging.
margins[[1]]))/length(bagging.margins[[1]]), type="l",xlim=c(-
1,1),main="Bagging: Margin cumulative distribution graph",
xlab="margin", ylab="% observations", col = "blue")

> lines(sort(bagging.pred.margins[[1]]), (1:length(bagging.pred.
margins[[1]]))/length(bagging.pred.margins[[1]]), type="l", col =
"green")

> abline(v=0, col="red",lty=2)
```

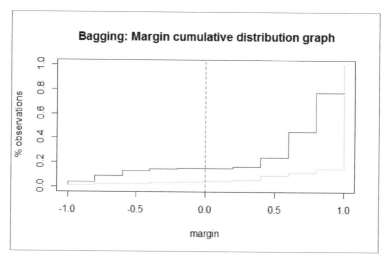

The margin cumulative distribution graph of the bagging method

6. Finally, you can then compute the percentage of negative margin matches training errors and the percentage of negative margin matches test errors:

```
> bagging.training.margin = table(bagging.margins[[1]] > 0)

> bagging.negative.training = as.numeric(bagging.training.
margin[1]/bagging.training.margin[2])

> bagging.negative.training

[1] 0.1733401
```

```
> bagging.testing.margin = table(bagging.pred.margins[[1]] > 0)

> bagging.negative.testing = as.numeric(bagging.testing.margin[1]/
bagging.testing.margin[2])

> bagging.negative.testing

[1] 0.04303279
```

How it works...

A margin is the measurement of certainty of the classification; it is computed by the support of the correct class and the maximum support of the incorrect class. The formula of margins can be formulated as:

$$\text{margin}(x_i) = support_c(x_i) - \max_{j \neq c} support_j(x_i)$$

Here, the margin of the xi sample equals the support of a correctly classified sample (c denotes the correct class) minus the maximum support of a sample that is classified to class j (where j≠c and j=1...k). Therefore, correctly classified examples will have positive margins and misclassified examples will have negative margins. If the margin value is close to one, it means that correctly classified examples have a high degree of confidence. On the other hand, examples of uncertain classifications will have small margins.

The `margins` function calculates the margins of AdaBoost.M1, AdaBoost-SAMME, or the bagging classifier, which returns a vector of a margin. To visualize the margin distribution, one can use a margin cumulative distribution graph. In these graphs, the x-axis shows the margin and the y-axis shows the percentage of observations where the margin is less than or equal to the margin value of the x-axis. If every observation is correctly classified, the graph will show a vertical line at the margin equal to 1 (where margin = 1).

For the margin cumulative distribution graph of the boosting classifiers, we can see that there are two lines plotted on the graph, in which the green line denotes the margin of the testing dataset, and the blue line denotes the margin of the training set. The figure shows about 6.39 percent of negative margins match the training error, and 6.26 percent of negative margins match the test error. On the other hand, we can find that 17.33% of negative margins match the training error and 4.3 percent of negative margins match the test error in the margin cumulative distribution graph of the bagging classifiers. Normally, the percentage of negative margins matching the training error should be close to the percentage of negative margins that match the test error. As a result of this, we should then examine the reason why the percentage of negative margins that match the training error is much higher than the negative margins that match the test error.

▸ If you are interested in more details on margin distribution graphs, please refer to the following source: *Kuncheva LI (2004), Combining Pattern Classifiers: Methods and Algorithms, John Wiley & Sons.*

Calculating the error evolution of the ensemble method

The `adabag` package provides the `errorevol` function for a user to estimate the ensemble method errors in accordance with the number of iterations. In this recipe, we will demonstrate how to use `errorevol` to show the evolution of errors of each ensemble classifier.

Getting ready

You need to have completed the previous recipe by storing the fitted bagging model in the variable, `churn.bagging`. Also, put the fitted boosting classifier in `churn.boost`.

How to do it...

Perform the following steps to calculate the error evolution of each ensemble learner:

1. First, use the `errorevol` function to calculate the error evolution of the boosting classifiers:

```
> boosting.evol.train = errorevol(churn.boost, trainset)
> boosting.evol.test = errorevol(churn.boost, testset)
> plot(boosting.evol.test$error, type = "l", ylim = c(0, 1),
+       main = "Boosting error versus number of trees", xlab =
"Iterations",
+       ylab = "Error", col = "red", lwd = 2)
> lines(boosting.evol.train$error, cex = .5, col = "blue", lty =
2, lwd = 2)
> legend("topright", c("test", "train"), col = c("red", "blue"),
lty = 1:2, lwd = 2)
```

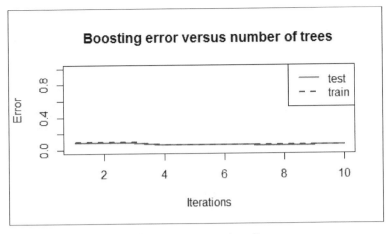

Boosting error versus number of trees

2. Next, use the `errorevol` function to calculate the error evolution of the bagging classifiers:

```
> bagging.evol.train = errorevol(churn.bagging, trainset)
> bagging.evol.test = errorevol(churn.bagging, testset)
> plot(bagging.evol.test$error, type = "l", ylim = c(0, 1),
+       main = "Bagging error versus number of trees", xlab =
"Iterations",
+       ylab = "Error", col = "red", lwd = 2)
> lines(bagging.evol.train$error, cex = .5, col = "blue", lty = 2,
lwd = 2)
> legend("topright", c("test", "train"), col = c("red", "blue"),
lty = 1:2, lwd = 2)
```

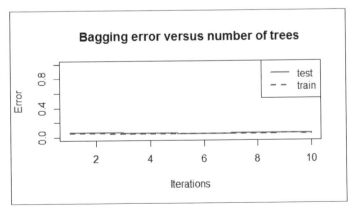

Bagging error versus number of trees

How it works...

The `errorest` function calculates the error evolution of AdaBoost.M1, AdaBoost-SAMME, or the bagging classifiers and returns a vector of error evolutions. In this recipe, we use the boosting and bagging models to generate error evolution vectors and graph the error versus number of trees.

The resulting graph reveals the error rate of each iteration. The trend of the error rate can help measure how fast the errors reduce, while the number of iterations increases. In addition to this, the graphs may show whether the model is over-fitted.

See also

  ▶   If the ensemble model is over-fitted, you can use the `predict.bagging` and `predict.boosting` functions to prune the ensemble model. For more information, please use the help function to refer to `predict.bagging` and `predict.boosting`:

```
> help(predict.bagging)
```

```
> help(predict.boosting)
```

Classifying data with random forest

Random forest is another useful ensemble learning method that grows multiple decision trees during the training process. Each decision tree will output its own prediction results corresponding to the input. The forest will use the voting mechanism to select the most voted class as the prediction result. In this recipe, we will illustrate how to classify data using the `randomForest` package.

Getting ready

In this recipe, we will continue to use the telecom `churn` dataset as the input data source to perform classifications with the random forest method.

How to do it...

Perform the following steps to classify data with random forest:

  1.   First, you have to install and load the `randomForest` package;

```
> install.packages("randomForest")
```

```
> library(randomForest)
```

2. You can then fit the random forest classifier with a training set:

```
> churn.rf = randomForest(churn ~ ., data = trainset, importance =
T)
> churn.rf
```

```
Call:
 randomForest(formula = churn ~ ., data = trainset, importance =
T)
               Type of random forest: classification
                     Number of trees: 500
No. of variables tried at each split: 4

        OOB estimate of  error rate: 4.88%
Confusion matrix:
     yes    no class.error
yes 247    95 0.277777778
no   18 1955 0.009123163
```

3. Next, make predictions based on the fitted model and testing dataset:

```
> churn.prediction = predict(churn.rf, testset)
```

4. Similar to other classification methods, you can obtain the classification table:

```
> table(churn.prediction, testset$churn)
```

```
churn.prediction yes   no
            yes 110    7
            no   31 870
```

5. You can use the `plot` function to plot the mean square error of the forest object:

```
> plot(churn.rf)
```

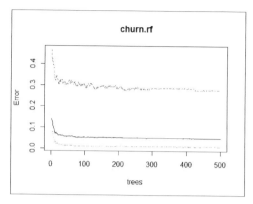

The mean square error of the random forest

6. You can then examine the importance of each attribute within the fitted classifier:

```
> importance(churn.rf)
```

	yes	no
international_plan	66.55206691	56.5100647
voice_mail_plan	19.98337191	15.2354970
number_vmail_messages	21.02976166	14.0707195
total_day_minutes	28.05190188	27.7570444

7. Next, you can use the `varImpPlot` function to obtain the plot of variable importance:

```
> varImpPlot(churn.rf)
```

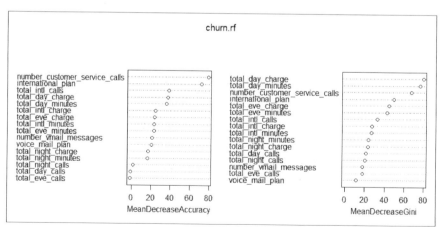

The visualization of variable importance

8. You can also use the `margin` function to calculate the margins and plot the margin cumulative distribution:

```
> margins.rf=margin(churn.rf,trainset)
```

```
> plot(margins.rf)
```

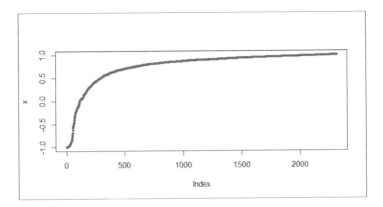

The margin cumulative distribution graph for the random forest method

9. Furthermore, you can use a histogram to visualize the margin distribution of the random forest:

```
> hist(margins.rf,main="Margins of Random Forest for churn
dataset")
```

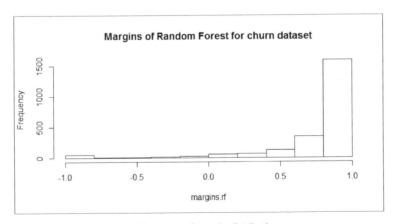

The histogram of margin distribution

10. You can also use `boxplot` to visualize the margins of the random forest by class:

```
> boxplot(margins.rf~trainset$churn, main="Margins of Random
Forest for churn dataset by class")
```

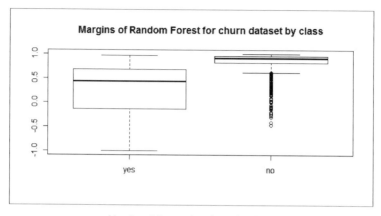

Margins of the random forest by class

How it works...

The purpose of random forest is to ensemble weak learners (for example, a single decision tree) into a strong learner. The process of developing a random forest is very similar to the bagging method, assuming that we have a training set containing *N* samples with *M* features. The process first performs bootstrap sampling, which samples *N* cases at random, with the replacement as the training dataset of each single decision tree. Next, in each node, the process first randomly selects *m* variables (where $m << M$), then finds the predictor variable that provides the best split among m variables. Next, the process grows the full tree without pruning. In the end, we can obtain the predicted result of an example from each single tree. As a result, we can get the prediction result by taking an average or weighted average (for regression) of an output or taking a majority vote (for classification):

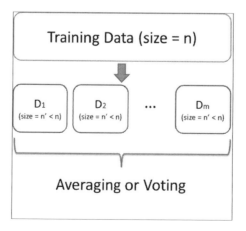

A random forest uses two parameters: **ntree** (the number of trees) and **mtry** (the number of features used to find the best feature), while the bagging method only uses ntree as a parameter. Therefore, if we set mtry equal to the number of features within a training dataset, then the random forest is equal to the bagging method.

The main advantages of random forest are that it is easy to compute, it can efficiently process data, and is fault tolerant to missing or unbalanced data. The main disadvantage of random forest is that it cannot predict the value beyond the range of a training dataset. Also, it is prone to over-fitting of noisy data.

In this recipe, we employ the random forest method adapted from the `randomForest` package to fit a classification model. First, we install and load `randomForest` into an R session. We then use the random forest method to train a classification model. We set `importance = T`, which will ensure that the importance of the predictor is assessed.

Similar to the bagging and boosting methods, once the model is fitted, one can perform predictions using a fitted model on the testing dataset, and furthermore, obtain the classification table.

In order to assess the importance of each attribute, the `randomForest` package provides the importance and `varImpPlot` functions to either list the importance of each attribute in the fitted model or visualize the importance using either mean decrease accuracy or mean decrease `gini`.

Similar to `adabag`, which contains a method to calculate the margins of the bagging and boosting methods, `randomForest` provides the `margin` function to calculate the margins of the forest object. With the `plot`, `hist`, and `boxplot` functions, you can visualize the margins in different aspects to the proportion of correctly classified observations.

There's more...

Apart from the `randomForest` package, the `party` package also provides an implementation of random forest. In the following steps, we illustrate how to use the `cforest` function within the `party` package to perform classifications:

1. First, install and load the `party` package:

```
> install.packages("party")
> library(party)
```

2. You can then use the `cforest` function to fit the classification model:

```
> churn.cforest = cforest(churn ~ ., data = trainset,
controls=cforest_unbiased(ntree=1000, mtry=5))
> churn.cforest
```

Random Forest using Conditional Inference Trees

Number of trees: 1000

Response: churn
Inputs: international_plan, voice_mail_plan, number_vmail_
messages, total_day_minutes, total_day_calls, total_day_charge,
total_eve_minutes, total_eve_calls, total_eve_charge, total_
night_minutes, total_night_calls, total_night_charge, total_intl_
minutes, total_intl_calls, total_intl_charge, number_customer_
service_calls

Number of observations: 2315

3. You can make predictions based on the built model and the testing dataset:

```
> churn.cforest.prediction = predict(churn.cforest, testset,
OOB=TRUE, type = "response")
```

4. Finally, obtain the classification table from the predicted labels and the labels of the testing dataset:

```
> table(churn.cforest.prediction, testset$churn)
```

```
churn.cforest.prediction yes   no
                     yes  91    3
                     no   50  874
```

Estimating the prediction errors of different classifiers

At the beginning of this chapter, we discussed why we use ensemble learning and how it can improve the prediction performance compared to using just a single classifier. We now validate whether the ensemble model performs better than a single decision tree by comparing the performance of each method. In order to compare the different classifiers, we can perform a 10-fold cross-validation on each classification method to estimate test errors using `errorest` from the `ipred` package.

Getting ready

In this recipe, we will continue to use the telecom `churn` dataset as the input data source to estimate the prediction errors of the different classifiers.

How to do it...

Perform the following steps to estimate the prediction errors of each classification method:

1. You can estimate the error rate of the bagging model:

   ```
   > churn.bagging= errorest(churn ~ ., data = trainset, model =
   bagging)
   > churn.bagging
   ```

   ```
   Call:
   errorest.data.frame(formula = churn ~ ., data = trainset, model =
   bagging)

           10-fold cross-validation estimator of misclassification error

   Misclassification error:   0.0583
   ```

2. You can then estimate the error rate of the boosting method:

   ```
   > install.packages("ada")
   > library(ada)
   > churn.boosting= errorest(churn ~ ., data = trainset, model =
   ada)
   > churn.boosting
   ```

   ```
   Call:
   errorest.data.frame(formula = churn ~ ., data = trainset, model =
   ada)

           10-fold cross-validation estimator of misclassification error

   Misclassification error:   0.0475
   ```

3. Next, estimate the error rate of the random forest model:

   ```
   > churn.rf= errorest(churn ~ ., data = trainset, model =
   randomForest)
   > churn.rf
   ```

   ```
   Call:
   ```

```
errorest.data.frame(formula = churn ~ ., data = trainset, model =
randomForest)
```

```
    10-fold cross-validation estimator of misclassification error
```

```
Misclassification error:   0.051
```

4. Finally, make a prediction function using `churn.predict`, and then use the function to estimate the error rate of the single decision tree:

```
> churn.predict = function(object, newdata) {predict(object,
newdata = newdata, type = "class")}
```

```
> churn.tree= errorest(churn ~ ., data = trainset, model =
rpart,predict = churn.predict)
```

```
> churn.tree
```

```
Call:
errorest.data.frame(formula = churn ~ ., data = trainset, model =
rpart,

    predict = churn.predict)
```

```
    10-fold cross-validation estimator of misclassification error
```

```
Misclassification error:   0.0674
```

How it works...

In this recipe, we estimate the error rates of four different classifiers using the `errorest` function from the `ipred` package. We compare the boosting, bagging, and random forest methods, and the single decision tree classifier. The `errorest` function performs a 10-fold cross-validation on each classifier and calculates the misclassification error. The estimation results from the four chosen models reveal that the boosting method performs the best with the lowest error rate (0.0475). The random forest method has the second lowest error rate (0.051), while the bagging method has an error rate of 0.0583. The single decision tree classifier, `rpart`, performs the worst among the four methods with an error rate equal to 0.0674. These results show that all three ensemble learning methods, boosting, bagging, and random forest, outperform a single decision tree classifier.

See also

▶ In this recipe we mentioned the `ada` package, which contains a method to perform stochastic boosting. For those interested in this package, please refer to: *Additive Logistic Regression: A Statistical View of Boosting by Friedman, et al. (2000)*.

9
Clustering

In this chapter, we will cover the following topics:

- ▶ Clustering data with hierarchical clustering
- ▶ Cutting a tree into clusters
- ▶ Clustering data with the k-means method
- ▶ Drawing a bivariate cluster plot
- ▶ Comparing clustering methods
- ▶ Extracting silhouette information from clustering
- ▶ Obtaining optimum clusters for k-means
- ▶ Clustering data with the density-based method
- ▶ Clustering data with the model-based method
- ▶ Visualizing a dissimilarity matrix
- ▶ Validating clusters externally

Introduction

Clustering is a technique used to group similar objects (close in terms of distance) together in the same group (cluster). Unlike supervised learning methods (for example, classification and regression) covered in the previous chapters, a clustering analysis does not use any label information, but simply uses the similarity between data features to group them into clusters.

Clustering can be widely adapted in the analysis of businesses. For example, a marketing department can use clustering to segment customers by personal attributes. As a result of this, different marketing campaigns targeting various types of customers can be designed.

The four most common types of clustering methods are hierarchical clustering, k-means clustering, model-based clustering, and density-based clustering:

▶ **Hierarchical clustering**: It creates a hierarchy of clusters, and presents the hierarchy in a dendrogram. This method does not require the number of clusters to be specified at the beginning.

▶ **k-means clustering**: It is also referred to as flat clustering. Unlike hierarchical clustering, it does not create a hierarchy of clusters, and it requires the number of clusters as an input. However, its performance is faster than hierarchical clustering.

▶ **Model-based clustering**: Both hierarchical clustering and k-means clustering use a heuristic approach to construct clusters, and do not rely on a formal model. Model-based clustering assumes a data model and applies an EM algorithm to find the most likely model components and the number of clusters.

▶ **Density-based clustering**: It constructs clusters in regard to the density measurement. Clusters in this method have a higher density than the remainder of the dataset.

In the following recipes, we will discuss how to use these four clustering techniques to cluster data. We discuss how to validate clusters internally, using within clusters the sum of squares, average silhouette width, and externally, with ground truth.

Clustering data with hierarchical clustering

Hierarchical clustering adopts either an agglomerative or divisive method to build a hierarchy of clusters. Regardless of which approach is adopted, both first use a distance similarity measure to combine or split clusters. The recursive process continues until there is only one cluster left or you cannot split more clusters. Eventually, we can use a dendrogram to represent the hierarchy of clusters. In this recipe, we will demonstrate how to cluster customers with hierarchical clustering.

Getting ready

In this recipe, we will perform hierarchical clustering on customer data, which involves segmenting customers into different groups. You can download the data from this Github page: https://github.com/ywchiu/ml_R_cookbook/tree/master/CH9.

How to do it...

Perform the following steps to cluster customer data into a hierarchy of clusters:

1. First, you need to load data from `customer.csv` and save it into `customer`:

```
> customer= read.csv('customer.csv', header=TRUE)
> head(customer)
```

```
    ID Visit.Time Average.Expense Sex Age
1   1          3             5.7   0  10
2   2          5            14.5   0  27
3   3         16            33.5   0  32
4   4          5            15.9   0  30
5   5         16            24.9   0  23
6   6          3            12.0   0  15
```

2. You can then examine the dataset structure:

    ```
    > str(customer)
    'data.frame':  60 obs. of  5 variables:
     $ ID              : int  1 2 3 4 5 6 7 8 9 10 ...
     $ Visit.Time      : int  3 5 16 5 16 3 12 14 6 3 ...
     $ Average.Expense: num  5.7 14.5 33.5 15.9 24.9 12 28.5 18.8 23.8
    5.3 ...
     $ Sex             : int  0 0 0 0 0 0 0 0 0 0 ...
     $ Age             : int  10 27 32 30 23 15 33 27 16 11 ...
    ```

3. Next, you should normalize the customer data into the same scale:

    ```
    > customer = scale(customer[,-1])
    ```

4. You can then use agglomerative hierarchical clustering to cluster the customer data:

    ```
    > hc = hclust(dist(customer, method="euclidean"), method="ward.
    D2")
    > hc


    Call:
    hclust(d = dist(customer, method = "euclidean"), method = "ward.
    D2")


    Cluster method   : ward.D2
    Distance         : euclidean
    Number of objects: 60
    ```

5. Lastly, you can use the `plot` function to plot the dendrogram:

```
> plot(hc, hang = -0.01, cex = 0.7)
```

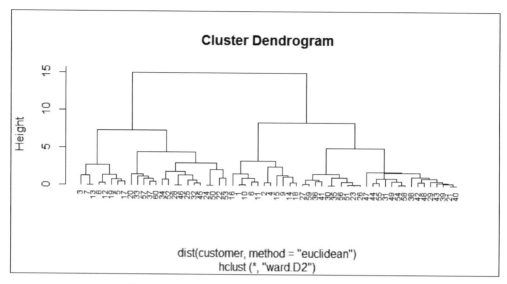

The dendrogram of hierarchical clustering using "ward.D2"

6. Additionally, you can use the single method to perform hierarchical clustering and see how the generated dendrogram differs from the previous:

```
> hc2 = hclust(dist(customer), method="single")
> plot(hc2, hang = -0.01, cex = 0.7)
```

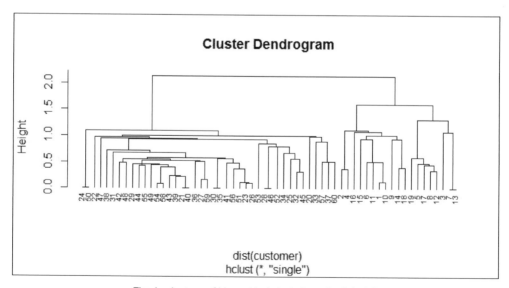

The dendrogram of hierarchical clustering using "single"

How it works...

Hierarchical clustering is a clustering technique that tries to build a hierarchy of clusters iteratively. Generally, there are two approaches to build hierarchical clusters:

- **Agglomerative hierarchical clustering**: This is a bottom-up approach. Each observation starts in its own cluster. We can then compute the similarity (or the distance) between each cluster and then merge the two most similar ones at each iteration until there is only one cluster left.

- **Divisive hierarchical clustering**: This is a top-down approach. All observations start in one cluster, and then we split the cluster into the two least dissimilar clusters recursively until there is one cluster for each observation:

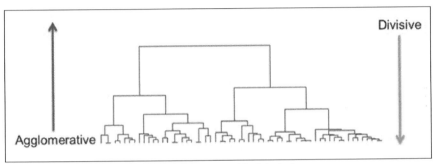

An illustration of hierarchical clustering

Before performing hierarchical clustering, we need to determine how similar the two clusters are. Here, we list some common distance functions used for the measurement of similarity:

- **Single linkage**: This refers to the shortest distance between two points in each cluster:

$$\text{dist}\left(C_i, C_j\right) = \min_{a \in C_i, b \in C_j} \; dist\left(a, b\right)$$

- **Complete linkage**: This refers to the longest distance between two points in each cluster:

$$\text{dist}\left(C_i, C_j\right) = \max_{a \in C_i, b \in C_j} \; dist\left(a, b\right)$$

▶ **Average linkage**: This refer to the average distance between two points in each cluster (where $|C_i|$ is the size of cluster C_i and $|C_j|$ is the size of cluster C_j):

$$\text{dist}\left(C_i, C_j\right) = \frac{1}{|C_i||C_j|} \sum_{a \in C_i, b \in C_j} \text{dist}\left(a, b\right)$$

▶ **Ward method**: This refers to the sum of the squared distance from each point to the mean of the merged clusters (where μ is the mean vector of $C_i \cup C_j$):

$$\text{dist}\left(C_i, C_j\right) = \sum_{a \in C_i \cup C_j} \|a - \mu\|$$

In this recipe, we perform hierarchical clustering on customer data. First, we load the data from `customer.csv`, and then load it into the customer data frame. Within the data, we find five variables of customer account information, which are ID, number of visits, average expense, sex, and age. As the scale of each variable varies, we use the scale function to normalize the scale.

After the scales of all the attributes are normalized, we perform hierarchical clustering using the `hclust` function. We use the Euclidean distance as distance metrics, and use Ward's minimum variance method to perform agglomerative clustering.

Finally, we use the `plot` function to plot the dendrogram of hierarchical clusters. We specify `hang` to display labels at the bottom of the dendrogram, and use `cex` to shrink the label to 70 percent of the normal size. In order to compare the differences using the `ward.D2` and `single` methods to generate a hierarchy of clusters, we draw another dendrogram using `single` in the preceding figure (step 6).

There's more...

You can choose a different distance measure and method while performing hierarchical clustering. For more details, you can refer to the documents for `dist` and `hclust`:

```
> ? dist
> ? hclust
```

In this recipe, we use `hclust` to perform agglomerative hierarchical clustering; if you would like to perform divisive hierarchical clustering, you can use the `diana` function:

1. First, you can use `diana` to perform divisive hierarchical clustering:

```
> dv = diana(customer, metric = "euclidean")
```

2. Then, you can use `summary` to obtain the summary information:

    ```
    > summary(dv)
    ```

3. Lastly, you can plot a dendrogram and banner with the `plot` function:

    ```
    > plot(dv)
    ```

If you are interested in drawing a horizontal dendrogram, you can use the `dendextend` package. Use the following procedure to generate a horizontal dendrogram:

1. First, install and load the `dendextend` and `magrittr` packages (if your R version is 3.1 and above, you do not have to install and load the `magrittr` package):

    ```
    > install.packages("dendextend")
    > library(dendextend)
    > install.packages("margrittr")
    > library(magrittr)
    ```

2. Set up the dendrogram:

    ```
    > dend = customer %>% dist %>% hclust %>% as.dendrogram
    ```

3. Finally, plot the horizontal dendrogram:

    ```
    dend %>% plot(horiz=TRUE, main = "Horizontal Dendrogram")
    ```

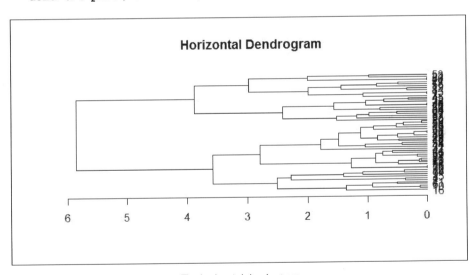

The horizontal dendrogram

Cutting trees into clusters

In a dendrogram, we can see the hierarchy of clusters, but we have not grouped data into different clusters yet. However, we can determine how many clusters are within the dendrogram and cut the dendrogram at a certain tree height to separate the data into different groups. In this recipe, we demonstrate how to use the `cutree` function to separate the data into a given number of clusters.

Getting ready

In order to perform the `cutree` function, you need to have the previous recipe completed by generating the hclust object, `hc`.

How to do it...

Perform the following steps to cut the hierarchy of clusters into a given number of clusters:

1. First, categorize the data into four groups:

   ```
   > fit = cutree(hc, k = 4)
   ```

2. You can then examine the cluster labels for the data:

   ```
   > fit
    [1] 1 1 2 1 2 1 2 2 1 1 1 2 2 1 1 1 2 1 2 3 4 3 4 3 3 4 4 3 4
   [30] 4 4 3 3 3 4 4 3 4 4 4 4 4 4 4 3 3 4 4 4 3 4 3 3 4 4 4 3 4
   [59] 4 3
   ```

3. Count the number of data within each cluster:

   ```
   > table(fit)
   fit
    1  2  3  4
   11  8 16 25
   ```

4. Finally, you can visualize how data is clustered with the red rectangle border:

   ```
   > plot(hc)
   > rect.hclust(hc, k = 4 , border="red")
   ```

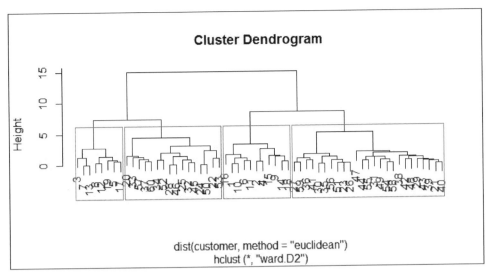

Cluster Dendrogram

dist(customer, method = "euclidean")
hclust (*, "ward.D2")

Using the red rectangle border to distinguish different clusters within the dendrogram

How it works...

We can determine the number of clusters from the dendrogram in the preceding figure. In this recipe, we determine there should be four clusters within the tree. Therefore, we specify the number of clusters as 4 in the `cutree` function. Besides using the number of clusters to cut the tree, you can specify the `height` as the cut tree parameter.

Next, we can output the cluster labels of the data and use the `table` function to count the number of data within each cluster. From the counting table, we find that most of the data is in cluster 4. Lastly, we can draw red rectangles around the clusters to show how data is categorized into the four clusters with the `rect.hclust` function.

There's more...

Besides drawing rectangles around all hierarchical clusters, you can place a red rectangle around a certain cluster:

```
> rect.hclust(hc, k = 4 , which =2, border="red")
```

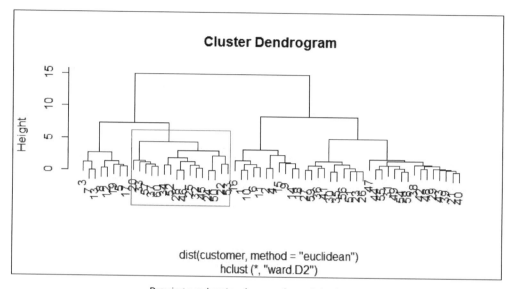

Drawing a red rectangle around a certain cluster.

Also, you can color clusters in different colors with a red rectangle around the clusters by using the dendextend package. You have to complete the instructions outlined in the *There's more* section of the previous recipe and perform the following steps:

1. Color the branch according to the cluster it belongs to:

   ```
   > dend %>% color_branches(k=4) %>% plot(horiz=TRUE, main =
   "Horizontal Dendrogram")
   ```

2. You can then add a red rectangle around the clusters:

   ```
   > dend %>% rect.dendrogram(k=4,horiz=TRUE)
   ```

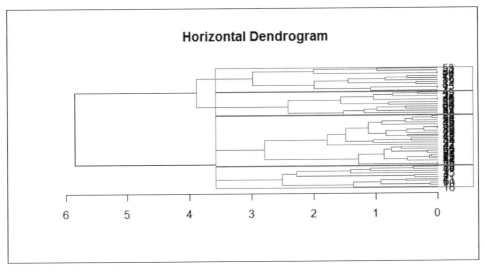

Drawing red rectangles around clusters within a horizontal dendrogram

3. Finally, you can add a line to show the tree cutting location:

```
> abline(v = heights_per_k.dendrogram(dend)["4"] + .1, lwd = 2,
lty = 2, col = "blue")
```

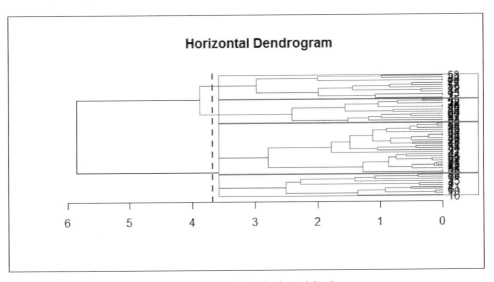

Drawing a cutting line within a horizontal dendrogram

Clustering data with the k-means method

k-means clustering is a flat clustering technique, which produces only one partition with *k* clusters. Unlike hierarchical clustering, which does not require a user to determine the number of clusters at the beginning, the k-means method requires this to be determined first. However, k-means clustering is much faster than hierarchical clustering as the construction of a hierarchical tree is very time consuming. In this recipe, we will demonstrate how to perform k-means clustering on the customer dataset.

Getting ready

In this recipe, we will continue to use the customer dataset as the input data source to perform k-means clustering.

How to do it...

Perform the following steps to cluster the `customer` dataset with the k-means method:

1. First, you can use `kmeans` to cluster the customer data:

```
> set.seed(22)
> fit = kmeans(customer, 4)
> fit
K-means clustering with 4 clusters of sizes 8, 11, 16, 25

Cluster means:
   Visit.Time Average.Expense        Sex        Age
1   1.3302016       1.0155226 -1.4566845  0.5591307
2  -0.7771737      -0.5178412 -1.4566845 -0.4774599
3   0.8571173       0.9887331  0.6750489  1.0505015
4  -0.6322632      -0.7299063  0.6750489 -0.6411604

Clustering vector:
 [1] 2 2 1 2 1 2 1 1 2 2 2 1 1 2 2 2 1 2 1 3 4 3 4 3 3 4 4 3
[29] 4 4 4 3 3 3 4 4 3 4 4 4 4 4 4 4 3 3 4 4 4 3 4 3 3 4 4 4
[57] 3 4 4 3

Within cluster sum of squares by cluster:
[1]   5.90040 11.97454 22.58236 20.89159
 (between_SS / total_SS =  74.0 %)

Available components:

[1] "cluster"      "centers"        "totss"
[4] "withinss"     "tot.withinss"   "betweenss"
[7] "size"         "iter"           "ifault
```

2. You can then inspect the center of each cluster using `barplot`:

```
> barplot(t(fit$centers), beside = TRUE,xlab="cluster",
ylab="value")
```

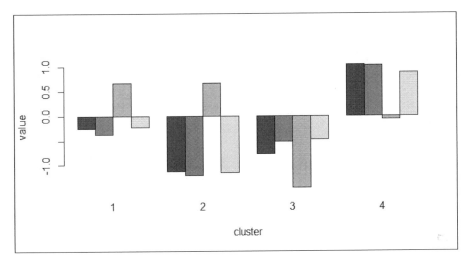

The barplot of centers of different attributes in four clusters

3. Lastly, you can draw a scatter plot of the data and color the points according to the clusters:

```
> plot(customer, col = fit$cluster)
```

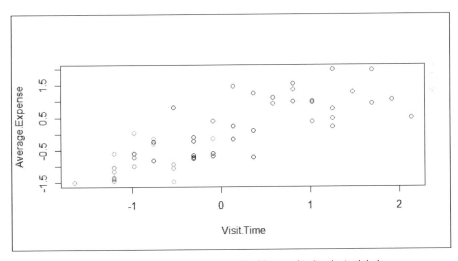

The scatter plot showing data colored with regard to its cluster label

How it works...

k-means clustering is a method of partitioning clustering. The goal of the algorithm is to partition n objects into *k* clusters, where each object belongs to the cluster with the nearest mean. The objective of the algorithm is to minimize the **within-cluster sum of squares** (**WCSS**). Assuming x is the given set of observations, S = $\{S_1, S_2 \cdots S_k\}$ denotes *k* partitions, and μ_i is the mean of S_i, then we can formulate the WCSS function as follows:

$$f = \sum_{i=1}^{k} \sum_{x \in S_i} \|x - \mu_i\|^2$$

The process of k-means clustering can be illustrated by the following five steps:

1. Specify the number of *k* clusters.
2. Randomly create k partitions.
3. Calculate the center of the partitions.
4. Associate objects closest to the cluster center.
5. Repeat steps 2, 3, and 4 until the WCSS changes very little (or is minimized).

In this recipe, we demonstrate how to use k-means clustering to cluster customer data. In contrast to hierarchical clustering, k-means clustering requires the user to input the number of *K*. In this example, we use *K=4*. Then, the output of a fitted model shows the size of each cluster, the cluster means of four generated clusters, the cluster vectors with regard to each data point, the within cluster sum of squares by the clusters, and other available components.

Further, you can draw the centers of each cluster in a bar plot, which will provide more details on how each attribute affects the clustering. Lastly, we plot the data point in a scatter plot and use the fitted cluster labels to assign colors with regard to the cluster label.

See also

▸ In k-means clustering, you can specify the algorithm used to perform clustering analysis. You can specify either Hartigan-Wong, Lloyd, Forgy, or MacQueen as the clustering algorithm. For more details, please use the help function to refer to the document for the kmeans function:

```
>help(kmeans)
```

Drawing a bivariate cluster plot

In the previous recipe, we employed the k-means method to fit data into clusters. However, if there are more than two variables, it is impossible to display how data is clustered in two dimensions. Therefore, you can use a bivariate cluster plot to first reduce variables into two components, and then use components, such as axis and circle, as clusters to show how data is clustered. In this recipe, we will illustrate how to create a bivariate cluster plot.

Getting ready

In this recipe, we will continue to use the `customer` dataset as the input data source to draw a bivariate cluster plot.

How to do it...

Perform the following steps to draw a bivariate cluster plot:

1. Install and load the cluster package:

   ```
   > install.packages("cluster")
   > library(cluster)
   ```

2. You can then draw a bivariate cluster plot:

   ```
   > clusplot(customer, fit$cluster, color=TRUE, shade=TRUE)
   ```

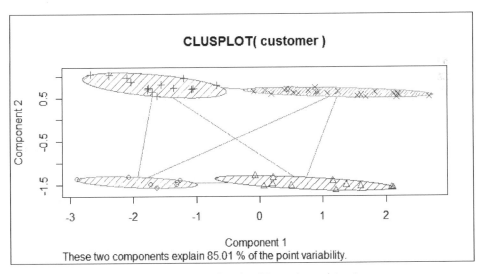

The bivariate clustering plot of the customer dataset

3. You can also zoom into the bivariate cluster plot:

```
> par(mfrow= c(1,2))
> clusplot(customer, fit$cluster, color=TRUE, shade=TRUE)
> rect(-0.7,-1.7, 2.2,-1.2, border = "orange", lwd=2)
> clusplot(customer, fit$cluster, color = TRUE, xlim = c(-
0.7,2.2), ylim = c(-1.7,-1.2))
```

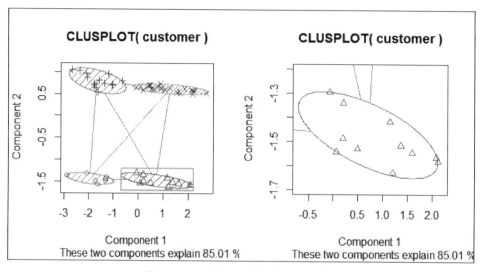

The zoom-in of the bivariate clustering plot

How it works...

In this recipe, we draw a bivariate cluster plot to show how data is clustered. To draw a bivariate cluster plot, we first need to install the cluster package and load it into R. We then use the clusplot function to draw a bivariate cluster plot from a customer dataset. In the clustplot function, we can set shade to TRUE and color to TRUE to display a cluster with colors and shades. As per the preceding figure (step 2) we found that the bivariate uses two components, which explains 85.01 percent of point variability, as the x-axis and y-axis. The data points are then scattered on the plot in accordance with component 1 and component 2. Data within the same cluster is circled in the same color and shade.

Besides drawing the four clusters in a single plot, you can use rect to add a rectangle around a specific area within a given x-axis and y-axis range. You can then zoom into the plot to examine the data within each cluster by using xlim and ylim in the clusplot function.

There's more

The `clusplot` function uses `princomp` and `cmdscale` to reduce the original feature dimension to the principal component. Therefore, one can see how data is clustered in a single plot with these two components as the x-axis and y-axis. To learn more about `princomp` and `cmdscale`, one can use the `help` function to view related documents:

```
> help(cmdscale)
> help(princomp)
```

For those interested in how to use `cmdscale` to reduce the dimensions, please perform the following steps:

```
> mds = cmdscale(dist(customer), k = 2)
> plot(mds, col = fit$cluster)
```

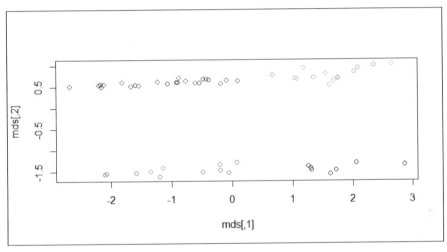

The scatter plot of data with regard to scaled dimensions

Comparing clustering methods

After fitting data into clusters using different clustering methods, you may wish to measure the accuracy of the clustering. In most cases, you can use either intracluster or intercluster metrics as measurements. We now introduce how to compare different clustering methods using `cluster.stat` from the `fpc` package.

Getting ready

In order to perform a clustering method comparison, one needs to have the previous recipe completed by generating the `customer` dataset.

How to do it...

Perform the following steps to compare clustering methods:

1. First, install and load the `fpc` package:

```
> install.packages("fpc")
> library(fpc)
```

2. You then need to use hierarchical clustering with the `single` method to cluster customer data and generate the object `hc_single`:

```
> single_c =  hclust(dist(customer), method="single")
> hc_single = cutree(single_c, k = 4)
```

3. Use hierarchical clustering with the `complete` method to cluster customer data and generate the object `hc_complete`:

```
> complete_c =  hclust(dist(customer), method="complete")
> hc_complete =  cutree(complete_c, k = 4)
```

4. You can then use k-means clustering to cluster customer data and generate the object `km`:

```
> set.seed(22)
> km = kmeans(customer, 4)
```

5. Next, retrieve the cluster validation statistics of either clustering method:

```
> cs = cluster.stats(dist(customer), km$cluster)
```

6. Most often, we focus on using `within.cluster.ss` and `avg.silwidth` to validate the clustering method:

```
> cs[c("within.cluster.ss","avg.silwidth")]
$within.cluster.ss
[1]  61.3489

$avg.silwidth
[1]  0.4640587
```

7. Finally, we can generate the cluster statistics of each clustering method and list them in a table:

```
> sapply(list(kmeans = km$cluster, hc_single = hc_single, hc_
complete = hc_complete), function(c) cluster.stats(dist(customer),
c)[c("within.cluster.ss","avg.silwidth")])
                   kmeans     hc_single hc_complete
within.cluster.ss 61.3489    136.0092   65.94076
avg.silwidth       0.4640587 0.2481926 0.4255961
```

How it works...

In this recipe, we demonstrate how to validate clusters. To validate a clustering method, we often employ two techniques: intercluster distance and intracluster distance. In these techniques, the higher the intercluster distance, the better it is, and the lower the intracluster distance, the better it is. In order to calculate related statistics, we can apply `cluster.stat` from the fpc package on the fitted clustering object.

From the output, the `within.cluster.ss` measurement stands for the within clusters sum of squares, and avg.silwidth represents the average silhouette width. The `within.cluster.ss` measurement shows how closely related objects are in clusters; the smaller the value, the more closely related objects are within the cluster. On the other hand, a silhouette is a measurement that considers how closely related objects are within the cluster and how clusters are separated from each other. Mathematically, we can define the silhouette width for each point x as follows:

$$\text{Silhouette}(x) = \frac{b(x) - a(x)}{\max\left(\left[b(x), a(x)\right]\right)}$$

In the preceding equation, $a(x)$ is the average distance between x and all other points within the cluster, and $b(x)$ is the minimum of the average distances between x and the points in the other clusters. The silhouette value usually ranges from 0 to 1; a value closer to 1 suggests the data is better clustered.

The summary table generated in the last step shows that the complete hierarchical clustering method outperforms a single hierarchical clustering method and k-means clustering in `within.cluster.ss` and `avg.silwidth`.

See also

▶ The `kmeans` function also outputs statistics (for example, `withinss` and `betweenss`) for users to validate a clustering method:

```
> set.seed(22)
> km = kmeans(customer, 4)
> km$withinss
[1]   5.90040 11.97454 22.58236 20.89159
> km$betweenss
[1] 174.6511
```

Extracting silhouette information from clustering

Silhouette information is a measurement to validate a cluster of data. In the previous recipe, we mentioned that the measurement of a cluster involves the calculation of how closely the data is clustered within each cluster, and measures how far different clusters are apart from each other. The silhouette coefficient combines the measurement of the intracluster and intercluster distance. The output value typically ranges from 0 to 1; the closer to 1, the better the cluster is. In this recipe, we will introduce how to compute silhouette information.

Getting ready

In order to extract the silhouette information from a cluster, you need to have the previous recipe completed by generating the `customer` dataset.

How to do it...

Perform the following steps to compute the silhouette information:

1. Use `kmeans` to generate a k-means object, `km`:

   ```
   > set.seed(22)
   > km = kmeans(customer, 4)
   ```

2. You can then compute the silhouette information:

   ```
   > kms = silhouette(km$cluster,dist(customer))
   > summary(kms)
   Silhouette of 60 units in 4 clusters from silhouette.default(x =
   km$cluster, dist = dist(customer))  :
    Cluster sizes and average silhouette widths:
            8          11          16          25
   0.5464597 0.4080823 0.3794910 0.5164434
   Individual silhouette widths:
      Min. 1st Qu.  Median    Mean 3rd Qu.    Max.
    0.1931  0.4030  0.4890  0.4641  0.5422  0.6333
   ```

3. Next, you can plot the silhouette information:

   ```
   > plot(kms)
   ```

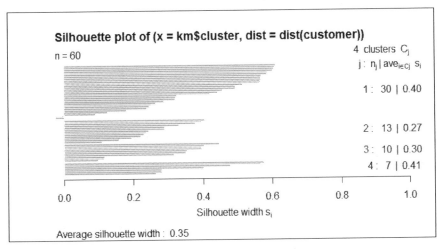

The silhouette plot of the k-means clustering result

How it works...

In this recipe, we demonstrate how to use the silhouette plot to validate clusters. You can first retrieve the silhouette information, which shows cluster sizes, the average silhouette widths, and individual silhouette widths. The silhouette coefficient is a value ranging from *0* to *1*; the closer to *1*, the better the quality of the cluster.

Lastly, we use the `plot` function to draw a silhouette plot. The left-hand side of the plot shows the number of horizontal lines, which represent the number of clusters. The right-hand column shows the mean similarity of the plot of its own cluster minus the mean similarity of the next similar cluster. The average silhouette width is presented at the bottom of the plot.

See also

▸   For those interested in how silhouettes are computed, please refer to the Wikipedia entry for **Silhouette Value**: `http://en.wikipedia.org/wiki/Silhouette_%28clustering%29`

Obtaining the optimum number of clusters for k-means

While k-means clustering is fast and easy to use, it requires *k* to be the input at the beginning. Therefore, we can use the sum of squares to determine which *k* value is best for finding the optimum number of clusters for k-means. In the following recipe, we will discuss how to find the optimum number of clusters for the k-means clustering method.

In order to find the optimum number of clusters, you need to have the previous recipe completed by generating the `customer` dataset.

Perform the following steps to find the optimum number of clusters for the k-means clustering:

1. First, calculate the within sum of squares (`withinss`) of different numbers of clusters:

```
> nk = 2:10
> set.seed(22)
> WSS = sapply(nk, function(k) {
+       kmeans(customer, centers=k)$tot.withinss
+ })
> WSS
[1] 123.49224  88.07028  61.34890  48.76431  47.20813
[6]  45.48114  29.58014  28.87519  23.21331
```

2. You can then use a line plot to plot the within sum of squares with a different number of k:

```
> plot(nk, WSS, type="l", xlab= "number of k", ylab="within sum of
squares")
```

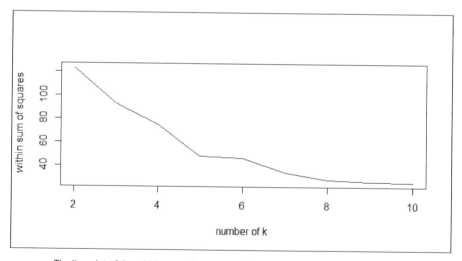

The line plot of the within sum of squares with regard to the different number of k

3. Next, you can calculate the average silhouette width (avg.silwidth) of different numbers of clusters:

```
> SW = sapply(nk, function(k) {
+    cluster.stats(dist(customer), kmeans(customer,
centers=k)$cluster)$avg.silwidth
+ })
> SW
[1] 0.4203896 0.4278904 0.4640587 0.4308448 0.3481157
[6] 0.3320245 0.4396910 0.3417403 0.4070539
```

4. You can then use a line plot to plot the average silhouette width with a different number of k:

```
> plot(nk, SW, type="l", xlab="number of clusers", ylab="average
silhouette width")
```

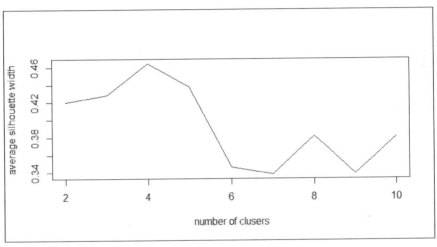

The line plot of average silhouette width with regard to the different number of k

5. Retrieve the maximum number of clusters:

```
> nk[which.max(SW)]
[1]  4
```

How it works...

In this recipe, we demonstrate how to find the optimum number of clusters by iteratively getting within the sum of squares and the average silhouette value. For the within sum of squares, lower values represent clusters with better quality. By plotting the within sum of squares in regard to different number of k, we find that the elbow of the plot is at k=4.

On the other hand, we also compute the average silhouette width based on the different numbers of clusters using `cluster.stats`. Also, we can use a line plot to plot the average silhouette width with regard to the different numbers of clusters. The preceding figure (step 4) shows the maximum average silhouette width appears at k=4. Lastly, we use `which.max` to obtain the value of k to determine the location of the maximum average silhouette width.

See also

▶ For those interested in how the within sum of squares is computed, please refer to the Wikipedia entry of **K-means clustering**: `http://en.wikipedia.org/wiki/K-means_clustering`

Clustering data with the density-based method

As an alternative to distance measurement, you can use a density-based measurement to cluster data. This method finds an area with a higher density than the remaining area. One of the most famous methods is DBSCAN. In the following recipe, we will demonstrate how to use DBSCAN to perform density-based clustering.

Getting ready

In this recipe, we will use simulated data generated from the `mlbench` package.

How to do it...

Perform the following steps to perform density-based clustering:

1. First, install and load the `fpc` and `mlbench` packages:

    ```
    > install.packages("mlbench")
    > library(mlbench)
    > install.packages("fpc")
    > library(fpc)
    ```

2. You can then use the `mlbench` library to draw a Cassini problem graph:

    ```
    > set.seed(2)
    > p = mlbench.cassini(500)
    > plot(p$x)
    ```

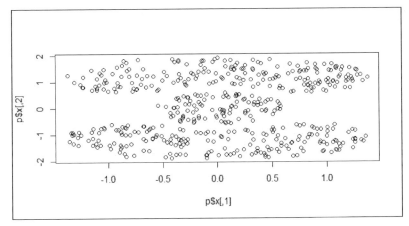

The Cassini problem graph

3. Next, you can cluster data with regard to its density measurement:

```
> ds = dbscan(dist(p$x),0.2, 2, countmode=NULL, method="dist")
> ds
dbscan Pts=500 MinPts=2 eps=0.2
          1   2   3
seed    200 200 100
total   200 200 100
```

4. Plot the data in a scatter plot with different cluster labels as the color:

```
> plot(ds, p$x)
```

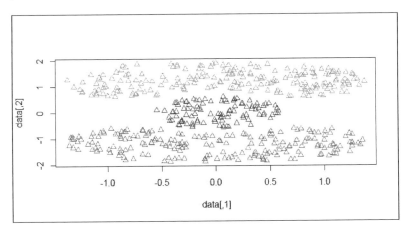

The data scatter plot colored with regard to the cluster label

5. You can also use `dbscan` to predict which cluster the data point belongs to. In this example, first make three inputs in the matrix `p`:

```
> y = matrix(0,nrow=3,ncol=2)
> y[1,] = c(0,0)
> y[2,] = c(0,-1.5)
> y[3,] = c(1,1)
> y
     [,1] [,2]
[1,]    0  0.0
[2,]    0 -1.5
[3,]    1  1.0
```

6. You can then predict which cluster the data belongs to:

```
> predict(ds, p$x, y)
[1] 3 1 2
```

How it works...

Density-based clustering uses the idea of density reachability and density connectivity, which makes it very useful in discovering a cluster in nonlinear shapes. Before discussing the process of density-based clustering, some important background concepts must be explained. Density-based clustering takes two parameters into account: `eps` and `MinPts`. `eps` stands for the maximum radius of the neighborhood; `MinPts` denotes the minimum number of points within the `eps` neighborhood. With these two parameters, we can define the core point as having points more than `MinPts` within `eps`. Also, we can define the board point as having points less than `MinPts`, but is in the neighborhood of the core points. Then, we can define the core object as if the number of points in the `eps`-neighborhood of p is more than `MinPts`.

Furthermore, we have to define the reachability between two points. We can say that a point, p, is directly density reachable from another point, q, if q is within the `eps`-neighborhood of p and p is a core object. Then, we can define that a point, p, is generic and density reachable from the point q, if there exists a chain of points, $p_1, p_2 \dots p_n$, where $p_1 = q$, $p_n = p$, and $p_i + 1$ is directly density reachable from pi with regard to Eps and `MinPts` for 1 <= i <= n:

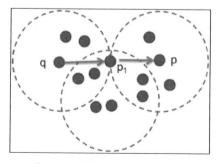

Point p and q is density reachable

With a preliminary concept of density-based clustering, we can then illustrate the process of DBSCAN, the most popular density-based clustering, as shown in these steps:

1. Randomly select a point, p.

2. Retrieve all the points that are density-reachable from p with regard to `Eps` and `MinPts`.

3. If p is a core point, then a cluster is formed. Otherwise, if it is a board point and no points are density reachable from p, the process will mark the point as noise and continue visiting the next point.

4. Repeat the process until all points have been visited.

In this recipe, we demonstrate how to use the DBSCAN density-based method to cluster customer data. First, we have to install and load the `mlbench` and `fpc` libraries. The `mlbench` package provides many methods to generate simulated data with different shapes and sizes. In this example, we generate a Cassini problem graph.

Next, we perform `dbscan` on a Cassini dataset to cluster the data. We specify the reachability distance as 0.2, the minimum reachability number of points to 2, the progress reporting as null, and use distance as a measurement. The clustering method successfully clusters data into three clusters with sizes of 200, 200, and 100. By plotting the points and cluster labels on the plot, we see that three sections of the Cassini graph are separated in different colors.

The `fpc` package also provides a `predict` function, and you can use this to predict the cluster labels of the input matrix. Point c(0,0) is classified into cluster 3, point c(0, -1.5) is classified into cluster 1, and point c(1,1) is classified into cluster 2.

See also

▶ The `fpc` package contains flexible procedures of clustering, and has useful clustering analysis functions. For example, you can generate a discriminant projection plot using the `plotcluster` function. For more information, please refer to the following document:

```
> help(plotcluster)
```

Clustering data with the model-based method

In contrast to hierarchical clustering and k-means clustering, which use a heuristic approach and do not depend on a formal model. Model-based clustering techniques assume varieties of data models and apply an EM algorithm to obtain the most likely model, and further use the model to infer the most likely number of clusters. In this recipe, we will demonstrate how to use the model-based method to determine the most likely number of clusters.

Getting ready

In order to perform a model-based method to cluster customer data, you need to have the previous recipe completed by generating the customer dataset.

How to do it...

Perform the following steps to perform model-based clustering:

1. First, please install and load the library `mclust`:

   ```
   > install.packages("mclust")
   > library(mclust)
   ```

2. You can then perform model-based clustering on the `customer` dataset:

   ```
   > mb = Mclust(customer)
   > plot(mb)
   ```

3. Then, you can press 1 to obtain the BIC against a number of components:

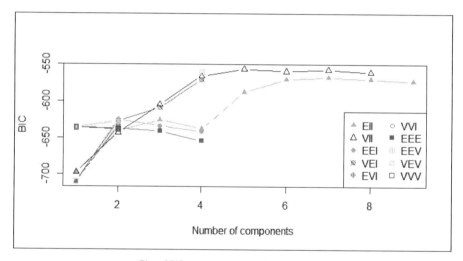

Plot of BIC against number of components

4. Then, you can press 2 to show the classification with regard to different combinations of features:

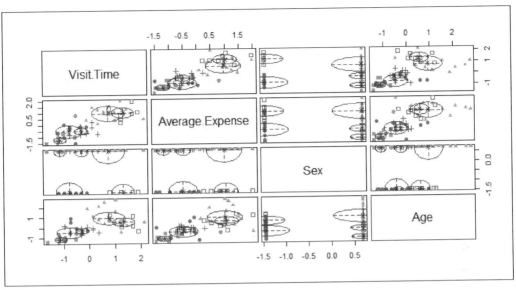

Plot showing classification with regard to different combinations of features

5. Press 3 to show the classification uncertainty with regard to different combinations of features:

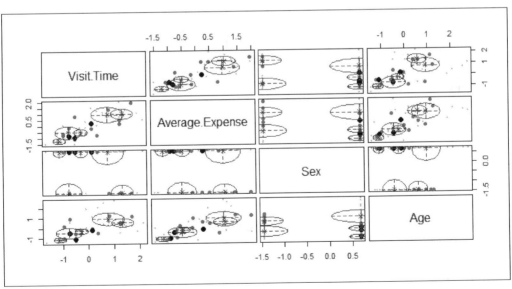

Plot showing classification uncertainty with regard to different combinations of features

6. Next, press 4 to plot the density estimation:

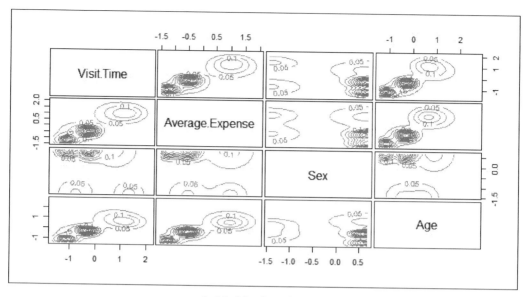

A plot of density estimation

7. Then, you can press 0 to plot density to exit the plotting menu.

8. Lastly, use the `summary` function to obtain the most likely model and number of clusters:

```
> summary(mb)
----------------------------------------------------------
Gaussian finite mixture model fitted by EM algorithm
----------------------------------------------------------

Mclust VII (spherical, varying volume) model with 5 components:

 log.likelihood  n df       BIC        ICL
     -218.6891 60 29 -556.1142 -557.2812

Clustering table:
  1   2   3   4   5
 11   8  17  14  10
```

How it works...

Instead of taking a heuristic approach to build a cluster, model-based clustering uses a probability-based approach. Model-based clustering assumes that the data is generated by an underlying probability distribution and tries to recover the distribution from the data. One common model-based approach is using finite mixture models, which provide a flexible modeling framework for the analysis of the probability distribution. Finite mixture models are a linearly weighted sum of component probability distribution. Assume the data $y=(y_1, y_2..y_n)$ contains n independent and multivariable observations; G is the number of components; the likelihood of finite mixture models can be formulated as:

$$ L_{MIX}\left(\theta_1, \cdots \theta_G \mid y\right) = \prod_{i=1}^{n} \prod_{k=1}^{G} \tau_k f_k\left(y_i \mid \theta_k\right) $$

Where f_k and θ_k are the density and parameters of the kth component in the mixture, and τ_k ($\tau_k \geq 0$ and $\sum_{k=1}^{G} \tau_k = 1$) is the probability that an observation belongs to the kth component.

The process of model-based clustering has several steps: First, the process selects the number and types of component probability distribution. Then, it fits a finite mixture model and calculates the posterior probabilities of a component membership. Lastly, it assigns the membership of each observation to the component with the maximum probability.

In this recipe, we demonstrate how to use model-based clustering to cluster data. We first install and load the `Mclust` library into R. We then fit the customer data into the model-based method by using the `Mclust` function.

After the data is fit into the model, we plot the model based on clustering results. There are four different plots: BIC, classification, uncertainty, and density plots. The BIC plot shows the BIC value, and one can use this value to choose the number of clusters. The classification plot shows how data is clustered in regard to different dimension combinations. The uncertainty plot shows the uncertainty of classifications in regard to different dimension combinations. The density plot shows the density estimation in contour.

You can also use the `summary` function to obtain the most likely model and the most possible number of clusters. For this example, the most possible number of clusters is five, with a BIC value equal to -556.1142.

See also

▸   For those interested in detail on how `Mclust` works, please refer to the following source: C. Fraley, A. E. Raftery, T. B. Murphy and L. Scrucca (2012). *mclust Version 4 for R: Normal Mixture Modeling for Model-Based Clustering, Classification, and Density Estimation*. Technical Report No. 597, Department of Statistics, University of Washington.

Visualizing a dissimilarity matrix

A dissimilarity matrix can be used as a measurement for the quality of a cluster. To visualize the matrix, we can use a heat map on a distance matrix. Within the plot, entries with low dissimilarity (or high similarity) are plotted darker, which is helpful to identify hidden structures in the data. In this recipe, we will discuss some techniques that are useful to visualize a dissimilarity matrix.

Getting ready

In order to visualize the dissimilarity matrix, you need to have the previous recipe completed by generating the customer dataset. In addition to this, a k-means object needs to be generated and stored in the variable km.

How to do it...

Perform the following steps to visualize the dissimilarity matrix:

1. First, install and load the seriation package:

   ```
   > install.packages("seriation")
   > library(seriation)
   ```

2. You can then use dissplot to visualize the dissimilarity matrix in a heat map:

   ```
   > dissplot(dist(customer), labels=km$cluster,
   options=list(main="Kmeans Clustering With k=4"))
   ```

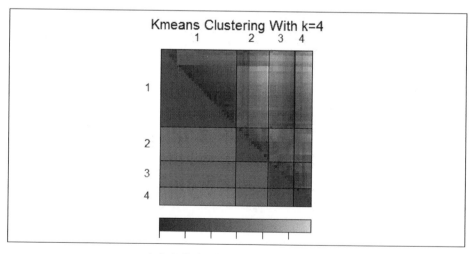

A dissimilarity plot of k-means clustering

3. Next, apply `dissplot` on hierarchical clustering in the heat map:

```
> complete_c =  hclust(dist(customer), method="complete")
> hc_complete =  cutree(complete_c, k = 4)
> dissplot(dist(customer), labels=hc_complete,
options=list(main="Hierarchical Clustering"))
```

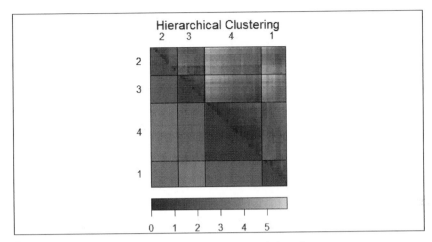

A dissimilarity plot of hierarchical clustering

How it works...

In this recipe, we use a dissimilarity plot to visualize the dissimilarity matrix. We first install and load the package `seriation`, and then apply the `dissplot` function on the k-means clustering output, generating the preceding figure (step 2).

It shows that clusters similar to each other are plotted darker, and dissimilar combinations are plotted lighter. Therefore, we can see clusters against their corresponding clusters (such as cluster 4 to cluster 4) are plotted diagonally and darker. On the other hand, clusters dissimilar to each other are plotted lighter and away from the diagonal.

Likewise, we can apply the `dissplot` function on the output of hierarchical clustering. The generated plot in the figure (step 3) shows the similarity of each cluster in a single heat map.

There's more...

Besides using `dissplot` to visualize the dissimilarity matrix, one can also visualize a distance matrix by using the `dist` and `image` functions. In the resulting graph, closely related entries are plotted in red. Less related entries are plotted closer to white:

```
> image(as.matrix(dist(customer)))
```

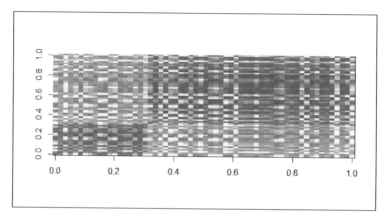

A distance matrix plot of customer dataset

In order to plot both a dendrogram and heat map to show how data is clustered, you can use the `heatmap` function:

```
> cd=dist(customer)
> hc=hclust(cd)
> cdt=dist(t(customer))
> hcc=hclust(cdt)
> heatmap(customer, Rowv=as.dendrogram(hc), Colv=as.dendrogram(hcc))
```

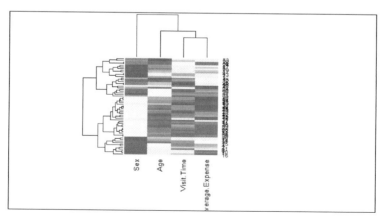

A heat map with dendrogram on the column and row side

Validating clusters externally

Besides generating statistics to validate the quality of the generated clusters, you can use known data clusters as the ground truth to compare different clustering methods. In this recipe, we will demonstrate how clustering methods differ with regard to data with known clusters.

Getting ready

In this recipe, we will continue to use handwriting digits as clustering inputs; you can find the figure on the author's Github page: `https://github.com/ywchiu/ml_R_cookbook/tree/master/CH9`.

How to do it...

Perform the following steps to cluster digits with different clustering techniques:

1. First, you need to install and load the package `png`:

```
> install.packages("png")
> library(png)
```

2. Then, please read images from `handwriting.png` and transform the read data into a scatter plot:

```
> img2 = readPNG("handwriting.png", TRUE)
> img3 = img2[,nrow(img2):1]
> b = cbind(as.integer(which(img3 < -1) %% 28), which(img3 < -1) / 28)
> plot(b, xlim=c(1,28), ylim=c(1,28))
```

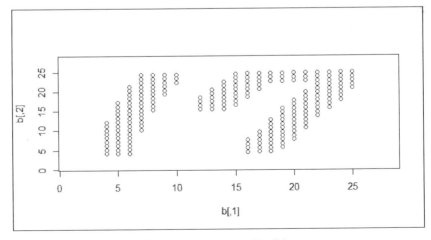

A scatter plot of handwriting digits

3. Perform a k-means clustering method on the handwriting digits:

```
> set.seed(18)
> fit = kmeans(b, 2)
> plot(b, col=fit$cluster)
> plot(b, col=fit$cluster,  xlim=c(1,28), ylim=c(1,28))
```

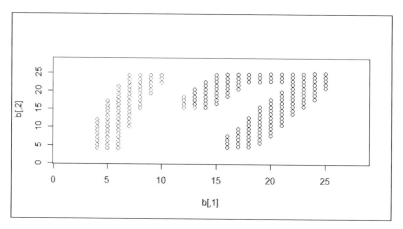

k-means clustering result on handwriting digits

4. Next, perform the dbscan clustering method on the handwriting digits:

```
> ds = dbscan(b, 2)
> ds
dbscan Pts=212 MinPts=5 eps=2
        1   2
seed   75 137
total  75 137
> plot(ds, b,  xlim=c(1,28), ylim=c(1,28))
```

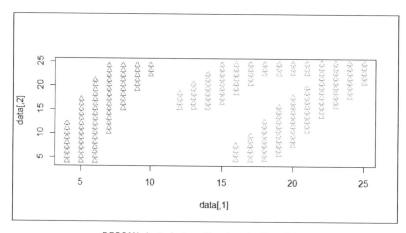

DBSCAN clustering result on handwriting digits

How it works...

In this recipe, we demonstrate how different clustering methods work in regard to a handwriting dataset. The aim of the clustering is to separate 1 and 7 into different clusters. We perform different techniques to see how data is clustered in regard to the k-means and DBSCAN methods.

To generate the data, we use the Windows application `paint.exe` to create a PNG file with dimensions of 28 x 28 pixels. We then read the PNG data using the `readPNG` function and transform the read PNG data points into a scatter plot, which shows the handwriting digits in 17.

After the data is read, we perform clustering techniques on the handwriting digits. First, we perform k-means clustering, where `k=2` on the dataset. Since k-means clustering employs distance measures, the constructed clusters cover the area of both the 1 and 7 digits. We then perform DBSCAN on the dataset. As DBSCAN is a density-based clustering technique, it successfully separates digit 1 and digit 7 into different clusters.

See also

▶ If you are interested in how to read various graphic formats in R, you may refer to the following document:

```
> help(package="png")
```

10

Association Analysis and Sequence Mining

In this chapter, we will cover the following topics:

- ▶ Transforming data into transactions
- ▶ Displaying transactions and associations
- ▶ Mining associations with the Apriori rule
- ▶ Pruning redundant rules
- ▶ Visualizing associations rules
- ▶ Mining frequent itemsets with Eclat
- ▶ Creating transactions with temporal information
- ▶ Mining frequent sequential patterns with cSPADE

Introduction

Enterprises accumulate a large amount of transaction data (for example, sales orders from retailers, invoices, and shipping documentations) from daily operations. Finding hidden relationships in the data can be useful, such as, "What products are often bought together?" or "What are the subsequent purchases after buying a cell phone?" To answer these two questions, we need to perform association analysis and frequent sequential pattern mining on a transaction dataset.

Association analysis is an approach to find interesting relationships within a transaction dataset. A famous association between products is that *customers who buy diapers also buy beer*. While this association may sound unusual, if retailers can use this kind of information or rule to cross-sell products to their customers, there is a high likelihood that they can increase their sales.

Association analysis is used to find a correlation between **itemsets**, but what if you want to find out the order in which items are frequently purchased? To achieve this, you can adopt frequent sequential pattern mining to find frequent subsequences from transaction datasets with temporal information. You can then use the mined frequent subsequences to predict customer shopping sequence orders, web click streams, biological sequences, and usages in other applications.

In this chapter, we will cover recipes to create and inspect transaction datasets, performing association analysis with an Apriori algorithm, visualizing associations in various graph formats, and finding frequent itemsets using the Eclat algorithm. Lastly, we will create transactions with temporal information and use the cSPADE algorithm to discover frequent sequential patterns.

Transforming data into transactions

Before creating a mining association rule, you need to transform the data into transactions. In the following recipe, we will introduce how to transform either a list, matrix, or data frame into transactions.

Getting ready

In this recipe, we will generate three different datasets in a list, matrix, or data frame. We can then transform the generated dataset into transactions.

How to do it...

Perform the following steps to transform different formats of data into transactions:

1. First, you have to install and load the package `arule`:

    ```
    > install.packages("arules")
    > library(arules)
    ```

2. You can then make a list with three vectors containing purchase records:

    ```
    > tr_list = list(c("Apple", "Bread", "Cake"),
    +                 c("Apple", "Bread", "Milk"),
    +                 c("Bread", "Cake", "Milk"))
    > names(tr_list) = paste("Tr",c(1:3), sep = "")
    ```

3. Next, you can use the `as` function to transform the data frame into transactions:

    ```
    > trans = as(tr_list, "transactions")
    > trans
    transactions in sparse format with
     3 transactions (rows) and
     4 items (columns)
    ```

4. You can also transform the matrix format data into transactions:

```
> tr_matrix = matrix(
+    c(1,1,1,0,
+      1,1,0,1,
+      0,1,1,1), ncol = 4)
> dimnames(tr_matrix) =  list(
+    paste("Tr",c(1:3), sep = ""),
+    c("Apple","Bread","Cake", "Milk")
+    )
> trans2 =  as(tr_matrix, "transactions")
> trans2
transactions in sparse format with
 3 transactions (rows) and
 4 items (columns)
```

5. Lastly, you can transform the data frame format datasets into transactions:

```
> Tr_df = data.frame(
+    TrID= as.factor(c(1,2,1,1,2,3,2,3,2,3)),
+    Item = as.factor(c("Apple","Milk","Cake","Bread",
+                       "Cake","Milk","Apple","Cake",
+                       "Bread","Bread"))
+ )
> trans3 = as(split(Tr_df[,"Item"], Tr_df[,"TrID"]),
"transactions")
> trans3
transactions in sparse format with
 3 transactions (rows) and
 4 items (columns)
```

How it works...

Before mining frequent itemsets or using the association rule, it is important to prepare the dataset by the class of transactions. In this recipe, we demonstrate how to transform a dataset from a list, matrix, and data frame format to transactions. In the first step, we generate the dataset in a list format containing three vectors of purchase records. Then, after we have assigned a transaction ID to each transaction, we transform the data into transactions using the `as` function.

Next, we demonstrate how to transform the data from the matrix format into transactions. To denote how items are purchased, one should use a binary incidence matrix to record the purchase behavior of each transaction with regard to different items purchased. Likewise, we can use an `as` function to transform the dataset from the matrix format into transactions.

Lastly, we illustrate how to transform the dataset from the data frame format into transactions. The data frame contains two factor-type vectors: one is a transaction ID named `TrID`, while the other shows purchased items (named in `Item`) with regard to different transactions. Also, one can use the `as` function to transform the data frame format data into transactions.

See also

▸ The `transactions` class is used to represent transaction data for rules or frequent pattern mining. It is an extension of the `itemMatrix` class. If you are interested in how to use the two different classes to represent transaction data, please use the `help` function to refer to the following documents:

```
> help(transactions)
> help(itemMatrix)
```

Displaying transactions and associations

The `arule` package uses its own `transactions` class to store transaction data. As such, we must use the generic function provided by `arule` to display transactions and association rules. In this recipe, we will illustrate how to display transactions and association rules via various functions in the `arule` package.

Getting ready

Ensure that you have completed the previous recipe by generating transactions and storing these in the variable, `trans`.

How to do it...

Perform the following steps to display transactions and associations:

1. First, you can obtain a LIST representation of the transaction data:

```
> LIST(trans)
$Tr1
[1] "Apple" "Bread" "Cake"

$Tr2
[1] "Apple" "Bread" "Milk"

$Tr3
[1] "Bread" "Cake"  "Milk"
```

2. Next, you can use the `summary` function to show a summary of the statistics and details of the transactions:

```
> summary(trans)
transactions as itemMatrix in sparse format with
 3 rows (elements/itemsets/transactions) and
 4 columns (items) and a density of 0.75

most frequent items:
  Bread    Apple    Cake    Milk (Other)
      3        2       2       2      0

element (itemset/transaction) length distribution:
sizes
3
3

    Min. 1st Qu. Median   Mean 3rd Qu.   Max.
      3       3      3      3       3      3

includes extended item information - examples:
  labels
1   Apple
2   Bread
3   Cake

includes extended transaction information - examples:
  transactionID
1           Tr1
2           Tr2
3           Tr3
```

3. You can then display transactions using the `inspect` function:

```
> inspect(trans)
  items    transactionID
1 {Apple,
   Bread,
   Cake}          Tr1
2 {Apple,
   Bread,
   Milk}          Tr2
3 {Bread,
   Cake,
   Milk}          Tr3
```

4. In addition to this, you can filter the transactions by size:

```
> filter_trains = trans[size(trans) >=3]
> inspect(filter_trains)
  items     transactionID
1 {Apple,
  Bread,
  Cake}          Tr1
2 {Apple,
  Bread,
  Milk}          Tr2
3 {Bread,
  Cake,
  Milk}          Tr3
```

5. Also, you can use the image function to visually inspect the transactions:

```
> image(trans)
```

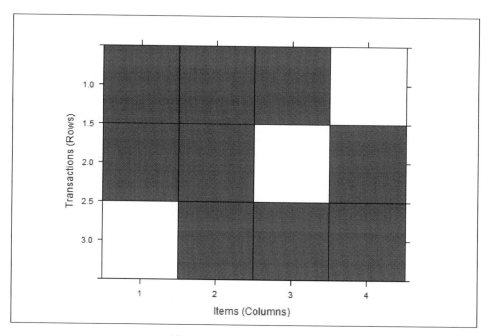

Visual inspection of transactions

6. To visually show the frequency/support bar plot, one can use `itemFrequenctPlot`:

```
> itemFrequencyPlot (trans)
```

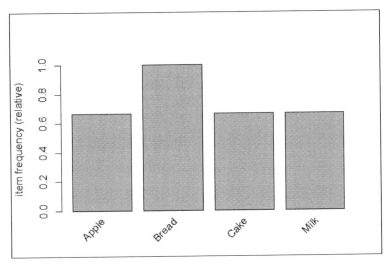

Item frequency bar plot of transactions

How it works...

As the transaction data is the base for mining associations and frequent patterns, we have to learn how to display the associations to gain insights and determine how associations are built. The `arules` package provides various methods to inspect transactions. First, we use the `LIST` function to obtain the list representation of the transaction data. We can then use the `summary` function to obtain information, such as basic descriptions, most frequent items, and the transaction length distribution.

Next, we use the `inspect` function to display the transactions. Besides displaying all transactions, one can first filter the transactions by size and then display the associations by using the `inspect` function. Furthermore, we can use the `image` function to visually inspect the transactions. Finally, we illustrate how to use the frequency/support bar plot to display the relative item frequency of each item.

See also

▶ Besides using `itemFrequencyPlot` to show the frequency/bar plot, you can use the `itemFrequency` function to show the support distribution. For more details, please use the `help` function to view the following document:

```
> help(itemFrequency)
```

Mining associations with the Apriori rule

Association mining is a technique that can discover interesting relationships hidden in transaction datasets. This approach first finds all frequent itemsets, and generates strong association rules from frequent itemsets. Apriori is the most well-known association mining algorithm, which identifies frequent individual items first and then performs a breadth-first search strategy to extend individual items to larger itemsets until larger frequent itemsets cannot be found. In this recipe, we will introduce how to perform association analysis using the Apriori rule.

Getting ready

In this recipe, we will use the built-in transaction dataset, `Groceries`, to demonstrate how to perform association analysis with the Apriori algorithm in the `arules` package. Please make sure that the `arules` package is installed and loaded first.

How to do it...

Perform the following steps to analyze the association rules:

1. First, you need to load the dataset `Groceries`:

   ```
   > data(Groceries)
   ```

2. You can then examine the summary of the `Groceries` dataset:

   ```
   > summary(Groceries)
   ```

3. Next, you can use `itemFrequencyPlot` to examine the relative item frequency of itemsets:

   ```
   > itemFrequencyPlot(Groceries, support = 0.1, cex.names=0.8,
   topN=5)
   ```

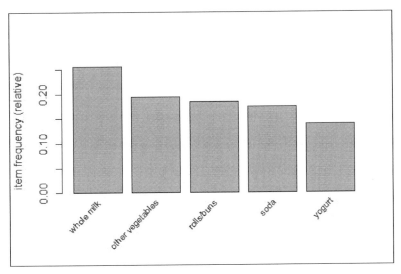

The top five item frequency bar plot of groceries transactions

4. Use `apriori` to discover rules with the support over 0.001 and confidence over 0.5:

```
> rules = apriori(Groceries, parameter = list(supp = 0.001, conf =
0.5, target= "rules"))
> summary(rules)
set of 5668 rules

rule length distribution (lhs + rhs):sizes
   2    3    4    5    6
  11 1461 3211  939   46

  Min. 1st Qu.  Median  Mean 3rd Qu.   Max.
  2.00    3.00    4.00  3.92    4.00   6.00

summary of quality measures:
     support           confidence          lift
Min.    :0.001017   Min.    :0.5000   Min.    : 1.957
1st Qu.:0.001118   1st Qu.:0.5455   1st Qu.: 2.464
Median :0.001322   Median :0.6000   Median : 2.899
Mean    :0.001668   Mean    :0.6250   Mean    : 3.262
3rd Qu.:0.001729   3rd Qu.:0.6842   3rd Qu.: 3.691
Max.    :0.022267   Max.    :1.0000   Max.    :18.996

mining info:
       data ntransactions support confidence
  Groceries          9835    0.001        0.5
```

5. We can then inspect the first few rules:

```
> inspect(head(rules))
  lhs                          rhs              support confidence
lift
1 {honey}               => {whole milk} 0.001118454   0.7333333
2.870009
2 {tidbits}             => {rolls/buns} 0.001220132   0.5217391
2.836542
3 {cocoa drinks}        => {whole milk} 0.001321810   0.5909091
2.312611
4 {pudding powder}      => {whole milk} 0.001321810   0.5652174
2.212062
5 {cooking chocolate}   => {whole milk} 0.001321810   0.5200000
2.035097
6 {cereals}             => {whole milk} 0.003660397   0.6428571
2.515917
```

6. You can sort rules by confidence and inspect the first few rules:

```
> rules=sort(rules, by="confidence", decreasing=TRUE)
> inspect(head(rules))
  lhs                          rhs                      support
confidence      lift
1 {rice,
   sugar}               => {whole milk}          0.001220132
1 3.913649
2 {canned fish,
   hygiene articles}    => {whole milk}          0.001118454
1 3.913649
3 {root vegetables,
   butter,
   rice}                => {whole milk}          0.001016777
1 3.913649
4 {root vegetables,
   whipped/sour cream,
   flour}               => {whole milk}          0.001728521
1 3.913649
5 {butter,
   soft cheese,
   domestic eggs}       => {whole milk}          0.001016777
1 3.913649
6 {citrus fruit,
   root vegetables,
   soft cheese}         => {other vegetables} 0.001016777
1 5.168156
```

How it works...

The purpose of association mining is to discover associations among items from the transactional database. Typically, the process of association mining proceeds by finding itemsets that have the support greater than the minimum support. Next, the process uses the frequent itemsets to generate strong rules (for example, `milk => bread`; a customer who buys milk is likely to buy bread) that have the confidence greater than minimum the confidence. By definition, an association rule can be expressed in the form of X=>Y, where X and Y are disjointed itemsets. We can measure the strength of associations between two terms: support and confidence. Support shows how much of the percentage of a rule is applicable within a dataset, while confidence indicates the probability of both X and Y appearing in the same transaction:

- Support = $\dfrac{\sigma(x \cup y)}{N}$

- Confidence = $\dfrac{\sigma(x \cup y)}{\sigma(x)}$

Here, σ refers to the frequency of a particular itemset; N denotes the populations.

As support and confidence are metrics for the strength rule only, you might still obtain many redundant rules with a high support and confidence. Therefore, we can use the third measure, lift, to evaluate the quality (ranking) of the rule. By definition, lift indicates the strength of a rule over the random co-occurrence of X and Y, so we can formulate lift in the following form:

Lift = $\dfrac{\sigma(x \cup y)}{\sigma(x) \times \sigma(y)}$

Apriori is the best known algorithm for mining associations, which performs a level-wise, breadth-first algorithm to count the candidate itemsets. The process of Apriori starts by finding frequent itemsets (a set of items that have minimum support) level-wisely. For example, the process starts with finding frequent 1-itemsets. Then, the process continues by using frequent 1-itemsets to find frequent 2-itemsets. The process iteratively discovers new frequent k+1-itemsets from frequent k-itemsets until no frequent itemsets are found.

Finally, the process utilizes frequent itemsets to generate association rules:

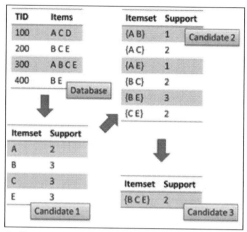

An illustration of Apriori algorithm (Where support = 2)

In this recipe, we use the Apriori algorithm to find association rules within transactions. We use the built-in `Groceries` dataset, which contains one month of real-world point-of-sale transaction data from a typical grocery outlet. We then use the `summary` function to obtain the summary statistics of the `Groceries` dataset. The summary statistics shows that the dataset contains 9,835 transactions, which are categorized into 169 categories. In addition to this, the summary shows information, such as most frequent items, itemset distribution, and example extended item information within the dataset. We can then use `itemFrequencyPlot` to visualize the five most frequent items with support over 0.1.

Next, we apply the Apriori algorithm to search for rules with support over 0.001 and confidence over 0.5. We then use the `summary` function to inspect detailed information on the generated rules. From the output summary, we find the Apriori algorithm generates 5,668 rules with support over 0.001 and confidence over 0.5. Further, we can find the rule length distribution, summary of quality measures, and mining information. In the summary of the quality measurement, we find descriptive statistics of three measurements, which are support, confidence, and lift. Support is the proportion of transactions containing a certain itemset. Confidence is the correctness percentage of the rule. Lift is the response target association rule divided by the average response.

To explore some generated rules, we can use the `inspect` function to view the first six rules of the 5,668 generated rules. Lastly, we can sort rules by confidence and list rules with the most confidence. Therefore, we find that `rich sugar` associated to `whole milk` is the most confident rule with the support equal to 0.001220132, confidence equal to 1, and lift equal to 3.913649.

See also

For those interested in the research results using the `Groceries` dataset, and how the support, confidence, and lift measurement are defined, you can refer to the following papers:

- Michael Hahsler, Kurt Hornik, and Thomas Reutterer (2006) *Implications of probabilistic data modeling for mining association rules. In M. Spiliopoulou, R. Kruse, C. Borgelt, A*
- Nuernberger, and W. Gaul, editors, *From Data and Information Analysis to Knowledge Engineering, Studies in Classification, Data Analysis, and Knowledge Organization, pages 598–605. Springer-Verlag*

Also, in addition to using the `summary` and `inspect` functions to inspect association rules, you can use `interestMeasure` to obtain additional interest measures:

```
> head(interestMeasure(rules, c("support", "chiSquare", "confidence",
"conviction","cosine", "coverage", "leverage", "lift","oddsRatio"),
Groceries))
```

Pruning redundant rules

Among the generated rules, we sometimes find repeated or redundant rules (for example, one rule is the super rule or subset of another rule). In this recipe, we will show you how to prune (or remove) repeated or redundant rules.

Getting ready

In this recipe, you have to complete the previous recipe by generating rules and have it stored in the variable `rules`.

How to do it...

Perform the following steps to prune redundant rules:

1. First, follow these steps to find redundant rules:
   ```
   > rules.sorted = sort(rules, by="lift")
   > subset.matrix = is.subset(rules.sorted, rules.sorted)
   > subset.matrix[lower.tri(subset.matrix, diag=T)] = NA
   > redundant = colSums(subset.matrix, na.rm=T) >= 1
   ```

2. You can then remove redundant rules:
   ```
   > rules.pruned = rules.sorted[!redundant]
   > inspect(head(rules.pruned))
   ```

```
    lhs                        rhs                    support
    confidence      lift
1 {Instant food products,
    soda}                  => {hamburger meat} 0.001220132
  0.6315789 18.99565
2 {soda,
    popcorn}               => {salty snack}    0.001220132
  0.6315789 16.69779
3 {flour,
    baking powder}         => {sugar}          0.001016777
  0.5555556 16.40807
4 {ham,
    processed cheese}      => {white bread}     0.001931876
  0.6333333 15.04549
5 {whole milk,
    Instant food products} => {hamburger meat} 0.001525165
  0.5000000 15.03823
6 {other vegetables,
    curd,
    yogurt,
    whipped/sour cream}    => {cream cheese }   0.001016777
  0.5882353 14.83409
```

How it works...

The two main constraints of association mining are to choose between the support and confidence. For example, if you use a high support threshold, you might remove rare item rules without considering whether these rules have a high confidence value. On the other hand, if you choose to use a low support threshold, the association mining can produce huge sets of redundant association rules, which make these rules difficult to utilize and analyze. Therefore, we need to prune redundant rules so we can discover meaningful information from these generated rules.

In this recipe, we demonstrate how to prune redundant rules. First, we search for redundant rules. We sort the rules by a lift measure, and then find subsets of the sorted rules using the is.subset function, which will generate an itemMatrix object. We can then set the lower triangle of the matrix to NA. Lastly, we compute colSums of the generated matrix, of which colSums >=1 indicates that the specific rule is redundant.

After we have found the redundant rules, we can prune these rules from the sorted rules. Lastly, we can examine the pruned rules using the `inspect` function.

See also

▶ In order to find subsets or supersets of rules, you can use the `is.superset` and `is.subset` functions on the association rules. These two methods may generate an `itemMatrix` object to show which rule is the superset or subset of other rules. You can refer to the `help` function for more information:

```
> help(is.superset)
> help(is.subset)
```

Visualizing association rules

Besides listing rules as text, you can visualize association rules, making it easier to find the relationship between itemsets. In the following recipe, we will introduce how to use the `aruleViz` package to visualize the association rules.

Getting ready

In this recipe, we will continue using the `Groceries` dataset. You need to have completed the previous recipe by generating the pruned rule `rules.pruned`.

How to do it...

Perform the following steps to visualize the association rule:

1. First, you need to install and load the package `arulesViz`:

```
> install.packages("arulesViz")
> library(arulesViz)
```

2. You can then make a scatter plot from the pruned rules:

```
> plot(rules.pruned)
```

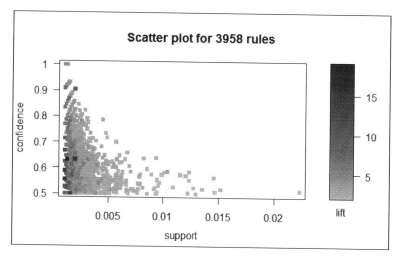

The scatter plot of pruned association rules

3. Additionally, to prevent overplotting, you can add jitter to the scatter plot:

```
> plot(rules.pruned, shading="order", control=list(jitter=6))
```

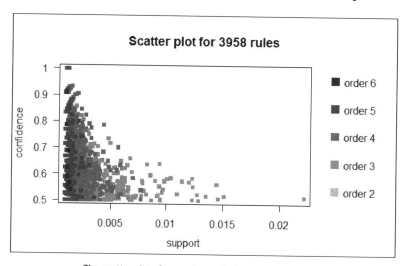

The scatter plot of pruned association rules with jitters

4. We then produce new rules with soda on the left-hand side using the Apriori algorithm:

```
> soda_rule=apriori(data=Groceries, parameter=list(supp=0.001,conf
= 0.1, minlen=2), appearance = list(default="rhs",lhs="soda"))
```

5. Next, you can plot `soda_rule` in a graph plot:

```
> plot(sort(soda_rule, by="lift"), method="graph",
control=list(type="items"))
```

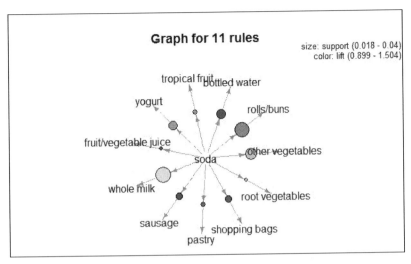

Graph plot of association rules

6. Also, the association rules can be visualized in a balloon plot:

```
> plot(soda_rule, method="grouped")
```

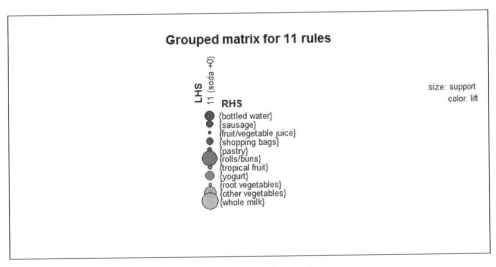

Balloon plot of association rules

How it works...

Besides presenting association rules as text, one can use `arulesViz` to visualize association rules. The `arulesViz` is an `arules` extension package, which provides many visualization techniques to explore association rules. To start using `arulesViz`, first install and load the package `arulesViz`. We then use the pruned rules generated in the previous recipe to make a scatter plot. As per the figure in step 2, we find the rules are shown as points within the scatter plot, with the x-axis in support and y-axis in confidence. The shade of color shows the lift of the rule; the darker the shade, the higher the lift. Next, in order to prevent overplotting points, we can include the jitter as an argument in the control list. The plot with the jitter added is provided in the figure in step 3.

In addition to plotting the rules in a scatter plot, `arulesViz` enables you to plot rules in a graph and grouped matrix. Instead of printing all the rules on a single plot, we choose to produce new rules with `soda` on the left-hand side. We then sort the rules by using the lift and visualize the rules in the graph in the figure in step 4. From the graph, every itemset is presented in a vertex and their relationship is presented in an edge. The figure (step 4) shows it is clear that the rule with `soda` on the left-handside to `whole milk` on the right-handside has the maximum support, for the size of the node is greatest. Also, the rule shows that `soda` on the left-hand side to `bottled water` on the right-hand side has the maximum lift as the shade of color in the circle is the darkest. We can then use the same data with `soda` on the left-handside to generate a grouped matrix, which is a balloon plot shown in the figure in step 5, with the left-handside rule as column labels and the right-handside as row labels. Similar to the graph plot in the figure in step 4, the size of the balloon in the figure in step 5 shows the support of the rule, and the color of the balloon shows the lift of the rule.

See also

▶ In this recipe, we introduced three visualization methods to plot association rules. However, `arulesViz` also provides features to plot parallel coordinate plots, double-decker plots, mosaic plots, and other related charts. For those who are interested in how these plots work, you may refer to: Hahsler, M., and Chelluboina, S. (2011). *Visualizing association rules: Introduction to the R-extension package arulesViz. R project module.*

▶ In addition to generating a static plot, you can generate an interactive plot by setting interactive equal to TRUE through the following steps:

```
> plot(rules.pruned,interactive=TRUE)
```

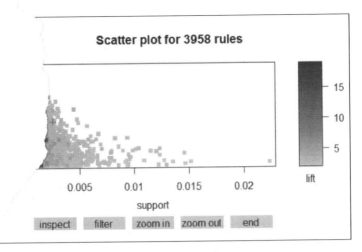

Scatter plot for 3958 rules

The interactive scatter plots

Mining frequent itemsets with Eclat

In addition to the Apriori algorithm, you can use the Eclat algorithm to generate frequent itemsets. As the Apriori algorithm performs a breadth-first search to scan the complete database, the support counting is rather time consuming. Alternatively, if the database fits into the memory, you can use the Eclat algorithm, which performs a depth-first search to count the supports. The Eclat algorithm, therefore, performs quicker than the Apriori algorithm. In this recipe, we introduce how to use the Eclat algorithm to generate frequent itemsets.

Getting ready

In this recipe, we will continue using the dataset Groceries as our input data source.

How to do it...

Perform the following steps to generate a frequent itemset using the Eclat algorithm:

1. Similar to the Apriori method, we can use the eclat function to generate the frequent itemset:

    ```
    > frequentsets=eclat(Groceries,parameter=list(support=0.05,maxl
    en=10))
    ```

2. We can then obtain the summary information from the generated frequent itemset:

    ```
    > summary(frequentsets)
    set of 31 itemsets
    ```

```
most frequent items:
       whole milk other vegetables            yogurt
              4                  2                 2
       rolls/buns          frankfurter        (Other)
              2                  1                23

element (itemset/transaction) length distribution:sizes
  1  2
 28  3

  Min. 1st Qu.  Median   Mean 3rd Qu.   Max.
 1.000   1.000   1.000  1.097   1.000  2.000

summary of quality measures:
    support
 Min.   :0.05236
 1st Qu.:0.05831
 Median :0.07565
 Mean   :0.09212
 3rd Qu.:0.10173
 Max.   :0.25552

includes transaction ID lists: FALSE

mining info:
        data ntransactions support
  Groceries         9835      0.05
```

3. Lastly, we can examine the top ten support frequent itemsets:

```
> inspect(sort(frequentsets,by="support")[1:10])
    items                support
1   {whole milk}        0.25551601
2   {other vegetables}  0.19349263
3   {rolls/buns}        0.18393493
4   {soda}              0.17437722
5   {yogurt}            0.13950178
6   {bottled water}     0.11052364
7   {root vegetables}   0.10899847
8   {tropical fruit}    0.10493137
9   {shopping bags}     0.09852567
10  {sausage}           0.09395018
```

How it works...

In this recipe, we introduce another algorithm, Eclat, to perform frequent itemset generation. Though Apriori is a straightforward and easy to understand association mining method, the algorithm has the disadvantage of generating huge candidate sets and performs inefficiently in support counting, for it takes multiple scans of databases. In contrast to Apriori, Eclat uses equivalence classes, depth-first searches, and set intersections, which greatly improves the speed in support counting.

In Apriori, the algorithm uses a horizontal data layout to store transactions. On the other hand, Eclat uses a vertical data layout to store a list of transaction IDs (`tid`) for each item. Then, Eclat determines the support of any k+1-itemset by intersecting tid-lists of two k-itemsets. Lastly, Eclat utilizes frequent itemsets to generate association rules:

An illustration of Eclat algorithm

Similar to the recipe using the Apriori algorithm, we can use the `eclat` function to generate a frequent itemset with a given support (assume support = 2 in this case) and maximum length.

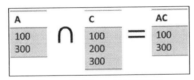

Generating frequent itemset

We can then use the `summary` function to obtain summary statistics, which include: most frequent items, itemset length distributions, summary of quality measures, and mining information. Finally, we can sort frequent itemsets by the support and inspect the top ten support frequent itemsets.

See also

▶ Besides Apriori and Eclat, another popular association mining algorithm is **FP-Growth**. Similar to Eclat, this takes a depth-first search to count supports. However, there is no existing R package that you can download from CRAN that contains this algorithm. However, if you are interested in knowing how to apply the FP-growth algorithm in your transaction dataset, you can refer to Christian Borgelt's page at `http://www.borgelt.net/fpgrowth.html` for more information.

Creating transactions with temporal information

In addition to mining interesting associations within the transaction database, we can mine interesting sequential patterns using transactions with temporal information. In the following recipe, we demonstrate how to create transactions with temporal information.

Getting ready

In this recipe, we will generate transactions with temporal information. We can use the generated transactions as the input source for frequent sequential pattern mining.

How to do it...

Perform the following steps to create transactions with temporal information:

1. First, you need to install and load the package `arulesSequences`:

```
> install.packages("arulesSequences")
> library(arulesSequences)
```

2. You can first create a list with purchasing records:

```
> tmp_data=list(c("A"),
+                c("A","B","C"),
+                c("A","C"),
+                c("D"),
+                c("C","F"),
+                c("A","D"),
+                c("C"),
+                c("B","C"),
+                c("A","E"),
+                c("E","F"),
+                c("A","B"),
+                c("D","F"),
+                c("C"),
+                c("B"),
+                c("E"),
+                c("G"),
+                c("A","F"),
+                c("C"),
+                c("B"),
+                c("C"))
```

3. You can then turn the list into transactions and add temporal information:

```
>names(tmp_data) = paste("Tr",c(1:20), sep = "")
>trans =  as(tmp_data,"transactions")
>transactionInfo(trans)$sequenceID
=c(1,1,1,1,1,2,2,2,2,3,3,3,3,3,4,4,4,4,4,4)
>transactionInfo(trans)$eventID=c(10,20,30,40,50,10,20,30,40,10,20
,30,40,50,10,20,30,40,50,60)
> trans
transactions in sparse format with
 20 transactions (rows) and
 7 items (columns)
```

4. Next, you can use the `inspect` function to inspect the transactions:

```
> inspect(head(trans))
   items transactionID sequenceID eventID
1 {A}              Tr1          1      10
2 {A,
   B,
   C}              Tr2          1      20
3 {A,
   C}              Tr3          1      30
4 {D}              Tr4          1      40
5 {C,
   F}              Tr5          1      50
6 {A,
   D}              Tr6          2      10
```

5. You can then obtain the summary information of the transactions with the temporal information:

```
> summary(trans)
transactions as itemMatrix in sparse format with
 20 rows (elements/itemsets/transactions) and
 7 columns (items) and a density of 0.2214286

most frequent items:
    C       A       B       F       D  (Other)
    8       7       5       4       3       4

element (itemset/transaction) length distribution:
sizes
 1  2  3
10  9  1

    Min. 1st Qu.  Median    Mean 3rd Qu.    Max.
```

```
     1.00      1.00      1.50      1.55      2.00      3.00
```

```
includes extended item information - examples:
   labels
1       A
2       B
3       C
```

```
includes extended transaction information - examples:
   transactionID sequenceID eventID
1              Tr1          1        10
2              Tr2          1        20
3              Tr3          1        30
```

6. You can also read the transaction data in a basket format:

```
> zaki=read_baskets(con = system.file("misc", "zaki.txt", package
= "arulesSequences"), info = c("sequenceID","eventID","SIZE"))
> as(zaki, "data.frame")
```

```
    transactionID.sequenceID transactionID.eventID transactionID.
SIZE      items
```

#	SIZE	items	eventID	transactionID
1	2	{C,D}	1	10
2	3	{A,B,C}	1	15
3	3	{A,B,F}	1	20
4	4	{A,C,D,F}	1	25
5	3	{A,B,F}	2	15
6	1	{E}	2	20
7	3	{A,B,F}	3	10
8	3	{D,G,H}	4	10
9	2	{B,F}	4	20
10	3	{A,G,H}	4	25

How it works...

Before mining frequent sequential patterns, you are required to create transactions with the temporal information. In this recipe, we introduce two methods to obtain transactions with temporal information. In the first method, we create a list of transactions, and assign a transaction ID for each transaction. We use the `as` function to transform the list data into a transaction dataset. We then add `eventID` and `sequenceID` as temporal information; `sequenceID` is the sequence that the event belongs to, and `eventID` indicates when the event occurred. After generating transactions with temporal information, one can use this dataset for frequent sequential pattern mining.

In addition to creating your own transactions with temporal information, if you already have data stored in a text file, you can use the `read_basket` function from `arulesSequences` to read the transaction data into the basket format. We can also read the transaction dataset for further frequent sequential pattern mining.

See also

> ▶ The `arulesSequences` function provides two additional data structures, `sequences` and `timedsequences`, to present pure sequence data and sequence data with the time information. For those who are interested in these two collections, please use the help function to view the following documents:
>
>   > help("sequences-class")
>
>   > help("timedsequences-class")

Mining frequent sequential patterns with cSPADE

In contrast to association mining, which only discovers relationships between itemsets, we may be interested in exploring patterns shared among transactions where a set of itemsets occurs sequentially.

One of the most famous frequent sequential pattern mining algorithms is the **Sequential PAttern Discovery using Equivalence classes (SPADE)** algorithm, which employs the characteristics of a vertical database to perform an intersection on an ID list with an efficient lattice search and allows us to place constraints on mined sequences. In this recipe, we will demonstrate how to use cSPADE to mine frequent sequential patterns.

Getting ready

In this recipe, you have to complete the previous recipes by generating transactions with the temporal information and have it stored in the variable `trans`.

How to do it...

Perform the following steps to mine the frequent sequential patterns:

1. First, you can use the `cspade` function to generate frequent sequential patterns:

```
> s_result=cspade(trans,parameter = list(support = 0.75),control =
list(verbose = TRUE))
```

2. You can then examine the summary of the frequent sequential patterns:

```
> summary(s_result)

set of 14 sequences with
```

most frequent items:

C	A	B	D	E	(Other)
8	5	5	2	1	1

most frequent elements:

{C}	{A}	{B}	{D}	{E}	(Other)
8	5	5	2	1	1

element (sequence) size distribution:

```
sizes
1 2 3
6 6 2
```

sequence length distribution:

```
lengths
1 2 3
6 6 2
```

summary of quality measures:

```
    support
Min.   :0.7500
1st Qu.:0.7500
Median :0.7500
Mean   :0.8393
3rd Qu.:1.0000
```

```
Max.    :1.0000


includes transaction ID lists: FALSE


mining info:
  data ntransactions nsequences support
  trans              20           4    0.75
```

3. Transform a generated sequence format data back to the data frame:

```
> as(s_result, "data.frame")
           sequence support
1            <{A}>    1.00
2            <{B}>    1.00
3            <{C}>    1.00
4            <{D}>    0.75
5            <{E}>    0.75
6            <{F}>    0.75
7        <{A},{C}>    1.00
8        <{B},{C}>    0.75
9        <{C},{C}>    0.75
10       <{D},{C}>    0.75
11   <{A},{C},{C}>    0.75
12       <{A},{B}>    1.00
13       <{C},{B}>    0.75
14   <{A},{C},{B}>    0.75
```

How it works...

The object of sequential pattern mining is to discover sequential relationships or patterns in transactions. You can use the pattern mining result to predict future events, or recommend items to users.

One popular method of sequential pattern mining is SPADE. SPADE uses a vertical data layout to store a list of IDs. In these, each input sequence in the database is called SID, and each event in a given input sequence is called EID. The process of SPADE is performed by generating patterns level-wisely by an Apriori candidate generation. In detail, SPADE generates subsequent n-sequences from joining (n-1)-sequences from the intersection of ID lists. If the number of sequences is greater than the **minimum support** (**minsup**), we can consider the sequence to be frequent enough. The algorithm stops until the process cannot find more frequent sequences:

Database			Frequent Sequences (minsup =2)		
SID	EID	Items	Frequent 1-Sequences		Frequent 3-Sequences
1	100	C D	A	4	ABF	3
1	150	A B C	B	4	BF->A	2
1	200	A B F	D	2	D->BF	2
1	250	A C D F	F	4	D->B->A	2
2	150	A B F	Frequent 2-Sequences		D->F->A	2
2	200	E	AB	3		
3	100	A B F	AF	3	Frequent 4-Sequences	
4	100	D G H	B->A	2	D->BF->A	2
4	200	B F	BF	4		
4	250	A G H	D->A	2		
			D->B	2		
			D->F	2		
			F->A	2		

An illustration of SPADE algorithm

In this recipe, we illustrate how to use a frequent sequential pattern mining algorithm, cSPADE, to mine frequent sequential patterns. First, as we have transactions with temporal information loaded in the variable `trans`, we can use the `cspade` function with the support over 0.75 to generate frequent sequential patterns in the `sequences` format. We can then obtain summary information, such as most frequent items, sequence size distributions, a summary of quality measures, and mining information. Lastly, we can transform the generated `sequence` information back to the data frame format, so we can examine the sequence and support of frequent sequential patterns with the support over 0.75.

See also

▸ If you are interested in the concept and design of the SPADE algorithm, you can refer to the original published paper: M. J. Zaki. (2001). *SPADE: An Efficient Algorithm for Mining Frequent Sequences. Machine Learning Journal*, 42, 31–60.

11
Dimension Reduction

In this chapter, we will cover the following topics:

- ▶ Performing feature selection with FSelector
- ▶ Performing dimension reduction with PCA
- ▶ Determining the number of principal components using a scree test
- ▶ Determining the number of principal components using the Kaiser method
- ▶ Visualizing multivariate data using biplot
- ▶ Performing dimension reduction with MDS
- ▶ Reducing dimensions with SVD
- ▶ Compressing images with SVD
- ▶ Performing nonlinear dimension reduction with ISOMAP
- ▶ Performing nonlinear dimension deduction with Local Linear Embedding

Introduction

Most datasets contain features (such as attributes or variables) that are highly redundant. In order to remove irrelevant and redundant data to reduce the computational cost and avoid overfitting, you can reduce the features into a smaller subset without a significant loss of information. The mathematical procedure of reducing features is known as dimension reduction.

The reduction of features can increase the efficiency of data processing. Dimension reduction is, therefore, widely used in the fields of pattern recognition, text retrieval, and machine learning. Dimension reduction can be divided into two parts: feature extraction and feature selection. Feature extraction is a technique that uses a lower dimension space to represent data in a higher dimension space. Feature selection is used to find a subset of the original variables.

The objective of feature selection is to select a set of relevant features to construct the model. The techniques for feature selection can be categorized into feature ranking and feature selection. Feature ranking ranks features with a certain criteria and then selects features that are above a defined threshold. On the other hand, feature selection searches the optimal subset from a space of feature subsets.

In feature extraction, the problem can be categorized as linear or nonlinear. The linear method searches an affine space that best explains the variation of data distribution. In contrast, the nonlinear method is a better option for data that is distributed on a highly nonlinear curved surface. Here, we list some common linear and nonlinear methods.

Here are some common linear methods:

- **PCA**: Principal component analysis maps data to a lower dimension, so that the variance of the data in a low dimension representation is maximized.

- **MDS**: Multidimensional scaling is a method that allows you to visualize how near (pattern proximities) objects are to each other and can produce a representation of your data with lower dimension space. PCA can be regarded as the simplest form of MDS if the distance measurement used in MDS equals the covariance of data.

- **SVD**: Singular value decomposition removes redundant features that are linear correlated from the perspective of linear algebra. PCA can also be regarded as a specific case of SVD.

Here are some common nonlinear methods:

- **ISOMAP**: ISOMAP can be viewed as an extension of MDS, which uses the distance metric of geodesic distances. In this method, geodesic distance is computed by graphing the shortest path distances.

- **LLE**: Locally linear embedding performs local PCA and global eigen-decomposition. LLE is a local approach, which involves selecting features for each category of the class feature. In contrast, ISOMAP is a global approach, which involves selecting features for all features.

In this chapter, we will first discuss how to perform feature ranking and selection. Next, we will focus on the topic of feature extraction and cover recipes in performing dimension reduction with both linear and nonlinear methods. For linear methods, we will introduce how to perform PCA, determine the number of principal components, and its visualization. We then move on to MDS and SVD. Furthermore, we will introduce the application of SVD to compress images. For nonlinear methods, we will introduce how to perform dimension reduction with ISOMAP and LLE.

Performing feature selection with FSelector

The `FSelector` package provides two approaches to select the most influential features from the original feature set. Firstly, rank features by some criteria and select the ones that are above a defined threshold. Secondly, search for optimum feature subsets from a space of feature subsets. In this recipe, we will introduce how to perform feature selection with the `FSelector` package.

Getting ready

In this recipe, we will continue to use the telecom `churn` dataset as the input data source to train the support vector machine. For those who have not prepared the dataset, please refer to *Chapter 5, Classification (I) – Tree, Lazy, and Probabilistic*, for detailed information.

How to do it...

Perform the following steps to perform feature selection on a `churn` dataset:

1. First, install and load the package, `FSelector`:

   ```
   > install.packages("FSelector")
   > library(FSelector)
   ```

2. Then, we can use `random.forest.importance` to calculate the weight for each attribute, where we set the importance type to 1:

   ```
   > weights = random.forest.importance(churn~., trainset,
   importance.type = 1)
   > print(weights)
                               attr_importance
   international_plan             96.3255882
   voice_mail_plan               24.8921239
   number_vmail_messages         31.5420332
   total_day_minutes             51.9365357
   total_day_calls               -0.1766420
   total_day_charge              53.7930096
   total_eve_minutes             33.2006078
   total_eve_calls               -2.2270323
   total_eve_charge              32.4317375
   total_night_minutes           22.0888120
   total_night_calls              0.3407087
   total_night_charge            21.6368855
   ```

total_intl_minutes	32.4984413
total_intl_calls	51.1154046
total_intl_charge	32.4855194
number_customer_service_calls	114.2566676

3. Next, we can use the `cutoff` function to obtain the attributes of the top five weights:

```
> subset = cutoff.k(weights, 5)
> f = as.simple.formula(subset, "Class")
> print(f)
Class ~ number_customer_service_calls + international_plan +
    total_day_charge + total_day_minutes + total_intl_calls
<environment: 0x00000000269a28e8>
```

4. Next, we can make an evaluator to select the feature subsets:

```
> evaluator = function(subset) {
+    k = 5
+    set.seed(2)
+    ind = sample(5, nrow(trainset), replace = TRUE)
+    results = sapply(1:k, function(i) {
+      train = trainset[ind ==i,]
+      test  = trainset[ind !=i,]
+      tree  = rpart(as.simple.formula(subset, "churn"), trainset)
+      error.rate = sum(test$churn != predict(tree, test,
type="class")) / nrow(test)
+      return(1 - error.rate)
+    })
+    return(mean(results))
+ }
```

5. Finally, we can find the optimum feature subset using a hill climbing search:

```
> attr.subset = hill.climbing.search(names(trainset)
[!names(trainset) %in% "churn"], evaluator)
> f = as.simple.formula(attr.subset, "churn")
> print(f)
churn ~ international_plan + voice_mail_plan + number_vmail_
messages +
    total_day_minutes + total_day_calls + total_eve_minutes +
```

```
total_eve_charge + total_intl_minutes + total_intl_calls +
total_intl_charge + number_customer_service_calls
<environment: 0x000000002224d3d0>
```

How it works...

In this recipe, we present how to use the `FSelector` package to select the most influential features. We first demonstrate how to use the feature ranking approach. In the feature ranking approach, the algorithm first employs a weight function to generate weights for each feature. Here, we use the random forest algorithm with the mean decrease in accuracy (where `importance.type = 1`) as the importance measurement to gain the weights of each attribute. Besides the random forest algorithm, you can select other feature ranking algorithms (for example, `chi.squared`, `information.gain`) from the `FSelector` package. Then, the process sorts attributes by their weight. At last, we can obtain the top five features from the sorted feature list with the `cutoff` function. In this case, `number_customer_service_calls`, `international_plan`, `total_day_charge`, `total_day_minutes`, and `total_intl_calls` are the five most important features.

Next, we illustrate how to search for optimum feature subsets. First, we need to make a five-fold cross-validation function to evaluate the importance of feature subsets. Then, we use the hill climbing searching algorithm to find the optimum feature subsets from the original feature sets. Besides the hill-climbing method, one can select other feature selection algorithms (for example, `forward.search`) from the `FSelector` package. Lastly, we can find that `international_plan + voice_mail_plan + number_vmail_messages + total_day_minutes + total_day_calls + total_eve_minutes + total_eve_charge + total_intl_minutes + total_intl_calls + total_intl_charge + number_customer_service_calls` are optimum feature subsets.

See also

▶ You can also use the `caret` package to perform feature selection. As we have discussed related recipes in the model assessment chapter, you can refer to *Chapter 7, Model Evaluation*, for more detailed information.

▶ For both feature ranking and optimum feature selection, you can explore the package, `FSelector`, for more related functions:

```
> help(package="FSelector")
```

Performing dimension reduction with PCA

Principal component analysis (**PCA**) is the most widely used linear method in dealing with dimension reduction problems. It is useful when data contains many features, and there is redundancy (correlation) within these features. To remove redundant features, PCA maps high dimension data into lower dimensions by reducing features into a smaller number of principal components that account for most of the variance of the original features. In this recipe, we will introduce how to perform dimension reduction with the PCA method.

Getting ready

In this recipe, we will use the `swiss` dataset as our target to perform PCA. The `swiss` dataset includes standardized fertility measures and socio-economic indicators from around the year 1888 for each of the 47 French-speaking provinces of Switzerland.

How to do it...

Perform the following steps to perform principal component analysis on the `swiss` dataset:

1. First, load the `swiss` dataset:

   ```
   > data(swiss)
   ```

2. Exclude the first column of the `swiss` data:

   ```
   > swiss = swiss[,-1]
   ```

3. You can then perform principal component analysis on the `swiss` data:

   ```
   > swiss.pca = prcomp(swiss,
   + center = TRUE,
   + scale  = TRUE)
   > swiss.pca
   Standard deviations:
   [1] 1.6228065 1.0354873 0.9033447 0.5592765 0.4067472


   Rotation:
                      PC1          PC2          PC3          PC4
   PC5
   Agriculture        0.52396452  -0.25834215   0.003003672  -0.8090741
   0.06411415
   Examination       -0.57185792  -0.01145981  -0.039840522  -0.4224580
   -0.70198942
   ```

```
Education          -0.49150243  0.19028476  0.539337412 -0.3321615
0.56656945

Catholic                       0.38530580  0.36956307  0.725888143 0.1007965
-0.42176895

Infant.Mortality 0.09167606 0.87197641 -0.424976789 -0.2154928
0.06488642
```

4. Obtain a summary from the PCA results:

   ```
   > summary(swiss.pca)
   Importance of components:
                           PC1    PC2    PC3    PC4     PC5
   Standard deviation     1.6228 1.0355 0.9033 0.55928 0.40675
   Proportion of Variance 0.5267 0.2145 0.1632 0.06256 0.03309
   Cumulative Proportion  0.5267 0.7411 0.9043 0.96691 1.00000
   ```

5. Lastly, you can use the `predict` function to output the value of the principal component with the first row of data:

   ```
   > predict(swiss.pca, newdata=head(swiss, 1))
                     PC1        PC2        PC3      PC4       PC5
   Courtelary -0.9390479 0.8047122 -0.8118681 1.000307 0.4618643
   ```

How it works...

Since the feature selection method may remove some correlated but informative features, you have to consider combining these correlated features into a single feature with the feature extraction method. PCA is one of the feature extraction methods, which performs orthogonal transformation to convert possibly correlated variables into principal components. Also, you can use these principal components to identify the directions of variance.

The process of PCA is carried on by the following steps: firstly, find the mean vector, $\mu = \frac{1}{n}\sum_{i=1}^{n}x_i$, where x_i indicates the data point, and n denotes the number of points. Secondly, compute the covariance matrix by the equation, $C = \frac{1}{n}\sum_{i=1}^{n}(x_i - \mu)(x_i - \mu)^T$. Thirdly, compute the eigenvectors, $\wp$, and the corresponding eigenvalues. In the fourth step, we rank and choose the top k eigenvectors. In the fifth step, we construct a $d \times k$ dimensional eigenvector matrix, U. Here, d is the number of original dimensions and k is the number of eigenvectors. Finally, we can transform data samples to a new subspace in the equation, $y = U^T \cdot x$.

In the following figure, it is illustrated that we can use two principal components, φ_1, and φ_2, to transform the data point from a two-dimensional space to new two-dimensional subspace:

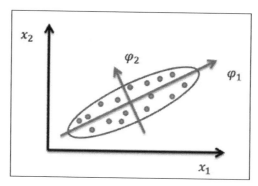

A sample illustration of PCA

In this recipe we use the prcomp function from the stats package to perform PCA on the swiss dataset. First, we remove the standardized fertility measures and use the rest of the predictors as input to the function, prcomp. In addition to this, we set swiss as an input dataset; the variable should be shifted to the zero center by specifying center=TRUE; scale variables into the unit variance with the option, scale=TRUE, and store the output in the variable, swiss.pca.

Then, as we print out the value stored in swiss.pca, we can find the standard deviation and rotation of the principal component. The standard deviation indicates the square root of the eigenvalues of the covariance/correlation matrix. On the other hand, the rotation of the principal components shows the coefficient of the linear combination of the input features. For example, PC1 equals *Agriculture * 0.524 + Examination * -0.572 + Education * -0.492 + Catholic* 0.385 + Infant.Mortality * 0.092*. Here, we can find that the attribute, *Agriculture*, contributes the most for PC1, for it has the highest coefficient.

Additionally, we can use the summary function to obtain the importance of components. The first row shows the standard deviation of each principal component, the second row shows the proportion of variance explained by each component, and the third row shows the cumulative proportion of the explained variance. Finally, you can use the predict function to obtain principal components from the input features. Here, we input the first row of the dataset, and retrieve five principal components.

There's more...

Another principal component analysis function is princomp. In this function, the calculation is performed by using eigen on a correlation or covariance matrix instead of a single value decomposition used in the prcomp function. In general practice, using prcomp is preferable; however, we cover how to use princomp here:

1. First, use `princomp` to perform PCA:

```
> swiss.princomp = princomp(swiss,
+ center = TRUE,
+ scale  = TRUE)
> swiss.princomp
Call:
princomp(x = swiss, center = TRUE, scale = TRUE)


Standard deviations:
    Comp.1     Comp.2    Comp.3     Comp.4     Comp.5
42.896335 21.201887  7.587978  3.687888   2.721105


 5 variables and 47 observations.
```

2. You can then obtain the summary information:

```
> summary(swiss.princomp)
Importance of components:
                              Comp.1      Comp.2     Comp.3
Comp.4        Comp.5
Standard deviation       42.8963346 21.2018868 7.58797830
3.687888330 2.721104713
Proportion of Variance  0.7770024   0.1898152 0.02431275
0.005742983 0.003126601
Cumulative Proportion    0.7770024   0.9668177 0.99113042
0.996873399 1.000000000
```

3. You can use the `predict` function to obtain principal components from the input features:

```
> predict(swiss.princomp, swiss[1,])
                Comp.1      Comp.2    Comp.3    Comp.4     Comp.5
Courtelary  -38.95923   -20.40504  12.45808  4.713234  -1.46634
```

In addition to the `prcomp` and `princomp` functions from the `stats` package, you can use the `principal` function from the `psych` package:

1. First, install and load the `psych` package:

```
> install.packages("psych")
> install.packages("GPArotation")
> library(psych)
```

2. You can then use the `principal` function to retrieve the principal components:

```
> swiss.principal = principal(swiss, nfactors=5, rotate="none")
> swiss.principal
Principal Components Analysis
Call: principal(r = swiss, nfactors = 5, rotate = "none")
Standardized loadings (pattern matrix) based upon correlation
matrix
```

	PC1	PC2	PC3	PC4	PC5	h2	u2
Agriculture	-0.85	-0.27	0.00	0.45	-0.03	1	-6.7e-16
Examination	0.93	-0.01	-0.04	0.24	0.29	1	4.4e-16
Education	0.80	0.20	0.49	0.19	-0.23	1	2.2e-16
Catholic	-0.63	0.38	0.66	-0.06	0.17	1	-2.2e-16
Infant.Mortality	-0.15	0.90	-0.38	0.12	-0.03	1	-8.9e-16

	PC1	PC2	PC3	PC4	PC5
SS loadings	2.63	1.07	0.82	0.31	0.17
Proportion Var	0.53	0.21	0.16	0.06	0.03
Cumulative Var	0.53	0.74	0.90	0.97	1.00
Proportion Explained	0.53	0.21	0.16	0.06	0.03
Cumulative Proportion	0.53	0.74	0.90	0.97	1.00

```
Test of the hypothesis that 5 components are sufficient.


The degrees of freedom for the null model are 10 and the objective
function was 2.13
The degrees of freedom for the model are -5  and the objective
function was  0
The total number of observations was  47  with MLE Chi Square =  0
with prob <  NA


Fit based upon off diagonal values = 1
```

Determining the number of principal components using the scree test

As we only need to retain the principal components that account for most of the variance of the original features, we can either use the Kaiser method, scree test, or the percentage of variation explained as the selection criteria. The main purpose of a scree test is to graph the component analysis results as a scree plot and find where the obvious change in the slope (elbow) occurs. In this recipe, we will demonstrate how to determine the number of principal components using a scree plot.

Getting ready

Ensure that you have completed the previous recipe by generating a principal component object and save it in the variable, `swiss.pca`.

How to do it...

Perform the following steps to determine the number of principal components with the scree plot:

1. First, you can generate a bar plot by using `screeplot`:

   ```
   > screeplot(swiss.pca, type="barplot")
   ```

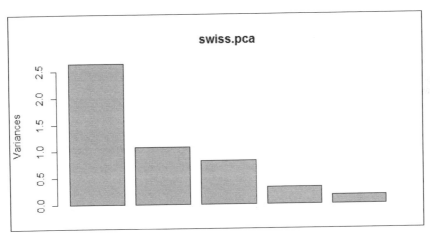

The scree plot in bar plot form

2. You can also generate a line plot by using `screeplot`:

```
> screeplot(swiss.pca, type="line")
```

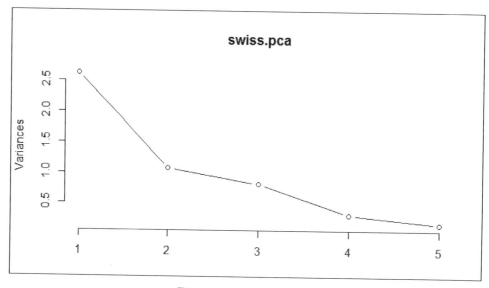

The scree plot in line plot form

How it works...

In this recipe, we demonstrate how to use a scree plot to determine the number of principal components. In a scree plot, there are two types of plots, namely, bar plots and line plots. As both generated scree plots reveal, the obvious change in slope (the so-called elbow or knee) occurs at component 2. As a result, we should retain component 1, where the component is in a steep curve before component 2, which is where the flat line trend commences. However, as this method can be ambiguous, you can use other methods (such as the Kaiser method) to determine the number of components.

There's more...

By default, if you use the `plot` function on a generated principal component object, you can also retrieve the scree plot. For more details on `screeplot`, please refer to the following document:

```
> help(screeplot)
```

You can also use `nfactors` to perform parallel analysis and nongraphical solutions to the Cattell scree test:

```
> install.packages("nFactors")
> library(nFactors)
> ev = eigen(cor(swiss))
> ap = parallel(subject=nrow(swiss),var=ncol(swiss),rep=100,cent=.05)
> nS = nScree(x=ev$values, aparallel=ap$eigen$qevpea)
> plotnScree(nS)
```

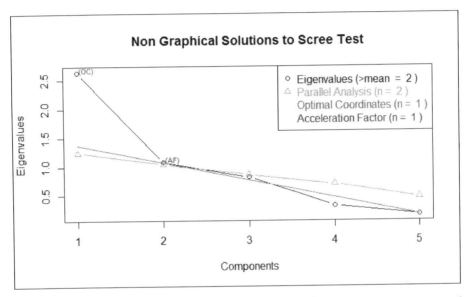

Non-graphical solution to scree test

Determining the number of principal components using the Kaiser method

In addition to the scree test, you can use the Kaiser method to determine the number of principal components. In this method, the selection criteria retains eigenvalues greater than 1. In this recipe, we will demonstrate how to determine the number of principal components using the Kaiser method.

Getting ready

Ensure that you have completed the previous recipe by generating a principal component object and save it in the variable, `swiss.pca`.

How to do it...

Perform the following steps to determine the number of principal components with the Kaiser method:

1. First, you can obtain the standard deviation from `swiss.pca`:

   ```
   > swiss.pca$sdev
   [1] 1.6228065 1.0354873 0.9033447 0.5592765 0.4067472
   ```

2. Next, you can obtain the variance from `swiss.pca`:

   ```
   > swiss.pca$sdev ^ 2
   [1] 2.6335008 1.0722340 0.8160316 0.3127902 0.1654433
   ```

3. Select components with a variance above 1:

   ```
   > which(swiss.pca$sdev ^ 2> 1)
   [1] 1 2
   ```

4. You can also use the scree plot to select components with a variance above 1:

   ```
   > screeplot(swiss.pca, type="line")
   > abline(h=1, col="red", lty= 3)
   ```

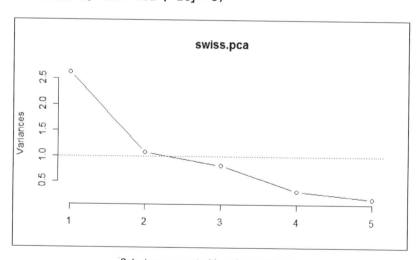

Select component with variance above 1

How it works...

You can also use the Kaiser method to determine the number of components. As the computed principal component object contains the standard deviation of each component, we can compute the variance as the standard deviation, which is the square root of variance. From the computed variance, we find both component 1 and 2 have a variance above 1. Therefore, we can determine the number of principal components as 2 (both component 1 and 2). Also, we can draw a red line on the scree plot (as shown in the preceding figure) to indicate that we need to retain component 1 and 2 in this case.

See also

In order to determine which principal components to retain, please refer to:

> ▸ Ledesma, R. D., and Valero-Mora, P. (2007). *Determining the Number of Factors to Retain in EFA: an easy-to-use computer program for carrying out Parallel Analysis. Practical Assessment, Research & Evaluation*, 12(2), 1-11.

Visualizing multivariate data using biplot

In order to find out how data and variables are mapped in regard to the principal component, you can use `biplot`, which plots data and the projections of original features on to the first two components. In this recipe, we will demonstrate how to use `biplot` to plot both variables and data on the same figure.

Getting ready

Ensure that you have completed the previous recipe by generating a principal component object and save it in the variable, `swiss.pca`.

How to do it...

Perform the following steps to create a biplot:

1. You can create a scatter plot using component 1 and 2:

```
> plot(swiss.pca$x[,1], swiss.pca$x[,2], xlim=c(-4,4))
> text(swiss.pca$x[,1], swiss.pca$x[,2], rownames(swiss.pca$x),
cex=0.7, pos=4, col="red")
```

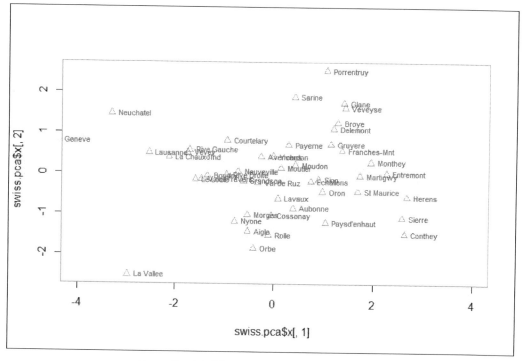

The scatter plot of first two components from PCA result

2. If you would like to add features on the plot, you can create biplot using the generated principal component object:

```
> biplot(swiss.pca)
```

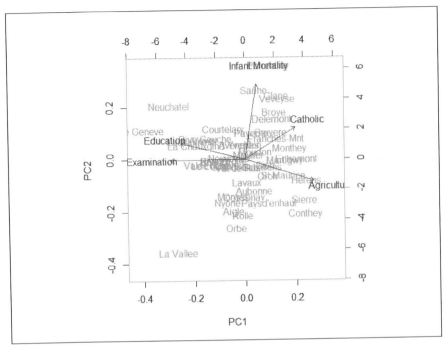

The biplot using PCA result

How it works...

In this recipe, we demonstrate how to use `biplot` to plot data and projections of original features on to the first two components. In the first step, we demonstrate that we can actually use the first two components to create a scatter plot. Furthermore, if you want to add variables on the same plot, you can use `biplot`. In `biplot`, you can see the provinces with higher indicators in the agriculture variable, lower indicators in the education variable, and examination variables scores that are higher in PC1. On the other hand, the provinces with higher infant mortality indicators and lower agriculture indicators score higher in PC2.

There's more...

Besides `biplot` in the `stats` package, you can also use `ggbiplot`. However, you may not find this package from CRAN; you have to first install `devtools` and then install `ggbiplot` from GitHub:

```
> install.packages("devtools")
```

```
> library(ggbiplot)
> g = ggbiplot(swiss.pca, obs.scale = 1, var.scale = 1,
+ ellipse = TRUE,
+ circle = TRUE)
> print(g)
```

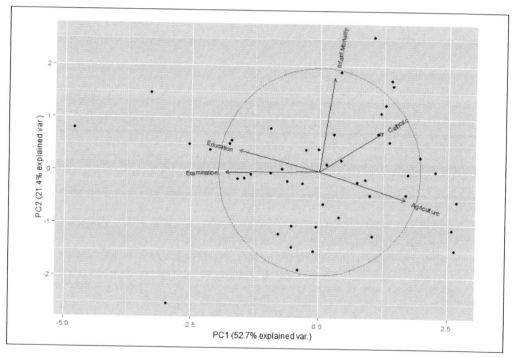

The ggbiplot using PCA result

Performing dimension reduction with MDS

Multidimensional scaling (**MDS**) is a technique to create a visual presentation of similarities or dissimilarities (distance) of a number of objects. The *multi* prefix indicates that one can create a presentation map in one, two, or more dimensions. However, we most often use MDS to present the distance between data points in one or two dimensions.

In MDS, you can either use a metric or a nonmetric solution. The main difference between the two solutions is that metric solutions try to reproduce the original metric, while nonmetric solutions assume that the ranks of the distance are known. In this recipe, we will illustrate how to perform MDS on the `swiss` dataset.

Getting ready

In this recipe, we will continue using the `swiss` dataset as our input data source.

How to do it...

Perform the following steps to perform multidimensional scaling using the metric method:

1. First, you can perform metric MDS with a maximum of two dimensions:

   ```
   > swiss.dist =dist(swiss)
   > swiss.mds = cmdscale(swiss.dist, k=2)
   ```

2. You can then plot the `swiss` data in a two-dimension scatter plot:

   ```
   > plot(swiss.mds[,1], swiss.mds[,2], type = "n", main = "cmdscale
   (stats)")
   > text(swiss.mds[,1], swiss.mds[,2], rownames(swiss), cex = 0.9,
   xpd = TRUE)
   ```

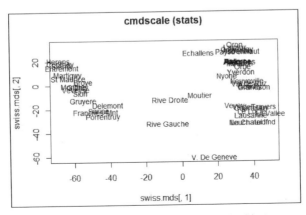

The 2-dimension scatter plot from cmdscale object

3. In addition, you can perform nonmetric MDS with `isoMDS`:

```
> library(MASS)
> swiss.nmmds = isoMDS(swiss.dist, k=2)
initial   value 2.979731
iter    5 value 2.431486
iter   10 value 2.343353
final   value 2.338839
converged
```

4. You can also plot the data points in a two-dimension scatter plot:

```
> plot(swiss.nmmds$points, type = "n", main = "isoMDS (MASS)")
> text(swiss.nmmds$points, rownames(swiss), cex = 0.9, xpd = TRUE)
```

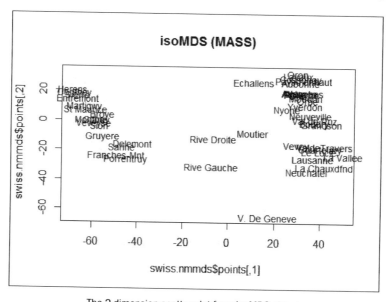

The 2-dimension scatter plot from isoMDS object

5. You can then plot the data points in a two-dimension scatter plot:

```
> swiss.sh = Shepard(swiss.dist, swiss.mds)
> plot(swiss.sh, pch = ".")
> lines(swiss.sh$x, swiss.sh$yf, type = "S")
```

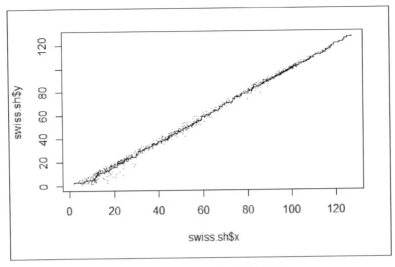

The Shepard plot from isoMDS object

How it works...

MDS reveals the structure of the data by providing a visual presentation of similarities among a set of objects. In more detail, MDS places an object in an n-dimensional space, where the distances between pairs of points corresponds to the similarities among the pairs of objects. Usually, the dimensional space is a two-dimensional Euclidean space, but it may be non-Euclidean and have more than two dimensions. In accordance with the meaning of the input matrix, MDS can be mainly categorized into two types: metric MDS, where the input matrix is metric-based, nonmetric MDS, where the input matrix is nonmetric-based.

Metric MDS is also known as principal coordinate analysis, which first transforms a distance into similarities. In the simplest form, the process linearly projects original data points to a subspace by performing principal components analysis on similarities. On the other hand, the process can also perform a nonlinear projection on similarities by minimizing the stress value, $S = \sum_{k \neq l} \left[d(k,l) - d'(k,l) \right]^2$, where $d(k,l)$ is the distance measurement between the two points, x_k and x_l, and $d'(k,l)$ is the similarity measure of two projected points, x'_k and x'_l. As a result, we can represent the relationship among objects in the Euclidean space.

In contrast to metric MDS, which use a metric-based input matrix, a nonmetric-based MDS is used when the data is measured at the ordinal level. As only the rank order of the distances between the vectors is meaningful, nonmetric MDS applies a monotonically increasing function, f, on the original distances and projects the distance to new values that preserve the rank order. The normalized equation can be formulated as

$$S = \frac{1}{\sum_{k \neq l} \left[d'(k,l) \right]^2} \sum_{k \neq l} \left[f(d(k,l)) - d'(k,l) \right]^2 .$$

In this recipe, we illustrate how to perform metric and nonmetric MDS on the `swiss` dataset. To perform metric MDS, we first need to obtain the distance metric from the `swiss` data. In this step, you can replace the distance measure to any measure as long as it produces a similarity/dissimilarity measure of data points. You can use `cmdscale` to perform metric multidimensional scaling. Here, we specify k = 2, so the maximum generated dimensions equals 2. You can also visually present the distance of the data points on a two-dimensional scatter plot.

Next, you can perform nonmetric MDS with `isoMDS`. In nonmetric MDS, we do not match the distances, but only arrange them in order. We also set `swiss` as an input dataset with maximum dimensions of two. Similar to the metric MDS example, we can plot the distance between data points on a two-dimensional scatter plot. Then, we use a Shepard plot, which shows how well the projected distances match those in the distance matrix. As per the figure in step 4, the projected distance matches well in the distance matrix.

There's more...

Another visualization method is to present an MDS object as a graph. A sample code is listed here:

```
> library(igraph)
> swiss.sample = swiss[1:10,]

> g = graph.full(nrow(swiss.sample))
> V(g)$label = rownames(swiss.sample)
> layout = layout.mds(g, dist = as.matrix(dist(swiss.sample)))
> plot(g, layout = layout, vertex.size = 3)
```

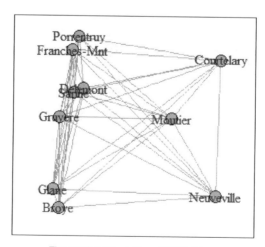

The graph presentation of MDS object

You can also compare differences between the generated results from MDS and PCA. You can compare their differences by drawing the projected dimensions on the same scatter plot. If you use a Euclidean distance on MDS, the projected dimensions are exactly the same as the ones projected from PCA:

```
> swiss.dist = dist(swiss)
> swiss.mds = cmdscale(swiss.dist, k=2)
> plot(swiss.mds[,1], swiss.mds[,2], type="n")
> text(swiss.mds[,1], swiss.mds[,2], rownames(swiss), cex = 0.9, xpd = TRUE)
> swiss.pca = prcomp(swiss)
> text(-swiss.pca$x[,1],-swiss.pca$x[,2], rownames(swiss),
+       ,col="blue", adj = c(0.2,-0.5),cex = 0.9, xpd = TRUE)
```

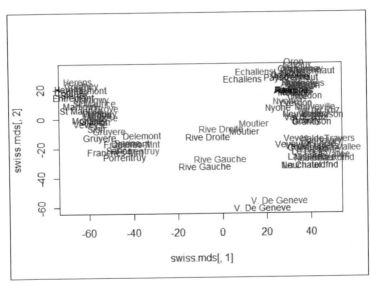

The comparison between MDS and PCA

Reducing dimensions with SVD

Singular value decomposition (**SVD**) is a type of matrix factorization (decomposition), which can factorize matrices into two orthogonal matrices and diagonal matrices. You can multiply the original matrix back using these three matrices. SVD can reduce redundant data that is linear dependent from the perspective of linear algebra. Therefore, it can be applied to feature selection, image processing, clustering, and many other fields. In this recipe, we will illustrate how to perform dimension reduction with SVD.

Getting ready

In this recipe, we will continue using the dataset, `swiss`, as our input data source.

How to do it...

Perform the following steps to perform dimension reduction using SVD:

1. First, you can perform `svd` on the `swiss` dataset:

   ```
   > swiss.svd = svd(swiss)
   ```

2. You can then plot the percentage of variance explained and the cumulative variance explained in accordance with the SVD column:

   ```
   > plot(swiss.svd$d^2/sum(swiss.svd$d^2), type="l", xlab=" Singular
   vector", ylab = "Variance explained")
   ```

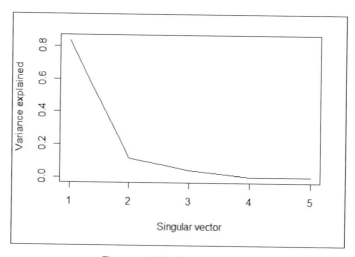

The percent of variance explained

   ```
   > plot(cumsum(swiss.svd$d^2/sum(swiss.svd$d^2)), type="l",
   xlab="Singular vector", ylab = "Cumulative percent of variance
   explained")
   ```

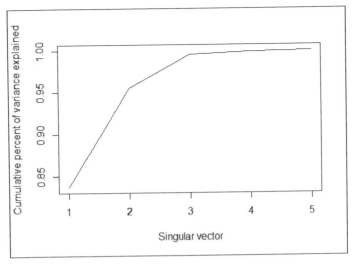

Cumulative percent of variance explained

3. Next, you can reconstruct the data with only one singular vector:

    ```
    > swiss.recon = swiss.svd$u[,1] %*% diag(swiss.svd$d[1],
    length(1), length(1)) %*% t(swiss.svd$v[,1])
    ```

4. Lastly, you can compare the original dataset with the constructed dataset in an image:

    ```
    > par(mfrow=c(1,2))
    ```
    ```
    > image(as.matrix(swiss), main="swiss data Image")
    ```
    ```
    > image(swiss.recon,  main="Reconstructed Image")
    ```

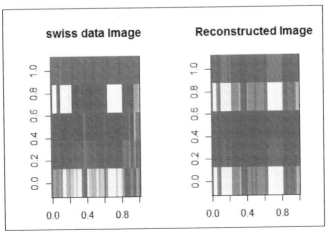

The comparison between original dataset and re-constructed dataset

How it works...

SVD is a factorization of a real or complex matrix. In detail, the SVD of m x n matrix, A, is the factorization of A into the product of three matrices, $A = UDV^T$. Here, U is an m x m orthonormal matrix, D has singular values and is an m x n diagonal matrix, and V^T is an n x n orthonormal matrix.

In this recipe, we demonstrate how to perform dimension reduction with SVD. First, you can apply the `svd` function on the `swiss` dataset to obtain factorized matrices. You can then generate two plots: one shows the variance explained in accordance to a singular vector, the other shows the cumulative variance explained in accordance to a singular vector.

The preceding figure shows that the first singular vector can explain 80 percent of variance. We now want to compare the differences from the original dataset and the reconstructed dataset with a single singular vector. We, therefore, reconstruct the data with a single singular vector and use the `image` function to present the original and reconstructed datasets side-by-side and see how they differ from each other. The next figure reveals that these two images are very similar.

See also

▸ As we mentioned earlier, PCA can be regarded as a specific case of SVD. Here, we generate the orthogonal vector from the `swiss` data from SVD and obtained the rotation from `prcomp`. We can see that the two generated matrices are the same:

```
> svd.m = svd(scale(swiss))
> svd.m$v
```

```
            [,1]        [,2]         [,3]        [,4]        [,5]
[1,]  0.52396452 -0.25834215  0.003003672 -0.8090741  0.06411415
[2,] -0.57185792 -0.01145981 -0.039840522 -0.4224580 -0.70198942
[3,] -0.49150243  0.19028476  0.539337412 -0.3321615  0.56656945
[4,]  0.38530580  0.36956307  0.725888143  0.1007965 -0.42176895
[5,]  0.09167606  0.87197641 -0.424976789 -0.2154928  0.06488642
```

```
> pca.m = prcomp(swiss,scale=TRUE)
> pca.m$rotation
```

```
                     PC1         PC2          PC3         PC4
PC5
Agriculture    0.52396452 -0.25834215  0.003003672 -0.8090741
0.06411415

Examination   -0.57185792 -0.01145981 -0.039840522 -0.4224580
-0.70198942
```

| Education | -0.49150243 | 0.19028476 | 0.539337412 | -0.3321615 |
| 0.56656945 | | | | |

| Catholic | 0.38530580 | 0.36956307 | 0.725888143 | 0.1007965 |
| -0.42176895 | | | | |

Infant.Mortality 0.09167606 0.87197641 -0.424976789 -0.2154928
0.06488642

Compressing images with SVD

In the previous recipe, we demonstrated how to factorize a matrix with SVD and then reconstruct the dataset by multiplying the decomposed matrix. Furthermore, the application of matrix factorization can be applied to image compression. In this recipe, we will demonstrate how to perform SVD on the classic image processing material, Lenna.

Getting ready

In this recipe, you should download the image of Lenna beforehand (refer to `http://www.ece.rice.edu/~wakin/images/lena512.bmp` for this), or you can prepare an image of your own to see how image compression works.

How to do it...

Perform the following steps to compress an image with SVD:

1. First, install and load `bmp`:

   ```
   > install.packages("bmp")
   ```
   ```
   > library(bmp)
   ```

2. You can then read the image of Lenna as a numeric matrix with the `read.bmp` function. When the reader downloads the image, the default name is `lena512.bmp`:

   ```
   > lenna = read.bmp("lena512.bmp")
   ```

3. Rotate and plot the image:

```
> lenna = t(lenna)[,nrow(lenna):1]
> image(lenna)
```

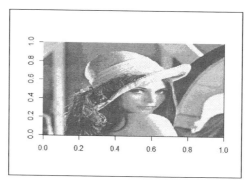

The picture of Lenna

4. Next, you can perform SVD on the read numeric matrix and plot the percentage of variance explained:

```
> lenna.svd = svd(scale(lenna))
> plot(lenna.svd$d^2/sum(lenna.svd$d^2), type="l", xlab=" Singular vector", ylab = "Variance explained")
```

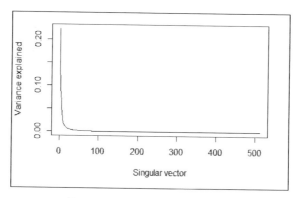

The percentage of variance explained

5. Next, you can obtain the number of dimensions to reconstruct the image:

```
> length(lenna.svd$d)
[1]  512
```

6. Obtain the point at which the singular vector can explain more than 90 percent of the variance:

```
> min(which(cumsum(lenna.svd$d^2/sum(lenna.svd$d^2))> 0.9))
[1]  18
```

7. You can also wrap the code into a function, `lenna_compression`, and you can then use this function to plot compressed Lenna:

```
> lenna_compression = function(dim){
+      u=as.matrix(lenna.svd$u[, 1:dim])
+      v=as.matrix(lenna.svd$v[, 1:dim])
+      d=as.matrix(diag(lenna.svd$d)[1:dim, 1:dim])
+      image(u%*%d%*%t(v))
+ }
```

8. Also, you can use 18 vectors to reconstruct the image:

```
> lenna_compression(18)
```

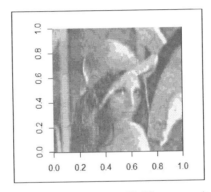

The reconstructed image with 18 components

9. You can obtain the point at which the singular vector can explain more than 99 percent of the variance;

```
> min(which(cumsum(lenna.svd$d^2/sum(lenna.svd$d^2))> 0.99))
[1] 92
> lenna_compression(92)
```

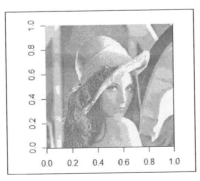

The reconstructed image with 92 components

How it works...

In this recipe, we demonstrate how to compress an image with SVD. In the first step, we use the package, `bmp`, to load the image, Lenna, to an R session. Then, as the read image is rotated, we can rotate the image back and use the `plot` function to plot Lenna in R (as shown in the figure in step 3). Next, we perform SVD on the image matrix to factorize the matrix. We then plot the percentage of variance explained in regard to the number of singular vectors.

Further, as we discover that we can use 18 components to explain 90 percent of the variance, we then use these 18 components to reconstruct Lenna. Thus, we make a function named `lenna_compression` with the purpose of reconstructing the image by matrix multiplication. As a result, we enter 18 as the input to the function, which returns a rather blurry Lenna image (as shown in the figure in step 8). However, we can at least see an outline of the image. To obtain a clearer picture, we discover that we can use 92 components to explain 99 percent of the variance. We, therefore, set the input to the function, `lenna_compression`, as 92. The figure in step 9 shows that this generates a clearer picture than the one constructed using merely 18 components.

See also

▶   The Lenna picture is one of the most widely used standard test images for compression algorithms. For more details on the Lenna picture, please refer to http://www.cs.cmu.edu/~chuck/lennapg/.

Performing nonlinear dimension reduction with ISOMAP

ISOMAP is one of the approaches for manifold learning, which generalizes linear framework to nonlinear data structures. Similar to MDS, ISOMAP creates a visual presentation of similarities or dissimilarities (distance) of a number of objects. However, as the data is structured in a nonlinear format, the Euclidian distance measure of MDS is replaced by the geodesic distance of a data manifold in ISOMAP. In this recipe, we will illustrate how to perform a nonlinear dimension reduction with ISOMAP.

Getting ready

In this recipe, we will use the `digits` data from `RnavGraphImageData` as our input source.

How to do it...

Perform the following steps to perform nonlinear dimension reduction with ISOMAP:

1. First, install and load the `RnavGraphImageData` and `vegan` packages:

   ```
   > install.packages("RnavGraphImageData")
   > install.packages("vegan")
   > library(RnavGraphImageData)
   > library(vegan)
   ```

2. You can then load the dataset, `digits`:

   ```
   > data(digits)
   ```

3. Rotate and plot the image:

   ```
   > sample.digit = matrix(digits[,3000],ncol = 16, byrow=FALSE)
   > image(t(sample.digit)[,nrow(sample.digit):1])
   ```

   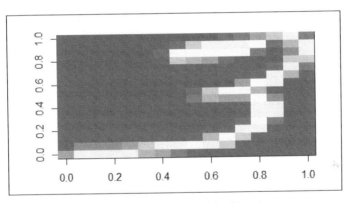

   A sample image from the digits dataset

4. Next, you can randomly sample 300 digits from the population:

   ```
   > set.seed(2)
   > digit.idx = sample(1:ncol(digits),size = 600)
   > digit.select = digits[,digit.idx]
   ```

5. Transpose the selected digit data and then compute the dissimilarity between objects using `vegdist`:

   ```
   > digits.Transpose = t(digit.select)
   > digit.dist = vegdist(digits.Transpose, method="euclidean")
   ```

6. Next, you can use `isomap` to perform dimension reduction:

```
> digit.isomap = isomap(digit.dist,k = 8, ndim=6, fragmentedOK =
TRUE)

> plot(digit.isomap)
```

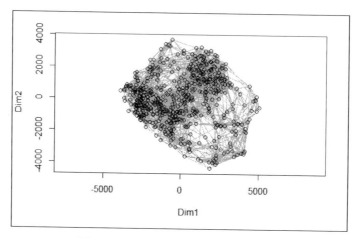

A 2-dimension scatter plot from ISOMAP object

7. Finally, you can overlay the scatter plot with the minimum spanning tree, marked in red;

```
> digit.st = spantree(digit.dist)
> digit.plot = plot(digit.isomap, main="isomap k=8")
> lines(digit.st, digit.plot, col="red")
```

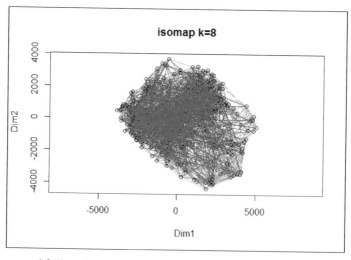

A 2-dimension scatter plot overlay with minimum spanning tree

How it works...

ISOMAP is a nonlinear dimension reduction method and a representative of isometric mapping methods. ISOMAP can be regarded as an extension of the metric MDS, where pairwise the Euclidean distance among data points is replaced by geodesic distances induced by a neighborhood graph.

The description of the ISOMAP algorithm is shown in four steps. First, determine the neighbor of each point. Secondly, construct a neighborhood graph. Thirdly, compute the shortest distance path between two nodes. At last, find a low dimension embedding of the data by performing MDS.

In this recipe, we demonstrate how to perform a nonlinear dimension reduction using ISOMAP. First, we load the digits data from `RnavGraphImageData`. Then, after we select one digit and plot its rotated image, we can see an image of the handwritten digit (the numeral 3, in the figure in step 3).

Next, we randomly sample 300 digits as our input data to ISOMAP. We then transpose the dataset to calculate the distance between each image object. Once the data is ready, we calculate the distance between each object and perform a dimension reduction. Here, we use `vegdist` to calculate the dissimilarities between each object using a Euclidean measure. We then use ISOMAP to perform a nonlinear dimension reduction on the `digits` data with the dimension set as `6`, number of shortest dissimilarities retained for a point as `8`, and ensure that you analyze the largest connected group by specifying `fragmentedOK` as `TRUE`.

Finally, we can use the generated ISOMAP object to make a two-dimension scatter plot (figure in step 6), and also overlay the minimum spanning tree with lines in red on the scatter plot (figure in step 7).

There's more...

You can also use the `RnavGraph` package to visualize high dimensional data (digits in this case) using graphs as a navigational infrastructure. For more information, please refer to http://www.icesi.edu.co/CRAN/web/packages/RnavGraph/vignettes/ RnavGraph.pdf.

Here is a description of how you can use `RnavGraph` to visualize high dimensional data in a graph:

1. First, install and load the `RnavGraph` and `graph` packages:

```
> install.packages("RnavGraph")
> source("http://bioconductor.org/biocLite.R")
> biocLite("graph")
> library(RnavGraph)
```

2. You can then create an `NG_data` object from the `digit` data:

```
> digit.group = rep(c(1:9,0), each = 1100)
> digit.ng_data = ng_data(name = "ISO_digits",
+ data = data.frame(digit.isomap$points),
+ shortnames = paste('i',1:6, sep = ''),
+ group = digit.group[digit.idx],
+ labels = as.character(digits.group[digit.idx]))
```

3. Create an `NG_graph` object from `NG_data`:

```
>   V = shortnames(digit.ng_data)
>   G = completegraph(V)
>   LG =linegraph(G)
>   LGnot = complement(LG)
>   ng.LG = ng_graph(name = "3D Transition", graph = LG)
> ng.LGnot = ng_graph(name = "4D Transition", graph = LGnot)
```

4. Finally, you can visualize the graph in the `tk2d` plot:

```
> ng.i.digits = ng_image_array_gray('USPS Handwritten Digits',
+ digit.select,16,16,invert = TRUE,
+ img_in_row = FALSE)
> vizDigits1 = ng_2d(data = digit.ng_data, graph = ng.LG, images =
ng.i.digits)
> vizDigits2 = ng_2d(data = digit.ng_data, graph = ng.LGnot,
images = ng.i.digits)
> nav = navGraph(data = digit.ng_data, graph = list(ng.LG,
ng.LGnot), viz = list(vizDigits1, vizDigits2))
```

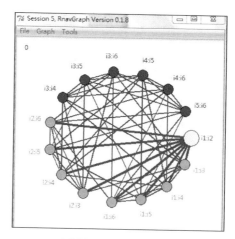

A 3-D Transition graph plot

5. One can also view a 4D transition graph plot:

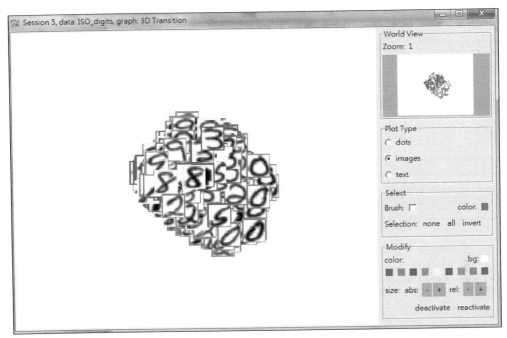

A 4D transition graph plot

Performing nonlinear dimension reduction with Local Linear Embedding

Locally linear embedding (**LLE**) is an extension of PCA, which reduces data that lies on a manifold embedded in a high dimensional space into a low dimensional space. In contrast to ISOMAP, which is a global approach for nonlinear dimension reduction, LLE is a local approach that employs a linear combination of the k-nearest neighbor to preserve local properties of data. In this recipe, we will give a short introduction of how to use LLE on an s-curve data.

Getting ready

In this recipe, we will use digit data from `lle_scurve_data` within the `lle` package as our input source.

How to do it...

Perform the following steps to perform nonlinear dimension reduction with LLE:

1. First, you need to install and load the package, `lle`:

   ```
   > install.packages("lle")
   > library(lle)
   ```

2. You can then load `ll_scurve_data` from `lle`:

   ```
   > data( lle_scurve_data )
   ```

3. Next, perform `lle` on `lle_scurve_data`:

   ```
   > X = lle_scurve_data
   > results = lle( X=X , m=2, k=12,  id=TRUE)
   finding neighbours
   calculating weights
   intrinsic dim: mean=2.47875, mode=2
   computing coordinates
   ```

4. Examine the result with the `str` and `plot` function:

   ```
   > str( results )
   List of 4
    $ Y     : num [1:800, 1:2] -1.586 -0.415 0.896 0.513 1.477 ...
    $ X     : num [1:800, 1:3] 0.955 -0.66 -0.983 0.954 0.958 ...
    $ choise: NULL
    $ id    : num [1:800] 3 3 2 3 2 2 2 3 3 3 ...
   >plot( results$Y, main="embedded data", xlab=expression(y[1]),
   ylab=expression(y[2]) )
   ```

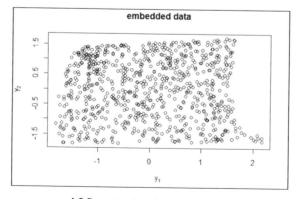

A 2-D scatter plot of embedded data

5. Lastly, you can use `plot_lle` to plot the LLE result:

```
> plot_lle( results$Y, X, FALSE, col="red", inter=TRUE )
```

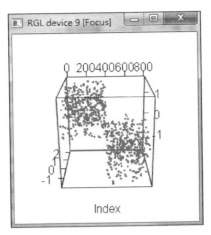

A LLE plot of LLE result

How it works...

LLE is a nonlinear dimension reduction method, which computes a low dimensional, neighborhood, preserving embeddings of high dimensional data. The algorithm of LLE can be illustrated in these steps: first, LLE computes the k-neighbors of each data point, x_i. Secondly, it computes a set of weights for each point, which minimizes the residual sum of errors, which can best reconstruct each data point from its neighbors. The residual sum of errors can be described as $RSS(w) = \sum_{i=1}^{n} \left\| x_i - \sum_{j \neq i} w_{ij} x_j \right\|^2$, where $w_{ij} = 0$ if x_j is not one of x_i's k-nearest neighbor, and for each i, $\sum_j w_{ij} = 1$. Finally, find the vector, Y, which is best reconstructed by the weight, W. The cost function can be illustrated as $\varphi(Y) = \sum_{i=1}^{n} \left\| y_i - \sum_{j \neq i} w_{ij} y_j \right\|^2$, with the constraint that $\sum_i Y_{ij} = 0$, and $Y^T Y = I$.

In this recipe, we demonstrate how to perform nonlinear dimension reduction using LLE. First, we load `lle_scurve_data` from `lle`. We then perform `lle` with two dimensions and 12 neighbors, and list the dimensions for every data point by specifying `id =TRUE`. The LLE has three steps, including: building a neighborhood for each point in the data, finding the weights for linearly approximating the data in that neighborhood, and finding the low dimensional coordinates.

Next, we can examine the data using the `str` and `plot` functions. The `str` function returns X,Y, choice, and ID. Here, X represents the input data, Y stands for the embedded data, choice indicates the index vector of the kept data, while subset selection and ID show the dimensions of every data input. The `plot` function returns the scatter plot of the embedded data. Lastly, we use `plot_lle` to plot the result. Here, we enable the interaction mode by setting the inter equal to `TRUE`.

See also

▶ Another useful package for nonlinear dimension reduction is `RDRToolbox`, which is a package for nonlinear dimension reduction with ISOMAP and LLE. You can use the following command to install `RDRToolbox`:

> `source("http://bioconductor.org/biocLite.R")`

> `biocLite("RDRToolbox")`

> `library(RDRToolbox)`

12

Big Data Analysis (R and Hadoop)

In this chapter, we will cover the following topics:

- ▶ Preparing the RHadoop environment
- ▶ Installing rmr2
- ▶ Installing rhdfs
- ▶ Operating HDFS with rhdfs
- ▶ Implementing a word count problem with RHadoop
- ▶ Comparing the performance between an R MapReduce program and a standard R program
- ▶ Testing and debugging the rmr2 program
- ▶ Installing plyrmr
- ▶ Manipulating data with plyrmr
- ▶ Conducting machine learning with RHadoop
- ▶ Configuring RHadoop clusters on Amazon EMR

Introduction

RHadoop is a collection of R packages that enables users to process and analyze big data with Hadoop. Before understanding how to set up RHadoop and put it in to practice, we have to know why we need to use machine learning to big-data scale.

In the previous chapters, we have mentioned how useful R is when performing data analysis and machine learning. In traditional statistical analysis, the focus is to perform analysis on historical samples (small data), which may ignore rarely occurring but valuable events and results to uncertain conclusions.

The emergence of Cloud technology has made real-time interaction between customers and businesses much more frequent; therefore, the focus of machine learning has now shifted to the development of accurate predictions for various customers. For example, businesses can provide real-time personal recommendations or online advertisements based on personal behavior via the use of a real-time prediction model.

However, if the data (for example, behaviors of all online users) is too large to fit in the memory of a single machine, you have no choice but to use a supercomputer or some other scalable solution. The most popular scalable big-data solution is Hadoop, which is an open source framework able to store and perform parallel computations across clusters. As a result, you can use RHadoop, which allows R to leverage the scalability of Hadoop, helping to process and analyze big data. In RHadoop, there are five main packages, which are:

- `rmr`: This is an interface between R and Hadoop MapReduce, which calls the Hadoop streaming MapReduce API to perform MapReduce jobs across Hadoop clusters. To develop an R MapReduce program, you only need to focus on the design of the map and reduce functions, and the remaining scalability issues will be taken care of by Hadoop itself.

- `rhdfs`: This is an interface between R and HDFS, which calls the HDFS API to access the data stored in HDFS. The use of `rhdfs` is very similar to the use of the Hadoop shell, which allows users to manipulate HDFS easily from the R console.

- `rhbase`: This is an interface between R and HBase, which accesses Hbase and is distributed in clusters through a Thrift server. You can use `rhbase` to read/write data and manipulate tables stored within HBase.

- `plyrmr`: This is a higher-level abstraction of MapReduce, which allows users to perform common data manipulation in a plyr-like syntax. This package greatly lowers the learning curve of big-data manipulation.

- `ravro`: This allows users to read `avro` files in R, or write `avro` files. It allows R to exchange data with HDFS.

In this chapter, we will start by preparing the Hadoop environment, so that you can install RHadoop. We then cover the installation of three main packages: `rmr`, `rhdfs`, and `plyrmr`. Next, we will introduce how to use `rmr` to perform MapReduce from R, operate an HDFS file through `rhdfs`, and perform a common data operation using `plyrmr`. Further, we will explore how to perform machine learning using RHadoop. Lastly, we will introduce how to deploy multiple RHadoop clusters on Amazon EC2.

Preparing the RHadoop environment

As RHadoop requires an R and Hadoop integrated environment, we must first prepare an environment with both R and Hadoop installed. Instead of building a new Hadoop system, we can use the **Cloudera QuickStart VM** (the VM is free), which contains a single node Apache Hadoop Cluster and R. In this recipe, we will demonstrate how to download the Cloudera QuickStart VM.

Getting ready

To use the Cloudera QuickStart VM, it is suggested that you should prepare a 64-bit guest OS with either VMWare or VirtualBox, or the KVM installed.

If you choose to use VMWare, you should prepare a player compatible with WorkStation 8.x or higher: Player 4.x or higher, ESXi 5.x or higher, or Fusion 4.x or higher.

Note, 4 GB of RAM is required to start VM, with an available disk space of at least 3 GB.

How to do it...

Perform the following steps to set up a Hadoop environment using the Cloudera QuickStart VM:

1. Visit the Cloudera QuickStart VM download site (you may need to update the link as Cloudera upgrades its VMs , the current version of CDH is 5.3) at `http://www.cloudera.com/content/cloudera/en/downloads/quickstart_vms/cdh-5-2-x.html`.

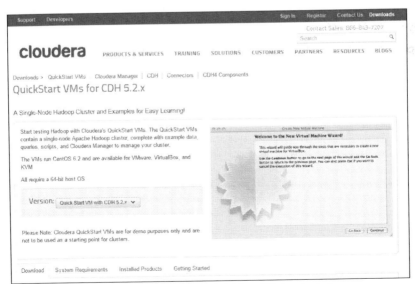

A screenshot of the Cloudera QuickStart VM download site

2. Depending on the virtual machine platform installed on your OS, choose the appropriate link (you may need to update the link as Cloudera upgrades its VMs) to download the VM file:

- **To download VMWare**: You can visit `https://downloads.cloudera.com/demo_vm/vmware/cloudera-quickstart-vm-5.2.0-0-vmware.7z`

- **To download KVM**: You can visit `https://downloads.cloudera.com/demo_vm/kvm/cloudera-quickstart-vm-5.2.0-0-kvm.7z`

- **To download VirtualBox**: You can visit `https://downloads.cloudera.com/demo_vm/virtualbox/cloudera-quickstart-vm-5.2.0-0-virtualbox.7z`

3. Next, you can start the QuickStart VM using the virtual machine platform installed on your OS. You should see the desktop of Centos 6.2 in a few minutes.

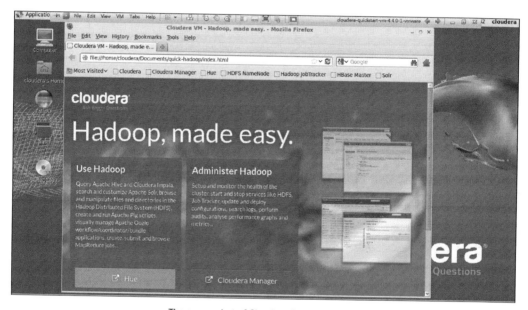

The screenshot of Cloudera QuickStart VM.

4. You can then open a terminal and type `hadoop`, which will display a list of functions that can operate a Hadoop cluster.

```
[cloudera@quickstart ~]$ hadoop
Usage: hadoop [--config confdir] COMMAND
       where COMMAND is one of:
  fs                    run a generic filesystem user client
  version               print the version
  jar <jar>             run a jar file
  checknative [-a|-h]   check native hadoop and compression libraries availa
bility
  distcp <srcurl> <desturl> copy file or directories recursively
  archive -archiveName NAME -p <parent path> <src>* <dest> create a hadoop
archive
  classpath             prints the class path needed to get the
                        Hadoop jar and the required libraries
  daemonlog             get/set the log level for each daemon
 or
  CLASSNAME             run the class named CLASSNAME

Most commands print help when invoked w/o parameters.
[cloudera@quickstart ~]$
```

The terminal screenshot after typing `hadoop`

5. Open a terminal and type `R`. Access an R session and check whether version 3.1.1 is already installed in the Cloudera QuickStart VM. If you cannot find R installed in the VM, please use the following command to install R:

```
$ yum install R R-core R-core-devel R-devel
```

How it works...

Instead of building a Hadoop system on your own, you can use the Hadoop VM application provided by Cloudera (the VM is free). The QuickStart VM runs on CentOS 6.2 with a single node Apache Hadoop cluster, Hadoop Ecosystem module, and R installed. This helps you to save time, instead of requiring you to learn how to install and use Hadoop.

The QuickStart VM requires you to have a computer with a 64-bit guest OS, at least 4 GB of RAM, 3 GB of disk space, and either VMWare, VirtualBox, or KVM installed. As a result, you may not be able to use this version of VM on some computers. As an alternative, you could consider using Amazon's Elastic MapReduce instead. We will illustrate how to prepare a RHadoop environment in EMR in the last recipe of this chapter.

Setting up the Cloudera QuickStart VM is simple. Download the VM from the download site and then open the built image with either VMWare, VirtualBox, or KVM. Once you can see the desktop of CentOS, you can then access the terminal and type `hadoop` to see whether Hadoop is working; then, type `R` to see whether R works in the QuickStart VM.

See also

▸ Besides using the Cloudera QuickStart VM, you may consider using a Sandbox VM provided by Hontonworks or MapR. You can find Hontonworks Sandbox at `http://hortonworks.com/products/hortonworks-sandbox/#install` and mapR Sandbox at `https://www.mapr.com/products/mapr-sandbox-hadoop/download`.

Installing rmr2

The `rmr2` package allows you to perform big data processing and analysis via MapReduce on a Hadoop cluster. To perform MapReduce on a Hadoop cluster, you have to install R and `rmr2` on every task node. In this recipe, we will illustrate how to install `rmr2` on a single node of a Hadoop cluster.

Getting ready

Ensure that you have completed the previous recipe by starting the Cloudera QuickStart VM and connecting the VM to the Internet, so that you can proceed with downloading and installing the `rmr2` package.

How to do it...

Perform the following steps to install `rmr2` on the QuickStart VM:

1. First, open the terminal within the Cloudera QuickStart VM.

2. Use the permission of the root to enter an R session:

   ```
   $ sudo R
   ```

3. You can then install dependent packages before installing `rmr2`:

   ```
   > install.packages(c("codetools", "Rcpp", "RJSONIO", "bitops",
   "digest", "functional", "stringr", "plyr", "reshape2", "rJava",
   "caTools"))
   ```

4. Quit the R session:

   ```
   > q()
   ```

5. Next, you can download `rmr-3.3.0` to the QuickStart VM. You may need to update the link if Revolution Analytics upgrades the version of `rmr2`:

   ```
   $ wget --no-check-certificate https://raw.githubusercontent.com/
   RevolutionAnalytics/rmr2/3.3.0/build/rmr2_3.3.0.tar.gz
   ```

6. You can then install `rmr-3.3.0` to the QuickStart VM:

   ```
   $ sudo R CMD INSTALL rmr2_3.3.0.tar.gz
   ```

7. Lastly, you can enter an R session and use the `library` function to test whether the library has been successfully installed:

   ```
   $ R
   > library(rmr2)
   ```

How it works...

In order to perform MapReduce on a Hadoop cluster, you have to install R and RHadoop on every task node. Here, we illustrate how to install `rmr2` on a single node of a Hadoop cluster. First, open the terminal of the Cloudera QuickStart VM. Before installing `rmr2`, we first access an R session with root privileges and install dependent R packages.

Next, after all the dependent packages are installed, quit the R session and use the `wget` command in the Linux shell to download `rmr-3.3.0` from GitHub to the local filesystem. You can then begin the installation of `rmr2`. Lastly, you can access an R session and use the library function to validate whether the package has been installed.

See also

- ▶ To see more information and read updates about RHadoop, you can refer to the RHadoop wiki page hosted on GitHub: `https://github.com/RevolutionAnalytics/RHadoop/wiki`

Installing rhdfs

The `rhdfs` package is the interface between R and HDFS, which allows users to access HDFS from an R console. Similar to `rmr2`, one should install `rhdfs` on every task node, so that one can access HDFS resources through R. In this recipe, we will introduce how to install `rhdfs` on the Cloudera QuickStart VM.

Getting ready

Ensure that you have completed the previous recipe by starting the Cloudera QuickStart VM and connecting the VM to the Internet, so that you can proceed with downloading and installing the `rhdfs` package.

How to do it...

Perform the following steps to install `rhdfs`:

1. First, you can download `rhdfs 1.0.8` from GitHub. You may need to update the link if Revolution Analytics upgrades the version of `rhdfs`:

   ```
   $wget --no-check-certificate https://raw.github.com/
   RevolutionAnalytics/rhdfs/master/build/rhdfs_1.0.8.tar.gz
   ```

2. Next, you can install `rhdfs` under the command-line mode:

   ```
   $ sudo HADOOP_CMD=/usr/bin/hadoop  R CMD INSTALL rhdfs_1.0.8.tar.
   gz
   ```

3. You can then set up `JAVA_HOME`. The configuration of `JAVA_HOME` depends on the installed Java version within the VM:

   ```
   $ sudo JAVA_HOME=/usr/java/jdk1.7.0_67-cloudera R CMD javareconf
   ```

4. Last, you can set up the system environment and initialize `rhdfs`. You may need to update the environment setup if you use a different version of QuickStart VM:

   ```
   $ R
   > Sys.setenv(HADOOP_CMD="/usr/bin/hadoop")
   > Sys.setenv(HADOOP_STREAMING="/usr/lib/hadoop-mapreduce/hadoop-
   streaming-2.5.0-cdh5.2.0.jar")
   > library(rhdfs)
   > hdfs.init()
   ```

How it works...

The package, `rhdfs`, provides functions so that users can manage HDFS using R. Similar to `rmr2`, you should install `rhdfs` on every task node, so that one can access HDFS through the R console.

To install `rhdfs`, you should first download `rhdfs` from GitHub. You can then install `rhdfs` in R by specifying where the `HADOOP_CMD` is located. You must configure R with Java support through the command, `javareconf`.

Next, you can access R and configure where `HADOOP_CMD` and `HADOOP_STREAMING` are located. Lastly, you can initialize `rhdfs` via the `rhdfs.init` function, which allows you to begin operating HDFS through `rhdfs`.

See also

▶ To find where HADOOP_CMD is located, you can use the `which hadoop` command in the Linux shell. In most Hadoop systems, HADOOP_CMD is located at `/usr/bin/hadoop`.

▶ As for the location of HADOOP_STREAMING, the streaming JAR file is often located in `/usr/lib/hadoop-mapreduce/`. However, if you cannot find the directory, `/usr/lib/Hadoop-mapreduce`, in your Linux system, you can search the streaming JAR by using the `locate` command. For example:

```
$ sudo updatedb
$ locate streaming | grep jar | more
```

Operating HDFS with rhdfs

The `rhdfs` package is an interface between Hadoop and R, which can call an HDFS API in the backend to operate HDFS. As a result, you can easily operate HDFS from the R console through the use of the `rhdfs` package. In the following recipe, we will demonstrate how to use the `rhdfs` function to manipulate HDFS.

Getting ready

To proceed with this recipe, you need to have completed the previous recipe by installing `rhdfs` into R, and validate that you can initial HDFS via the `hdfs.init` function.

How to do it...

Perform the following steps to operate files stored on HDFS:

1. Initialize the `rhdfs` package:

    ```
    > Sys.setenv(HADOOP_CMD="/usr/bin/hadoop")
    ```

    ```
    > Sys.setenv(HADOOP_STREAMING="/usr/lib/hadoop-mapreduce/hadoop-streaming-2.5.0-cdh5.2.0.jar")
    ```

    ```
    > library(rhdfs)
    ```

    ```
    > hdfs.init ()
    ```

2. You can then manipulate files stored on HDFS, as follows:

    ❑ `hdfs.put`: Copy a file from the local filesystem to HDFS:

    ```
    > hdfs.put('word.txt', './')
    ```

    ❑ `hdfs.ls`: Read the list of directory from HDFS:

    ```
    > hdfs.ls('./')
    ```

❑ hdfs.copy: Copy a file from one HDFS directory to another:

```
> hdfs.copy('word.txt', 'wordcnt.txt')
```

❑ hdfs.move : Move a file from one HDFS directory to another:

```
> hdfs.move('wordcnt.txt', './data/wordcnt.txt')
```

❑ hdfs.delete: Delete an HDFS directory from R:

```
> hdfs.delete('./data/')
```

❑ hdfs.rm: Delete an HDFS directory from R:

```
> hdfs.rm('./data/')
```

❑ hdfs.get: Download a file from HDFS to a local filesystem:

```
> hdfs.get(word.txt', '/home/cloudera/word.txt')
```

❑ hdfs.rename: Rename a file stored on HDFS:

```
hdfs.rename('./test/q1.txt','./test/test.txt')
```

❑ hdfs.chmod: Change the permissions of a file or directory:

```
> hdfs.chmod('test', permissions= '777')
```

❑ hdfs.file.info: Read the meta information of the HDFS file:

```
> hdfs.file.info('./')
```

3. Also, you can write stream to the HDFS file:

```
> f = hdfs.file("iris.txt","w")
> data(iris)
> hdfs.write(iris,f)
> hdfs.close(f)
```

4. Lastly, you can read stream from the HDFS file:

```
> f = hdfs.file("iris.txt", "r")
> dfserialized = hdfs.read(f)
> df = unserialize(dfserialized)
> df
> hdfs.close(f)
```

How it works...

In this recipe, we demonstrate how to manipulate HDFS using the rhdfs package. Normally, you can use the Hadoop shell to manipulate HDFS, but if you would like to access HDFS from R, you can use the rhdfs package.

Before you start using `rhdfs`, you have to initialize `rhdfs` with `hdfs.init()`. After initialization, you can operate HDFS through the functions provided in the `rhdfs` package.

Besides manipulating HDFS files, you can exchange streams to HDFS through `hdfs.read` and `hdfs.write`. We, therefore, demonstrate how to write a data frame in R to an HDFS file, `iris.txt`, using `hdfs.write`. Lastly, you can recover the written file back to the data frame using the `hdfs.read` function and the `unserialize` function.

See also

> ► To initialize `rhdfs`, you have to set `HADOOP_CMD` and `HADOOP_STREAMING` in the system environment. Instead of setting the configuration each time you're using `rhdfs`, you can put the configurations in the `.rprofile` file. Therefore, every time you start an R session, the configuration will be automatically loaded.

Implementing a word count problem with RHadoop

To demonstrate how MapReduce works, we illustrate the example of a word count, which counts the number of occurrences of each word in a given input set. In this recipe, we will demonstrate how to use `rmr2` to implement a word count problem.

Getting ready

In this recipe, we will need an input file as our word count program input. You can download the example input from `https://github.com/ywchiu/ml_R_cookbook/tree/master/CH12`.

How to do it...

Perform the following steps to implement the word count program:

1. First, you need to configure the system environment, and then load `rmr2` and `rhdfs` into an R session. You may need to update the use of the JAR file if you use a different version of QuickStart VM:

    ```
    > Sys.setenv(HADOOP_CMD="/usr/bin/hadoop")
    ```

    ```
    > Sys.setenv(HADOOP_STREAMING="/usr/lib/hadoop-mapreduce/hadoop-
    streaming-2.5.0-cdh5.2.0.jar ")
    ```

    ```
    > library(rmr2)
    ```

    ```
    > library(rhdfs)
    ```

    ```
    > hdfs.init()
    ```

2. You can then create a directory on HDFS and put the input file into the newly created directory:

```
> hdfs.mkdir("/user/cloudera/wordcount/data")
> hdfs.put("wc_input.txt", "/user/cloudera/wordcount/data")
```

3. Next, you can create a `map` function:

```
> map = function(.,lines) { keyval(
+    unlist(
+      strsplit(
+        x = lines,
+          split = " +")),
+    1)}
```

4. Create a `reduce` function:

```
> reduce = function(word, counts) {
+    keyval(word, sum(counts))
+ }
```

5. Call the `MapReduce` program to count the words within a document:

```
> hdfs.root = 'wordcount'
> hdfs.data = file.path(hdfs.root, 'data')
> hdfs.out = file.path(hdfs.root, 'out')
> wordcount = function (input, output=NULL) {
+    mapreduce(input=input, output=output, input.format="text", map=map,
+    reduce=reduce)
+ }
> out = wordcount(hdfs.data, hdfs.out)
```

6. Lastly, you can retrieve the top 10 occurring words within the document:

```
> results = from.dfs(out)
> results$key[order(results$val, decreasing = TRUE)][1:10]
```

How it works...

In this recipe, we demonstrate how to implement a word count using the `rmr2` package. First, we need to configure the system environment and load `rhdfs` and `rmr2` into R. Then, we specify the input of our word count program from the local filesystem into the HDFS directory, `/user/cloudera/wordcount/data`, via the `hdfs.put` function.

Next, we begin implementing the MapReduce program. Normally, we can divide the MapReduce program into the `map` and `reduce` functions. In the `map` function, we first use the `strsplit` function to split each line into words. Then, as the `strsplit` function returns a list of words, we can use the `unlist` function to character vectors. Lastly, we can return key-value pairs with each word as a key and the value as one. As the `reduce` function receives the key-value pair generated from the `map` function, the `reduce` function sums the count and returns the number of occurrences of each word (or key).

After we have implemented the `map` and `reduce` functions, we can submit our job via the `mapreduce` function. Normally, the `mapreduce` function requires four inputs, which are the HDFS input path, the HDFS output path, the map function, and the reduce function. In this case, we specify the input as `wordcount/data`, output as `wordcount/out`, map function as `map`, reduce function as `reduce`, and wrap the `mapreduce` call in function, `wordcount`. Lastly, we call the function, `wordcount` and store the output path in the variable, `out`.

We can use the `from.dfs` function to load the HDFS data into the `results` variable, which contains the mapping of words and number of occurrences. We can then generate the top 10 occurring words from the `results` variable.

See also

▶ In this recipe, we demonstrate how to write an R MapReduce program to solve a word count problem. However, if you are interested in how to write a native Java MapReduce program, you can refer to `http://hadoop.apache.org/docs/current/hadoop-mapreduce-client/hadoop-mapreduce-client-core/MapReduceTutorial.html`.

Comparing the performance between an R MapReduce program and a standard R program

Those not familiar with how Hadoop works may often see Hadoop as a remedy for big data processing. Some might believe that Hadoop can return the processed results for any size of data within a few milliseconds. In this recipe, we will compare the performance between an R MapReduce program and a standard R program to demonstrate that Hadoop does not perform as quickly as some may believe.

Getting ready

In this recipe, you should have completed the previous recipe by installing `rmr2` into the R environment.

How to do it...

Perform the following steps to compare the performance of a standard R program and an R MapReduce program:

1. First, you can implement a standard R program to have all numbers squared:

   ```
   > a.time = proc.time()
   > small.ints2=1:100000
   > result.normal = sapply(small.ints2, function(x) x^2)
   > proc.time() - a.time
   ```

2. To compare the performance, you can implement an R MapReduce program to have all numbers squared:

   ```
   > b.time = proc.time()
   > small.ints= to.dfs(1:100000)
   > result = mapreduce(input = small.ints, map = function(k,v)
   cbind(v,v^2))
   > proc.time() - b.time
   ```

How it works...

In this recipe, we implement two programs to square all the numbers. In the first program, we use a standard R function, `sapply`, to square the sequence from 1 to 100,000. To record the program execution time, we first record the processing time before the execution in `a.time`, and then subtract `a.time` from the current processing time after the execution. Normally, the execution takes no more than 10 seconds. In the second program, we use the `rmr2` package to implement a program in the R MapReduce version. In this program, we also record the execution time. Normally, this program takes a few minutes to complete a task.

The performance comparison shows that a standard R program outperforms the MapReduce program when processing small amounts of data. This is because a Hadoop system often requires time to spawn daemons, job coordination between daemons, and fetching data from data nodes. Therefore, a MapReduce program often takes a few minutes to a couple of hours to finish the execution. As a result, if you can fit your data in the memory, you should write a standard R program to solve the problem. Otherwise, if the data is too large to fit in the memory, you can implement a MapReduce solution.

See also

▶ In order to check whether a job will run smoothly and efficiently in Hadoop, you can run a MapReduce benchmark, MRBench, to evaluate the performance of the job:

```
$ hadoop jar /usr/lib/hadoop-0.20-mapreduce/hadoop-test.jar
mrbench -numRuns 50
```

Testing and debugging the rmr2 program

Since running a MapReduce program will require a considerable amount of time, varying from a few minutes to several hours, testing and debugging become very important. In this recipe, we will illustrate some techniques you can use to troubleshoot an R MapReduce program.

Getting ready

In this recipe, you should have completed the previous recipe by installing rmr2 into an R environment.

How to do it...

Perform the following steps to test and debug an R MapReduce program:

1. First, you can configure the backend as local in rmr.options:

   ```
   > rmr.options(backend = 'local')
   ```

2. Again, you can execute the number squared MapReduce program mentioned in the previous recipe:

   ```
   > b.time = proc.time()
   > small.ints= to.dfs(1:100000)
   > result = mapreduce(input = small.ints, map = function(k,v)
   cbind(v,v^2))
   > proc.time() - b.time
   ```

3. In addition to this, if you want to print the structure information of any variable in the MapReduce program, you can use the rmr.str function:

   ```
   > out = mapreduce(to.dfs(1), map = function(k, v) rmr.str(v))
   Dotted pair list of 14
    $ : language mapreduce(to.dfs(1), map = function(k, v) rmr.
   str(v))
   ```

```
$ : language mr(map = map, reduce = reduce, combine =
combine, vectorized.reduce, in.folder = if (is.list(input)) {
lapply(input, to.dfs.path) ...

$ : language c.keyval(do.call(c, lapply(in.folder,
function(fname) {     kv = get.data(fname) ...

$ : language do.call(c, lapply(in.folder, function(fname) {
kv = get.data(fname) ...

$ : language lapply(in.folder, function(fname) {     kv = get.
data(fname) ...

$ : language FUN("/tmp/Rtmp813BFJ/file25af6e85cfde"[[1L]], ...)

$ : language unname(tapply(1:lkv, ceiling((1:lkv)/(lkv/(object.
size(kv)/10^6))), function(r) {     kvr = slice.keyval(kv, r) ...

$ : language tapply(1:lkv, ceiling((1:lkv)/(lkv/(object.
size(kv)/10^6))), function(r) {     kvr = slice.keyval(kv, r) ...

$ : language lapply(X = split(X, group), FUN = FUN, ...)

$ : language FUN(X[[1L]], ...)

$ : language as.keyval(map(keys(kvr), values(kvr)))

$ : language is.keyval(x)

$ : language map(keys(kvr), values(kvr))

$ :length 2 rmr.str(v)

 ..- attr(*, "srcref")=Class 'srcref'  atomic [1:8] 1 34 1 58 34
58 1 1

 .. .. ..- attr(*, "srcfile")=Classes 'srcfilecopy', 'srcfile'
<environment: 0x3f984f0>

v

num 1
```

How it works...

In this recipe, we introduced some debugging and testing techniques you can use while implementing the MapReduce program. First, we introduced the technique to test a MapReduce program in a local mode. If you would like to run the MapReduce program in a pseudo distributed or fully distributed mode, it would take you a few minutes to several hours to complete the task, which would involve a lot of wastage of time while troubleshooting your MapReduce program. Therefore, you can set the backend to the local mode in rmr.options so that the program will be executed in the local mode, which takes lesser time to execute.

Another debugging technique is to list the content of the variable within the map or reduce function. In an R program, you can use the str function to display the compact structure of a single variable. In rmr2, the package also provides a function named rmr.str, which allows you to print out the content of a single variable onto the console. In this example, we use rmr.str to print the content of variables within a MapReduce program.

See also

▶ For those who are interested in the `option` settings for the `rmr2` package, you can refer to the help document of `rmr.options`:

```
> help(rmr.options)
```

Installing plyrmr

The `plyrmr` package provides common operations (as found in `plyr` or `reshape2`) for users to easily perform data manipulation through the MapReduce framework. In this recipe, we will introduce how to install `plyrmr` on the Hadoop system.

Getting ready

Ensure that you have completed the previous recipe by starting the Cloudera QuickStart VM and connecting the VM to the Internet. Also, you need to have the `rmr2` package installed beforehand.

How to do it...

Perform the following steps to install `plyrmr` on the Hadoop system:

1. First, you should install `libxml2-devel` and `curl-devel` in the Linux shell:
   ```
   $ yum install libxml2-devel
   $ sudo yum install curl-devel
   ```

2. You can then access R and install the dependent packages:
   ```
   $ sudo R
   > Install.packages(c(" Rcurl", "httr"), dependencies = TRUE
   > Install.packages("devtools", dependencies = TRUE)
   > library(devtools)
   > install_github("pryr", "hadley")
   > install.packages(c(" R.methodsS3", "hydroPSO"), dependencies = TRUE)
   > q()
   ```

3. Next, you can download `plyrmr 0.5.0` and install it on Hadoop VM. You may need to update the link if Revolution Analytics upgrades the version of `plyrmr`:
   ```
   $ wget -no-check-certificate https://raw.github.com/RevolutionAnalytics/plyrmr/master/build/plyrmr_0.5.0.tar.gz
   $ sudo R CMD INSTALL plyrmr_0.5.0.tar.gz
   ```

4. Lastly, validate the installation:

```
$ R
> library(plyrmr)
```

How it works...

Besides writing an R MapReduce program using the `rmr2` package, you can use the `plyrmr` to manipulate data. The `plyrmr` package is similar to hive and pig in the Hadoop ecosystem, which is the abstraction of the MapReduce program. Therefore, we can implement an R MapReduce program in `plyr` style instead of implementing the map f and `reduce` functions.

To install `plyrmr`, first install the package of `libxml2-devel` and `curl-devel`, using the `yum install` command. Then, access R and install the dependent packages. Lastly, download the file from GitHub and install `plyrmr` in R.

See also

▸ To read more information about `plyrmr`, you can use the `help` function to refer to the following document:

```
> help(package=plyrmr)
```

Manipulating data with plyrmr

While writing a MapReduce program with `rmr2` is much easier than writing a native Java version, it is still hard for nondevelopers to write a MapReduce program. Therefore, you can use `plyrmr`, a high-level abstraction of the MapReduce program, so that you can use plyr-like operations to manipulate big data. In this recipe, we will introduce some operations you can use to manipulate data.

Getting ready

In this recipe, you should have completed the previous recipes by installing `plyrmr` and `rmr2` in R.

How to do it...

Perform the following steps to manipulate data with `plyrmr`:

1. First, you need to load both `plyrmr` and `rmr2` into R:

```
> library(rmr2)
> library(plyrmr)
```

2. You can then set the execution mode to the local mode:

```
> plyrmr.options(backend="local")
```

3. Next, load the Titanic dataset into R:

```
> data(Titanic)
> titanic = data.frame(Titanic)
```

4. Begin the operation by filtering the data:

```
> where(
+     Titanic,
+ Freq >=100)
```

5. You can also use a pipe operator to filter the data:

```
> titanic %|% where(Freq >=100)
```

6. Put the Titanic data into HDFS and load the path of the data to the variable, `tidata`:

```
> tidata = to.dfs(data.frame(Titanic), output = '/tmp/titanic')
> tidata
```

7. Next, you can generate a summation of the frequency from the Titanic data:

```
> input(tidata) %|% transmute(sum(Freq))
```

8. You can also group the frequency by sex:

```
> input(tidata) %|% group(Sex) %|% transmute(sum(Freq))
```

9. You can then sample 10 records out of the population:

```
> sample(input(tidata), n=10)
```

10. In addition to this, you can use plyrmr to join two datasets:

```
> convert_tb = data.frame(Label=c("No","Yes"), Symbol=c(0,1))
ctb = to.dfs(convert_tb, output = 'convert')
> as.data.frame(plyrmr::merge(input(tidata), input(ctb),
by.x="Survived", by.y="Label"))
> file.remove('convert')
```

How it works...

In this recipe, we introduce how to use `plyrmr` to manipulate data. First, we need to load the `plyrmr` package into R. Then, similar to `rmr2`, you have to set the backend option of `plyrmr` as the local mode. Otherwise, you will have to wait anywhere between a few minutes to several hours if `plyrmr` is running on Hadoop mode (the default setting).

Next, we can begin the data manipulation with data filtering. You can choose to call the function nested inside the other function call in step 4. On the other hand, you can use the pipe operator, `%|%`, to chain multiple operations. Therefore, we can filter data similar to step 4, using pipe operators in step 5.

Next, you can input the dataset into either the HDFS or local filesystem, using `to.dfs` in accordance with the current running mode. The function will generate the path of the dataset and save it in the variable, `tidata`. By knowing the path, you can access the data using the `input` function. Next, we illustrate how to generate a summation of the frequency from the Titanic dataset with the `transmute` and `sum` functions. Also, `plyrmr` allows users to sum up the frequency by gender.

Additionally, in order to sample data from a population, you can also use the `sample` function to select 10 records out of the Titanic dataset. Lastly, we demonstrate how to join two datasets using the `merge` function from `plyrmr`.

See also

Here we list some functions that can be used to manipulate data with `plyrmr`. You may refer to the `help` function for further details on their usage and functionalities:

- Data manipulation:
  - `bind.cols`: This adds new columns
  - `select`: This is used to select columns
  - `where`: This is used to select rows
  - `transmute`: This uses all of the above plus their summaries

- From `reshape2`:
  - `melt` and `dcast`: It converts long and wide data frames

- Summary:
  - `count`
  - `quantile`
  - `sample`

- Extract:
  - `top.k`
  - `bottom.k`

Conducting machine learning with RHadoop

In the previous chapters, we have demonstrated how powerful R is when used to solve machine learning problems. Also, we have shown that the use of Hadoop allows R to process big data in parallel. At this point, some may believe that the use of RHadoop can easily solve machine learning problems of big data via numerous existing machine learning packages. However, you cannot use most of these to solve machine learning problems as they cannot be executed in the MapReduce mode. In the following recipe, we will demonstrate how to implement a MapReduce version of linear regression and compare this version with the one using the `lm` function.

Getting ready

In this recipe, you should have completed the previous recipe by installing `rmr2` into the R environment.

How to do it...

Perform the following steps to implement a linear regression in MapReduce:

1. First, load the `cats` dataset from the `MASS` package:

   ```
   > library(MASS)
   > data(cats)
   > X = matrix(cats$Bwt)
   > y = matrix(cats$Hwt)
   ```

2. You can then generate a linear regression model by calling the `lm` function:

   ```
   > model = lm(y~X)
   > summary(model)


   Call:
   lm(formula = y ~ X)


   Residuals:
       Min      1Q  Median      3Q     Max
   -3.5694 -0.9634 -0.0921  1.0426  5.1238


   Coefficients:
                 Estimate Std. Error t value Pr(>|t|)
   ```

```
(Intercept)   -0.3567      0.6923   -0.515     0.607
X              4.0341      0.2503   16.119    <2e-16 ***
---
Signif. codes:
0 '***' 0.001 '**' 0.01 '*' 0.05 '.' 0.1 ' ' 1


Residual standard error: 1.452 on 142 degrees of freedom
Multiple R-squared:  0.6466,  Adjusted R-squared:  0.6441
F-statistic: 259.8 on 1 and 142 DF,  p-value: < 2.2e-16
```

3. You can now make a regression plot with the given data points and model:

```
> plot(y~X)
> abline(model, col="red")
```

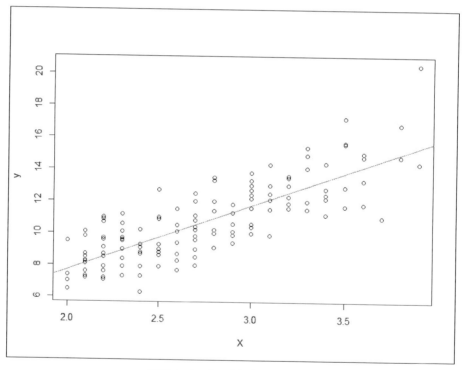

Linear regression plot of cats dataset

4. Load `rmr2` into R:

```
> Sys.setenv(HADOOP_CMD="/usr/bin/hadoop")
> Sys.setenv(HADOOP_STREAMING="/usr/lib/hadoop-mapreduce/hadoop->
streaming-2.5.0-cdh5.2.0.jar")
> library(rmr2)
> rmr.options(backend="local")
```

5. You can then set up X and y values:

```
> X = matrix(cats$Bwt)
> X.index = to.dfs(cbind(1:nrow(X), X))
> y = as.matrix(cats$Hwt)
```

6. Make a Sum function to sum up the values:

```
> Sum =
+    function(., YY)
+       keyval(1, list(Reduce('+', YY)))
```

7. Compute Xtx in MapReduce, Job1:

```
> XtX =
+    values(
+       from.dfs(
+          mapreduce(
+             input = X.index,
+             map =
+                function(., Xi) {
+                   Xi = Xi[,-1]
+                   keyval(1, list(t(Xi) %*% Xi))},
+             reduce = Sum,
+             combine = TRUE)))[[1]]
```

8. You can then compute `Xty` in MapReduce, `Job2`:

```
Xty =
+     values (
+        from.dfs (
+           mapreduce (
+              input = X.index,
+              map = function(., Xi) {
+                 yi = y[Xi[,1],]
+                 Xi = Xi[,-1]
+                 keyval(1, list(t(Xi) %*% yi))},
+              reduce = Sum,
+              combine = TRUE))) [[1]]
```

9. Lastly, you can derive the coefficient from `XtX` and `Xty`:

```
> solve(XtX, Xty)
         [,1]
[1,]  3.907113
```

How it works...

In this recipe, we demonstrate how to implement linear logistic regression in a MapReduce fashion in R. Before we start the implementation, we review how traditional linear models work. We first retrieve the `cats` dataset from the `MASS` package. We then load X as the body weight (`Bwt`) and y as the heart weight (`Hwt`).

Next, we begin to fit the data into a linear regression model using the `lm` function. We can then compute the fitted model and obtain the summary of the model. The summary shows that the coefficient is 4.0341 and the intercept is -0.3567. Furthermore, we draw a scatter plot in accordance with the given data points and then draw a regression line on the plot.

As we cannot perform linear regression using the `lm` function in the MapReduce form, we have to rewrite the regression model in a MapReduce fashion. Here, we would like to implement a MapReduce version of linear regression in three steps, which are: calculate the `XtX` value with the MapReduce, job1, calculate the `Xty` value with MapReduce, `job2`, and then derive the coefficient value:

▸ In the first step, we pass the matrix, X, as the input to the `map` function. The `map` function then calculates the cross product of the transposed matrix, X, and, X. The `reduce` function then performs the sum operation defined in the previous section.

- In the second step, the procedure of calculating Xty is similar to calculating XtX. The procedure calculates the cross product of the transposed matrix, X, and, y. The `reduce` function then performs the sum operation.

- Lastly, we use the `solve` function to derive the coefficient, which is 3.907113.

As the results show, the coefficients computed by `lm` and MapReduce differ slightly. Generally speaking, the coefficient computed by the `lm` model is more accurate than the one calculated by MapReduce. However, if your data is too large to fit in the memory, you have no choice but to implement linear regression in the MapReduce version.

See also

- You can access more information on machine learning algorithms at: `https://github.com/RevolutionAnalytics/rmr2/tree/master/pkg/tests`

Configuring RHadoop clusters on Amazon EMR

Until now, we have only demonstrated how to run a RHadoop program in a single Hadoop node. In order to test our RHadoop program on a multi-node cluster, the only thing you need to do is to install RHadoop on all the task nodes (nodes with either task tracker for mapreduce version 1 or node manager for map reduce version 2) of Hadoop clusters. However, the deployment and installation is time consuming. On the other hand, you can choose to deploy your RHadoop program on Amazon EMR, so that you can deploy multi-node clusters and RHadoop on every task node in only a few minutes. In the following recipe, we will demonstrate how to configure RHadoop cluster on an Amazon EMR service.

Getting ready

In this recipe, you must register and create an account on AWS, and you also must know how to generate a EC2 key-pair before using Amazon EMR.

For those who seek more information on how to start using AWS, please refer to the tutorial provided by Amazon at `http://docs.aws.amazon.com/AWSEC2/latest/UserGuide/EC2_GetStarted.html`.

How to do it...

Perform the following steps to configure RHadoop on Amazon EMR:

1. First, you can access the console of the Amazon Web Service (refer to `https://us-west-2.console.aws.amazon.com/console/`) and find EMR in the analytics section. Then, click on **EMR**.

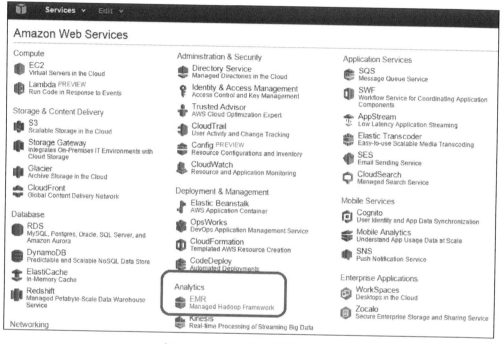

Access EMR service from **AWS** console.

2. You should find yourself in the cluster list of the EMR dashboard (refer to `https://us-west-2.console.aws.amazon.com/elasticmapreduce/home?region=us-west-2#cluster-list::`); click on **Create cluster**.

Cluster list of EMR

3. Then, you should find yourself on the **Create Cluster** page (refer to `https://us-west-2.console.aws.amazon.com/elasticmapreduce/home?region=us-west-2#create-cluster:`).

4. Next, you should specify **Cluster name** and **Log folder S3 location** in the cluster configuration.

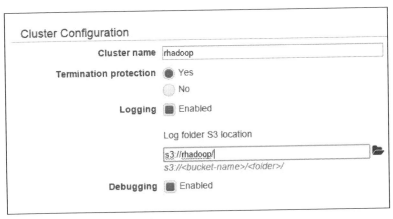

Cluster configuration in the create cluster page

5. You can then configure the Hadoop distribution on **Software Configuration**.

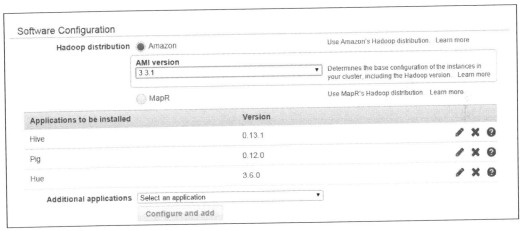

Configure the software and applications

6. Next, you can configure the number of nodes within the Hadoop cluster.

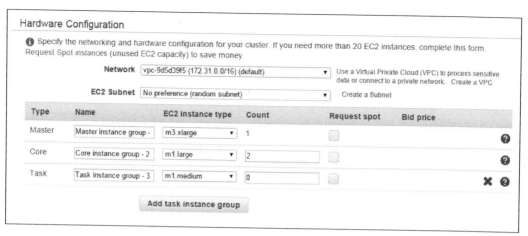

Configure the hardware within Hadoop cluster

7. You can then specify the EC2 key-pair for the master node login.

Security and Access

Configure the hardware within Hadoop cluster

Security and access to the master node of the EMR cluster

8. To set up RHadoop, one has to perform bootstrap actions to install RHadoop on every task node. Please write a file named `bootstrapRHadoop.sh`, and insert the following lines within the file:

```
echo 'install.packages(c("codetools", "Rcpp", "RJSONIO", "bitops",
"digest", "functional", "stringr", "plyr", "reshape2", "rJava",
"caTools"), repos="http://cran.us.r-project.org")' > /home/hadoop/
installPackage.R
sudo Rscript /home/hadoop/installPackage.R
wget --no-check-certificate https://raw.githubusercontent.com/
RevolutionAnalytics/rmr2/master/build/rmr2_3.3.0.tar.gz
sudo R CMD INSTALL rmr2_3.3.0.tar.gz
wget --no-check-certificate https://raw.github.com/
RevolutionAnalytics/rhdfs/master/build/rhdfs_1.0.8.tar.gz
sudo HADOOP_CMD=/home/hadoop/bin/hadoop R CMD INSTALL
rhdfs_1.0.8.tar.gz
```

9. You should upload `bootstrapRHadoop.sh` to S3.

10. You now need to add the bootstrap action with `Custom action`, and add `s3://<location>/bootstrapRHadoop.sh` within the S3 location.

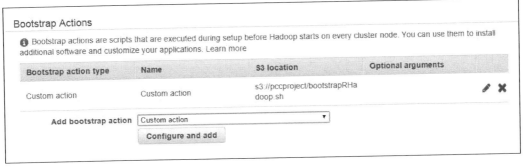

Set up the bootstrap action

11. Next, you can click on **Create cluster** to launch the Hadoop cluster.

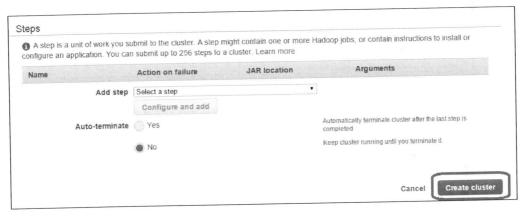

Create the cluster

12. Lastly, you should see the master public DNS when the cluster is ready. You can now access the terminal of the master node with your EC2-key pair:

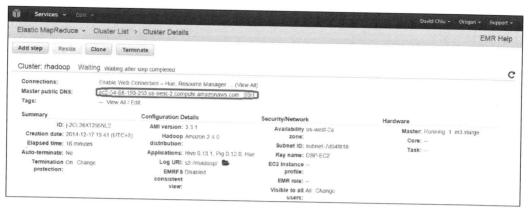

A screenshot of the created cluster

How it works...

In this recipe, we demonstrate how to set up RHadoop on Amazon EMR. The benefit of this is that you can quickly create a scalable, on demand Hadoop with just a few clicks within a few minutes. This helps save you time from building and deploying a Hadoop application. However, you have to pay for the number of running hours for each instance. Before using Amazon EMR, you should create an AWS account and know how to set up the EC2 key-pair and the S3. You can then start installing RHadoop on Amazon EMR.

In the first step, access the EMR cluster list and click on **Create cluster**. You can see a list of configurations on the **Create cluster** page. You should then set up the cluster name and log folder in the S3 location in the cluster configuration.

Next, you can set up the software configuration and choose the Hadoop distribution you would like to install. Amazon provides both its own distribution and the MapR distribution. Normally, you would skip this section unless you have concerns about the default Hadoop distribution.

You can then configure the hardware by specifying the master, core, and task node. By default, there is only one master node, and two core nodes. You can add more core and task nodes if you like. You should then set up the key-pair to login to the master node.

You should next make a file containing all the start scripts named `bootstrapRHadoop.sh`. After the file is created, you should save the file in the S3 storage. You can then specify `custom action` in **Bootstrap Action** with `bootstrapRHadoop.sh` as the Bootstrap script. Lastly, you can click on `Create cluster` and wait until the cluster is ready. Once the cluster is ready, one can see the master public DNS and can use the EC2 key-pair to access the terminal of the master node.

Beware! Terminate the running instance if you do not want to continue using the EMR service. Otherwise, you will be charged per instance for every hour you use.

See also

▶ Google also provides its own cloud solution, the Google compute engine. For those who would like to know more, please refer to `https://cloud.google.com/compute/`.

A

Resources for R and Machine Learning

The following table lists all the resources for R and machine learning:

R introduction		
Title	**Link**	**Author**
R in Action	`http://www.amazon.com/R-Action-Robert-Kabacoff/dp/1935182390`	Robert Kabacoff
The Art of R Programming: A Tour of Statistical Software Design	`http://www.amazon.com/The-Art-Programming-Statistical-Software/dp/1593273843`	Norman Matloff
An Introduction to R	`http://cran.r-project.org/doc/manuals/R-intro.pdf`	W. N. Venables, D. M. Smith, and the R Core Team
Quick-R	`http://www.statmethods.net/`	Robert I. Kabacoff, PhD
Online courses		
Title	**Link**	**Instructor**
Computing for Data Analysis (with R)	`https://www.coursera.org/course/compdata`	Roger D. Peng, Johns Hopkins University
Data Analysis	`https://www.coursera.org/course/dataanalysis`	Jeff Leek, Johns Hopkins University
Data Analysis and Statistical Inference	`https://www.coursera.org/course/statistics`	Mine Çetinkaya-Rundel, Duke University

Machine learning		
Title	**Link**	**Author**
Machine Learning for Hackers	`http://www.amazon.com/dp/144930371` `4?tag=inspiredalgor-20`	Drew Conway and John Myles White
Machine Learning with R	`http://www.packtpub.com/machine-` `learning-with-r/book`	Brett Lantz
Online blog		
Title	**Link**	
R-bloggers	`http://www.r-bloggers.com/`	
The R Journal	`http://journal.r-project.org/`	
CRAN task view		
Title	**Link**	
CRAN Task View: Machine Learning and Statistical Learning	`http://cran.r-project.org/web/views/` `MachineLearning.html`	

B

Dataset – Survival of Passengers on the Titanic

Before the exploration process, we would like to introduce the example adopted here. It is the demographic information on passengers aboard the RMS Titanic, provided by Kaggle (`https://www.kaggle.com/`, a platform for data prediction competitions). The result we are examining is whether passengers on board would survive the shipwreck or not.

There are two reasons to apply this dataset:

- ▶ RMS Titanic is considered as the most infamous shipwreck in history, with a death toll of up to 1,502 out of 2,224 passengers and crew. However, after the ship sank, the passengers' chance of survival was not by chance only; actually, the cabin class, sex, age, and other factors might also have affected their chance of survival.

- ▶ The dataset is relatively simple; you do not need to spend most of your time on data munging (except when dealing with some missing values), but you can focus on the application of exploratory analysis.

The following chart is the variables' descriptions of the target dataset:

Variable descriptions:

Variable	Description
survival	Survival (0 = No; 1 = Yes)
pclass	Passenger class (1 = 1st; 2 = 2nd; 3 = 3rd)
name	Name
sex	Sex
age	Age
sicbsp	Number of siblings/spouses aboard
parch	Number of parents/children aboard
ticket	Ticket number
fare	Passenger fare
cabin	Cabin
embarked	Port of embarkation (C = Cherbourg; Q = Queenstown; S = Southampton)

Special notes:

Pclass is a proxy for **socio-economic status (SES)**
1st ~ Upper; 2nd ~ Middle; 3rd ~ Lower

Age is in years; it is fractional if the age is less than one (1), and if the age is estimated, it is in the form, xx.5.

With respect to the family relation variables (that is, sibsp and parch), some relations were ignored. The following are the definitions used for sibsp and parch:

Sibling: Brother, sister, stepbrother, or stepsister of a passenger aboard the Titanic
Spouse: Husband or wife of a passenger aboard the Titanic (mistresses and fiancés are ignored)
Parent: Mother or father of a passenger aboard the Titanic
Child: Son, daughter, stepson, or stepdaughter of a passenger aboard the Titanic

Other family relatives excluded from this study include, cousins, nephews/nieces, aunts/uncles, and in-laws. Some children travelled only with a nanny, therefore, parch=0 for them. Also, some travelled with very close friends or neighbors from the same village; however, the definitions do not support such relations.

Judging from the description of the variables, one might have some questions in mind, such as, "Are there any missing values in this dataset?", "What was the average age of the passengers on the Titanic?", "What proportion of the passengers survived the disaster?", "What social class did most passengers on board belong to?". All these questions presented here will be answered in *Chapter 2, Data Exploration with RMS Titanic*.

Beyond questions relating to descriptive statistics, the eventual object of *Chapter 2, Data Exploration with RMS Titanic*, is to generate a model to predict the chance of survival given by the input parameters. In addition to this, we will assess the performance of the generated model to determine whether the model is suited for the problem.

Index

linear regression model
case study 131-137
conducting, for multivariate analysis 92-95
fitting, with lm function 118, 119
information obtaining, summary function
used 120-122
used, for predicting unknown
values 123, 124

LLE (locally linear embedding)
about 350
nonlinear dimension reduction,
performing 383-385

lm function
used, for fitting linear regression
model 118, 119
used, for fitting polynomial regression
model 127, 128

logistic regression
advantages 185
disadvantages 185
used, for classifying data 175-181

M

machine learning
about 13
dataset, obtaining 44-47
reference link, for algorithms 411
with R 13-15
with RHadoop 407-410

Mann-Whitney-Wilcoxon. *See* **Wilcoxon**
Signed Rank test

mapR Sandbox
URL 392

margin
about 268
calculating, of classifier 268-271

mboost package 266

MDS
about 350
used, for performing dimension
reduction 367-371

minimum support (minsup) 348

missing values
detecting 56-58
imputing 59-61

model assessment 51
model-based clustering
about 284
used, for clustering data 309-313

model evaluation 219

multidimensional scaling. *See* **MDS**

multivariate analysis
linear regression, conducting 92-95
performing 90, 91

multivariate data
visualizing, biplot used 363-365

N

Naïve Bayes classifier
advantages 185
data, classifying 182-186
disadvantages 185

NaN (not a number) 56

NA (not available) 56

neuralnet
labels, predicting of trained neural
networks 211-213
neural networks (NN), training 205-208
neural networks (NN), visualizing 209, 210

neural networks (NN)
about 187
advantages 208
training, with neuralnet 205-208
training, with nnet package 214, 215
versus SVM 188
visualizing, by neuralnet 209, 210

nnet package
about 214
labels, predicting of trained neural
network 216-218
used, for training neural
networks (NN) 214, 215

nominal variables 55

nonlinear dimension reduction
performing, with ISOMAP 378-382
performing, with LLE 383-385

nonlinear methods
ISOMAP 350
LLE 350

null hypothesis (H0) 97

Thank you for buying
Machine Learning with R Cookbook

About Packt Publishing

Packt, pronounced 'packed', published its first book, *Mastering phpMyAdmin for Effective MySQL Management*, in April 2004, and subsequently continued to specialize in publishing highly focused books on specific technologies and solutions.

Our books and publications share the experiences of your fellow IT professionals in adapting and customizing today's systems, applications, and frameworks. Our solution-based books give you the knowledge and power to customize the software and technologies you're using to get the job done. Packt books are more specific and less general than the IT books you have seen in the past. Our unique business model allows us to bring you more focused information, giving you more of what you need to know, and less of what you don't.

Packt is a modern yet unique publishing company that focuses on producing quality, cutting-edge books for communities of developers, administrators, and newbies alike. For more information, please visit our website at www.packtpub.com.

About Packt Open Source

In 2010, Packt launched two new brands, Packt Open Source and Packt Enterprise, in order to continue its focus on specialization. This book is part of the Packt open source brand, home to books published on software built around open source licenses, and offering information to anybody from advanced developers to budding web designers. The Open Source brand also runs Packt's open source Royalty Scheme, by which Packt gives a royalty to each open source project about whose software a book is sold.

Writing for Packt

We welcome all inquiries from people who are interested in authoring. Book proposals should be sent to author@packtpub.com. If your book idea is still at an early stage and you would like to discuss it first before writing a formal book proposal, then please contact us; one of our commissioning editors will get in touch with you.

We're not just looking for published authors; if you have strong technical skills but no writing experience, our experienced editors can help you develop a writing career, or simply get some additional reward for your expertise.

R Graph Essentials [Video]

ISBN: 978-1-78216-546-0   Duration: 01:57 hours

A visual and practical approach to learning how to create statistical graphs using R

1. Learn the basics of R graphs and how to make them.

2. Customize your graphs according to your specific needs without using overcomplicated techniques/packages.

3. Step-by-step instructions to create a wide range of professional-looking graphs.

Data Manipulation with R

ISBN: 978-1-78328-109-1   Paperback: 102 pages

Perform group-wise data manipulation and deal with large datasets using R efficiently and effectively

1. Perform factor manipulation and string processing.

2. Learn group-wise data manipulation using plyr.

3. Handle large datasets, interact with database software, and manipulate data using sqldf.

Please check **www.PacktPub.com** for information on our titles

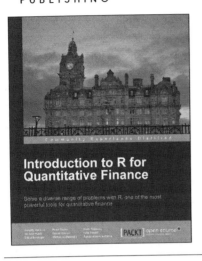

[PACKT] open source ✿
community experience distilled
PUBLISHING

Introduction to R for Quantitative Finance

ISBN: 978-1-78328-093-3   Paperback: 164 pages

Solve a diverse range of problems with R, one of the most powerful tools for quantitive finance

1. Use time series analysis to model and forecast house prices.

2. Estimate the term structure of interest rates using prices of government bonds.

3. Detect systemically important financial institutions by employing financial network analysis.

Machine Learning with R

ISBN: 978-1-78216-214-8   Paperback: 396 pages

Learn how to use R to apply powerful machine learning methods and gain an insight into real-world applications

1. Harness the power of R for statistical computing and data science.

2. Use R to apply common machine learning algorithms with real-world applications.

3. Prepare, examine, and visualize data for analysis.

Please check **www.PacktPub.com** for information on our titles

Made in the USA
San Bernardino, CA
16 July 2017